McGraw-Hill Books by H. James Harrington

- *The Improvement Process: How America's Leading Companies Improve Quality* (1987)
- *Business Process Improvement: The Breakthrough Strategy for Total Quality, Productivity, and Competitiveness* (1991)
- *Total Improvement Management: The Next Generation in Performance Improvement*, written with James S. Harrington (1995)
- *High Performance Benchmarking: 20 Steps to Success*, written with James S. Harrington (1996)
- *The Complete Benchmarking Implementation Guide: Total Benchmarking Management* (1996)
- *ISO 9000 and Beyond: From Compliance to Performance Improvement* (1997)
- *Business Process Improvement Workbook*, written with Erik K.C. Esseling and Harm van Ninwegen (1997)
- *The Creativity Toolkit: Provoking Creativity in Individuals and Organizations*, with Glen D. Hoffherr and Robert P. Reid (1998)*
- *Statistical Analysis Simplified: The Easy-to-Understand Guide to SPC and Data Analysis*, written with Glen D. Hoffherr and Robert P. Reid (1998)*
- *Reliability Simplified: Going Beyond Quality to Keep Customers for Life*, written with Les Anderson (1998)*
- *Area Activity Analysis: Aligning Work Group's Goals to Business Objectives*, written with Glen D. Hoffherr and Robert P. Reid (1998)*
- *ISO 14000 Implementation: Upgrading Your EMS Effectively*, written with Alan Knight (1999)*
- *Simulation Modeling Methods: To Reduce Risks and Increase Performance*, written with Kerim Tumay (1999)*
- *Project Change Management: Applying Change Management to Improve Projects*, written with Daryl R. Conner and Nicholas Horney (1999)*

*Titles in the Harrington Performance Improvement Series

Othe

Performa
Improvei
Methods

Performance Improvement Methods

Fighting the War on Waste

H. James Harrington
International Quality Advisor
Ernst & Young LLP

Kenneth C. Lomax
Founder and Managing Partner
Lomax Consulting Group

McGraw-Hill

New York San Francisco Washington, D.C. Auckland Bogotá
Caracas Lisbon London Madrid Mexico City Milan
Montreal New Delhi San Juan Singapore
Sydney Tokyo Toronto

McGraw-Hill

*A Division of The **McGraw·Hill** Companies*

1 2 3 4 5 6 7 8 9 0 DOC 9 0 1 0 9 8 7 6

ISBN 0-07-027141-0

Library of Congress Cataloging-in-Publication Data

Harrington, H.J. (H. James)
    Performance improvement methods: fighting the war on waste / by H. James Harrington, Kenneth C. Lomax
    p.   cm.
    ISBN 0-07-027141-0

The sponsoring editor for this book was Roger Marsh. Manuscript development and production by CWL Publishing Enterprises, Madison, WI, John A. Woods, President (www.execpc.com/cwlpubent).

McGraw-Hill books are available at special quantity discounts to use as premiums and sales promotions, or for use in corporate training programs. For more information, please write to the Director of Special Sales, McGraw-Hill, 11 West 19th Street, New York, NY 10011. Or contact your local bookstore.

Contents

6 Basic Action/Execution Weapons 247

About the Series

Performance Improvement Methods: *Fighting the War on Waste* is one title in McGraw-Hill's Harrington's Performance Improvement Series. The series is designed to meet an organization's need to understand the most useful approaches now available to bring about improvements in organizational performance as measured by:

- ► Return on investment,
- ► Value-added per employee, and
- ► Customer satisfaction

Each title in the series is written in an easy-to-read, user-friendly style designed to reach employees at all levels of an organization. Our goal is to present complex methodologies in a way that is simple but not simplistic. The following are other subjects covered in the books in this series:

- ► Statistical process controls
- ► Process redesign
- ► Process reengineering
- ► Establishing a balanced scorecard
- ► Reliability analysis
- ► Fostering teamwork
- ► Simulation modeling
- ► Rewards and recognition
- ► Managing the change process
- ► Creativity tools
- ► Statistical analysis simplified
- ► Area activity analysis

We believe that the books in this series will provide an effective way to learn about these practices as well as a training tool for use in any type of organization. In each title in the series, you'll find icons in the margins that call your attention to different points. Use these icons to guide your reading and study:

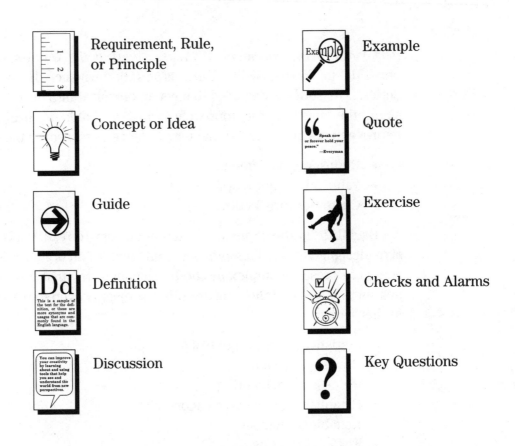

Requirement, Rule, or Principle

Example

Concept or Idea

Quote

Guide

Exercise

Definition

Checks and Alarms

Discussion

Key Questions

It is our hope that you will find this series of Performance Improvement books enjoyable and useful.

H. James Harrington
Principal, Ernst & Young LLP
International Quality Advisor

About the Authors

Dr. H. James Harrington is one of the world's leading process improvement gurus with more than 45 years of experience. He has been involved in developing management systems in Europe, South America, North America, and Asia. He currently serves as principal with Ernst & Young LLP and is their international quality advisor. He is also chairman of Emergency Technology Ltd., a high-tech software and hardware manufacturer and developer.

Before joining Ernst & Young LLP, he was president of the consulting firm Harrington, Hurd, and Rieker. He was a senior engineer and project manager for IBM, and for almost 40 years, he worked in IBM's quality function. He was chairman and president of the prestigious International Academy for quality and the American Society for Quality. He has released a series of videos and CD-ROM programs that cover ISO 9000 and QS-9000. He has also authored a computer program on benchmarking, plus members' videotapes on performance improvement. He has written 14 books on performance improvement and hundreds of technical reports.

The Harrington/Ishikawa Medal was named after him in recognition of his support to developing nations in implementing quality systems. The Harrington/Neron Medal was also named after him to recognize his contribution to the quality movement in Canada. China named him their Honorary Quality Advisor, and he has been elected honorary member of eight quality professional societies and has received numerous awards and medals for his work. Recently, Dr. Harrington was elected into Singapore's Hall of Fame.

Dr. Kenneth C. Lomax is the Founder and Managing Partner of the Lomax Consulting Group and leads a group of professionals in helping organizations to improve. Their focus is on general organizational improvement.

Ken has more than 27 years of experience in Total Quality Management, Quality Assurance, and Quality Control. Thirteen of those years have been spent as a quality consultant specializing in organizational improvement services for manufacturing, service, government, and nonprofit organizations.

After leaving the U.S. Air Force in 1975, Dr. Lomax was a Senior Quality Assurance Engineer on the Trans-Alaska Pipeline. He played a major role in developing the construction and operation inspection procedures for that operation. Later, while working for ARCO Oil and Gas Co. as their Senior Quality Assurance Coordinator, he designed the quality assurance process for ARCO's Kuparuk Oil Field, located on the North Slope of Alaska. Prior to starting his own consulting firm he was an executive for one of the world's largest consulting firms, Ernst & Young LLP.

For the past few years Dr. Lomax has worked with government, commercial, and non-profit organizations in recognizing and accepting the need for quality change. His efforts include strategic quality planning, quality process development, managing the quality process, organization-wide assessments, opinion surveys, employee involvement, leadership training, and managing the change process.

Dr. Lomax holds a Bachelor of Science degree in Quality Engineering, a Master of Science in Business Administration, and a Doctorate in Business Administration with a focus on Organizational Improvement. He lectures often and has authored numerous papers on quality. He is married and has two grown children and four grandchildren. He and his wife live in Roseville, California.

Dedication

This book is dedicated to my father and mother, Kenneth A. and Aileen Lomax. To my father, who taught me that "anything worth doing is worth doing right," and to my mother, who always told me, "You can succeed at anything in life as long as you're willing to try."

Thanks folks—you were both right.

—Ken Lomax

Preface

It's war! The U.S. has been invaded by Japan, China, Mexico, and Canada, with their products.

"It's war! The U.S. has been invaded by Japan, China, Mexico, and Canada, with their products."

We are engaged in a great World War III, testing whether this nation or any other nation so conceived and so dedicated can long endure. World War III is the first war since our Civil War that has been fought within the fifty states. It is a war that is not being fought with bombs, bullets, or battleships. It is an economic war that is destroying our financial structure rather than our buildings. It is a war in which countries like Japan, China, Mexico, and Canada are winning and we are losing.

To win this war, we need to have better processes, products, and practices than any other country in the world. We need to be able to produce cheaper, higher-quality, more reliable products and services than can be produced in China, Germany, Mexico, Canada, South Africa, Japan, or any other country. If we are going to pay our employees twice as much as the people in the countries we are competing against, we need to be twice as productive, and we are not. The U.S. share of the world export market continues to decrease (see Figure 0-1). We cannot even compete with foreign competition within our own domestic market. For example, the U.S. share of passenger cars in the United States continues to erode year after year (see Figure 0-2). If we cannot compete on our own soil, how can we hope to compete in the export market?

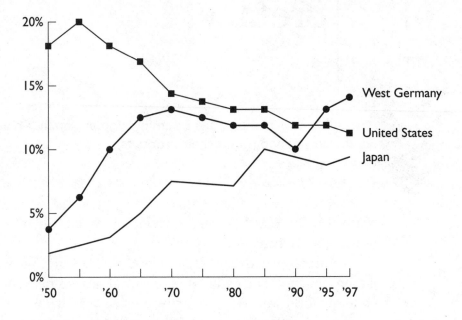

FIGURE 0-1. Exports as a percent of world total

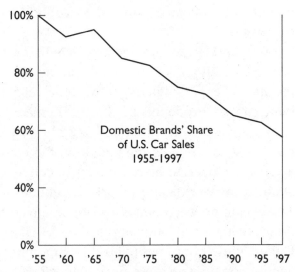

FIGURE 0-2. U.S. manufacturers' share of the U.S. passenger car market

Our buying power peaked in the 1970s and, since that date, has continued to decrease (see Figure 0-3). In the 1950s, one parent working was able to provide the family with a comfortable lifestyle. Today, both parents need to work. Our government's expenses have gone out of control. We now need to work an average of 128 days to pay our taxes when in 1950, we needed to work only 93 days. That's a one-third increase in the percentage of American wealth that is going into supporting the government and not into providing improved living conditions for our people.

Today, the federal government alone absorbs 24% of our gross national product. We have turned from the world's wealthiest nation to the world's most indebted nation, both from a government and individual standpoint (see Figure 0-4).

There is no doubt about it. We are losing World War III. The Pearl Harbor of World War III is our TV and radio industries. The equivalent to our loss of the Philippines is our losing the steel and shipbuilding industries. We are now in the middle of the battle for Midway—the battles for our automobile and aircraft industries and, at this point in time, we're also losing those battles.

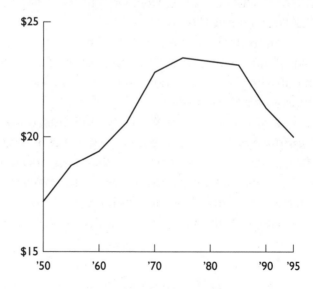

FIGURE 0-3. Average annual U.S. earnings in thousands of 1991 dollars for nonfarm, full-time, nonsupervisory workers

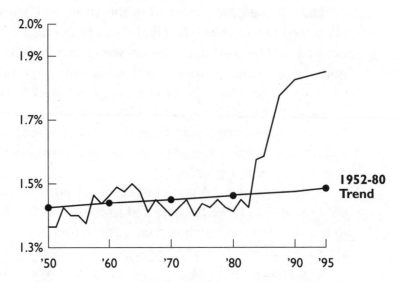

FIGURE 0-4. Total U.S. public and private debt-to-GNP ratio

Our headquarters in World War III is not the Pentagon; it is Wall Street. Our strategists are not generals and admirals; they are presidents and CEOs. People like Louis Gerstner, CEO of IBM; Jeff Ropows, CEO of Lotus; Desi De Simone, CEO of 3M; and John Welch, CEO of General Electric.

If there ever was a time for the U.S. to regroup and make better use of its weapons, now is that time. That's what this book is all about—helping you understand and learn to use the key performance improvement weapons.

We were originally going to call this book *Basic Performance Improvement Tools*, but when we got through writing it we found that the content went way beyond the *basic* tools so we eliminated the word "basic." Then when we went to *Webster's New World College Dictionary*, Third Edition, to look up the word "tool," we found the following definition:

Tool—Any implement, instrument, or utensil held in the hand and used for cutting, hitting, digging, rubbing, etc.; anything that serves in the manner of a tool; a means [books are the scholar's tools].

Somehow, this did not exactly fit the content of the book. We then looked up the word "method":

Method—A way of doing anything; a mode; a procedure; a process; a regular, orderly, defined procedure.

We then looked up "methodology":

Methodology—The science of methods, or orderly arrangements; the branch of logic concerned with the application of principles of reasoning to scientific and philosophical inquiry; or a system of methods.

Well, "methods" certainly comes a lot closer to what we were trying to accomplish in preparing this book. But we went one step further to check on how Webster's defined "system."

System—A set of facts, principles, rules, etc. classified or arranged in regular, orderly form so as to show a logical plan linking the various parts or any established way of doing something.

An established way of doing something. That's really what we're going to be presenting—a number of established ways to improve an organization's performance. As the authors discussed different book titles, we felt that using the word "system" would be misleading and to call things like brainstorming, fishbone diagramming, and Pareto analysis "systems" was incorrect because "systems" are generally perceived as being much more complex. We then looked up synonyms for "method." As we ran through the list, the word "weapon" jumped out at us as the correct descriptive word, because we are truly in a war to eliminate waste and to maximize the use of an organization's limited resources. Although we decided to call the book *Performance*

You need an established way of doing things.

Improvement Methods, what we are going to do is arm the reader with a number of weapons that can be used to fight his or her war on waste. We have divided the weapons into five categories according to how they are used:

Battle Plans—Combination of weapons to meet specific performance improvement objectives.

Data-Analysis Weapons—Methods used to organize data so that they are easy to analyze and use.

Idea-Generation Weapons—Methods used to generate new, creative ideas and concepts to solve problems and take advantage of opportunities.

Decision-Making Weapons—Methods used to help employees and management make correct decisions.

Action/Execution Weapons—Methods used to implement performance improvement.

Our database reveals that there are more than 1,001 different, or not so different, performance improvement weapons and battle plans in use today throughout the world and the list continues to grow (see Appendix B). Many of them use the same basic approach with only very slight modifications, so that an individual consulting organization can establish its own name brand or are the result of a different name that an organization gave to an established approach. For example, GM's Workout, Ernst & Young's Express, and Ford's RAPID are basically all the same approach. Other weapons are unique and very different from each other, although many people think they are the same. For example, process reengineering and process redesign are very different methodologies. Due to the large number of weapons in use today, we will present only 85 of the most effective and commonly used weapons. This is less than 10% of the over 1,001 performance improvement weapons listed in Appendix B.

This book serves as a arsenal of WOW weapons (performance improvement methods) for the other books in this series. It presents weapons that are frequently referred to and used in the other books, but are not discussed in detail there.

The WOW weapons of performance improvement vary all the way from the very simple to the very complex. As a result, we have subdivided the weapons into four categories based upon their complexity or who uses them. Each WOW weapon is classified in a 5x4 matrix based on complexity and use (see Figure 0-5).

Use	Type of WOW Weapon			
	Basic	**Specialized**	**Mass-Destruction**	**Strategic**
Battle Plans				
Data-Analysis				
Idea-Generation				
Decision-Making				
Action/Execution				

FIGURE 0-5. WOW weapon classification matrix

In this book, we will be discussing in detail only the *basic* WOW weapons. Due to their complexity, *specialized, mass-destruction*, and *strategic* weapons will be covered only briefly. It would take individual books dedicated to each of them to do an adequate job of presenting the methodologies. You will find a number of these mass-destruction and strategic weapons included in other books in this performance improvement series (such as simulation modeling, creative thinking, organizational change management, process reengineering, process redesign, and reliability analysis). The tables on pages xxx-xxxi list the 85 WOW weapons in this book and CD-ROM combination, in alphabetical order

The world is looking for a silver bullet that will kill the beast called "Waste." Unfortunately, there is no one bullet or weapon that will do the job. It takes a well-designed arsenal of weapons to fight and win the war on waste (WOW). In addition, it requires an army and navy of soldiers and sailors who are trained to use these weapons. Today, no general would consider fighting a war with only rifles or only airplanes or only bazookas or only tanks. No admiral would go to war with only PT boats or only battleships or only aircraft carriers. No—it takes the correct combination of weapons based on things like the terrain, the enemy, and the distance from the supply source. Likewise, a good general or admiral does not scrap his or her bombers because a supplier designs a new missile. A good general or admiral selects his or her weapons and resources carefully, with a mixture of weapons and trained personnel that provide a number of options for each particular battle. This allows him or her to select the best combination of weapons and personnel to win.

Unfortunately, in business today, most of our generals and admirals (top management) are not as familiar with the WOW weapons as they should be. They try to fight their war on waste using one or two weapons. Even if they win some battles, they don't win the war. As a result, they discard the weapons they are using and start looking for a new flavor of the month. Organizations have been unsuccessful with weapons like TQM, reengineering, redesign, six-sigma, empowerment, self-managed work teams, and quality circles—not because the

weapons are no good, but because they were deployed and used improperly. A bomber loaded with bombs is a powerful weapon, but it could get shot down if its guns are not loaded to ward off the enemy's fighter planes.

The authors don't recommend that every organization use all of the WOW weapons defined in this book, but we do believe that every organization should, at a minimum, evaluate all of these weapons before stocking its arsenal.

Too many managers act like children in a candy store when it comes to performance improvement tools. They take so many they get sick. They may get full but not well.

No.	Weapon Name	Page No.
1	5 S's	265
2	5 W's and 2 H's	176
3	Activity-Based Costing	CD-ROM
4	Affinity Diagram	CD-ROM
5	Area Activity Analysis	29
6	Arrow Diagram/Activity Network Diagrams	CD-ROM
7	Ask "Why" 5 Times	181
8	Assumption Evaluation	CD-ROM
9	Attributes Control Charts	CD-ROM
10	Best-Value Future-State Solution (BVFS)	CD-ROM
11	Brainstorming	184
12	Bureaucracy Elimination Methods	CD-ROM
13	Business Plans	CD-ROM
14	Cause-and-Effect Diagrams (Fishbone Diagrams)	191
15	Checksheets	96
16	Comparative Analysis	CD-ROM
17	Consensus	215
18	Creative Thinking	CD-ROM
19	Cycle-Time Analysis and Reduction	252
20	Creative Thinking	CD-ROM
21	Design of Experiments	CD-ROM
22	Error Proofing	CD-ROM
23	Executive Error-Rate Reduction (E^2R^2)	259
24	Failure Mode and Effect Analysis	CD-ROM
25	Fast Action Solution Teams (FAST)	CD-ROM
26	Flowcharts	CD-ROM
27	Force-Field Analysis	199
28	Function Diagrams	CD-ROM
29	Graphs	103
30	Histograms	124

No.	Weapon Name	Page No.
31	High-Impact Teams (HIT)	CD-ROM
32	Interrelationship Diagrams	CD-ROM
33	Interviewing Techniques	CD-ROM
34	Just-In-Time (JIT)	CD-ROM
35	Management Presentations	227
36	Matrix Data Analysis	CD-ROM
37	Matrix Diagrams/Decision Matrices	236
38	Mind Maps	207
39	Negative Analysis	CD-ROM
40	Nominal Group Technique	CD-ROM
41	Opportunity Cycle	CD-ROM
42	Organizational Change Management (OCM)	CD-ROM
43	Other Points of View	CD-ROM
44	Pareto Diagrams	134
45	Performance Improvement Plan (PIP)	CD-ROM
46	Performance Standards	56
47	Plus-Minus-Interesting	243
48	Policy Deployment (PD)	CD-ROM
49	Poor-Quality Costs (PQC)	CD-ROM
50	Problem-Tracking Logs	272
51	Process Benchmarking	CD-ROM
52	Process Capability Studies	CD-ROM
53	Process Decision Program Charts	CD-ROM
54	Process Qualification	CD-ROM
55	Process Redesign	CD-ROM
56	Process Reengineering	CD-ROM
57	Process Simplification	278
58	Project Management	CD-ROM
59	Quality Function Deployment (QFD)	CD-ROM
60	Quality Management Systems-ISO 9000	CD-ROM

Use your tools to take aim and destroy the waste monster

Acknowledgments

We would like to acknowledge the many contributions to this book made by the team at Ernst & Young LLP. In particular, thanks to Pravesh Mehra for his technical input and to Terry Ozan and George W. Alexander for their support of this project. It was a team effort, with Teu Feagai and Vi Nguyen always there to help get this book out on schedule.

We would particularly like to acknowledge the excellent work and effort put in by Stacey Burkholder and John Osborne, who created the storyboard for the CD-ROM, and converted and edited endless hours of dictation into this final product. John Woods and Bob Magnan of CWL Publishing Enterprises have worked closely with me in giving the manuscript one final review and managing the production, turning it into the book you now hold. Dale Mann prepared the cartoons that capture various concepts. We would also like to acknowledge the efforts put forth by the personnel at SystemCorp in preparing the CD-ROM. Richard Rosenblum, who brought the storyboard to life, and Ari Kugler, who provided the resources to create the CD-ROM free of charge. And last, but not least, Jaime Benchimol, who managed and followed the process that created the CD-ROM. We would also like to recognize the support and understanding provided by our wives, Sheila and Marguerite, who unselfishly allowed us to devote so much time to preparing this book and CD-ROM.

—H. James Harrington

1

Introduction to WOW (War on Waste)

Individuals make a major breakthrough when they stop looking for problems to solve and start taking advantage of the opportunities they have to contribute to the success of the organization.

Introduction

Most organizations are continuously upset because they have so many problems that they cannot see the light at the end of the tunnel. As new problems are identified, management gets more and more annoyed and demands to know who is causing all these problems. People soon become afraid to highlight problems and, instead, live with them until they get out of control. We need to look at problems differently than we have in the past. We need to look at each problem as an opportunity to stop the flow of wasted effort and costs.

We are continually faced by great opportunities brilliantly disguised as unsolvable problems.
　　—Anonymous

Although there are numerous opportunities to reduce waste by solving problems, there are even more opportunities for improving the ways our present processes operate that are not necessarily causing problems. Poor-quality cost in manufacturing runs about 20% of a product's cost. In our support processes, this cost can run as high as 85% of a function's total budget. Today, more than ever before, we need to attack the waste in our support processes and eliminate the waste related to the ineffectiveness that is designed into them. Our war on waste must attack both the problems and the ineffectiveness that are part of all organizations.

Waging a War on Waste

This book is designed to assist the reader in developing a systematic approach to problem solving, problem prevention, and continuous improvement, focusing on eliminating waste. The greatest resources of any organization are its individual employees, if management can get them involved and harness their creativity.

Use your skills and the weapons in this book to slay the waste monster.

There are many things managers can do, or not do, to encourage maximum employee participation and to elicit their ideas to wage a war on waste. Some of the weapons (tools and techniques) presented here for use in your performance improvement activities will enhance your efforts to encourage participation in a meaningful and constructive way. These weapons are nothing more than structured approaches to making decisions and are based upon the concept that empowered teams and individuals can make a major contribution to improving processes and correcting problems. These weapons will help you get participation, gather information, and examine it in a logical sequence as you work to resolve organizational issues and thus improve the work you do and the services you provide.

There are two well-known and widely used sets of problem-solving tools and process-improvement tools.

▶ Seven Basic Problem-Solving Tools[1]
The Seven Basic Weapons used to solve problems are:
1. Brainstorming
2. Cause-and-Effect Diagrams
3. Check Sheets
4. Pareto Diagrams
5. Scatter Diagrams
6. Histograms
7. Data Stratification

▶ Seven Management Tools[2]
These are more advanced weapons than the Seven Basic Problem-Solving Tools.
1. Matrix Charts–Decision Matrices
2. Affinity Diagrams
3. Arrow Diagrams
4. Interrelationship Diagrams
5. Matrix Data Analysis
6. Process Design Program Charts
7. Tree Diagrams

---

[1]Ishikawa, Kaoru. *Guide to Quality Control.*
[2]Akao, Yoji. *Hoshin Kanri.*

There are also two sets of business process improvement (BPI) weapons widely used today.

▶ Business Process Improvement's Ten Fundamental Tools[3]
The fundamental weapons used to improve business processes. They are:
1. BPI Concepts
2. Flowcharting
3. Comparative Analysis
4. BPI Measurement Methods (Cost, Cycle Time, Efficiency, Effectiveness, and Adaptability)
5. Non-Value-Added Activity and Bureaucracy Elimination Methods
6. Process Walk-Through Methods
7. Simulation Modeling
8. Organizational Change Management
9. Cost and Cycle-Time Analysis (Activity-Based Costing-ABC)
10. Simplification Analysis (Process, Paperwork and Language)

▶ BPI's Ten Sophisticated Tools[4]
These are advanced weapons used to improve business processes. They are:
1. Quality Function Deployment (QFD)
2. Program Evaluation and Review Technique (PERT) Charting
3. Business Systems Planning (BSP)
4. Process Analysis Technique (PAT)
5. Structured Analysis/Design (SA/SD)
6. Value Analysis and Control
7. Information Engineering
8. Poor-Quality Cost
9. Interviewing Techniques
10. Process Visioning

---

[3]Harrington, H. James, *Business Process Improvement*.
[4]Harrington, *Ibid.*

Most of the weapons included in these four will be discussed in this book or CD-ROM. As we have mentioned, there are hundreds of different WOW weapons. Appendix B lists more than 1,001 WOW weapons and this list is growing every month. What we have tried to do in this book is to highlight the weapons that have proven over the years to be the most effective in most cases. The problems and goals facing your organization will require you to mix and match these weapons to your particular battle.

Roadblocks to Performance Improvement

If you think about it, any time an organization identifies a problem area, in reality it has an improvement opportunity. You can look at these improvement opportunities in three ways:

1. You can think of them as a burden that has been put on your shoulders.
2. You can ignore them, hoping they will go away.
3. You can look at them as an opportunity to contribute to the success of your organization.

The right way to view problems and change is as opportunities to improve. In our minds we may know this but has it reached our hearts? Management and employees alike put up roadblocks in their own paths to success. There are ten roadblocks that inhibit successful problem solving.

1. **Lack of time.** "I don't have the time now." The reason we don't have the time to fix it today is that we didn't take the time to do it right yesterday.

2. **Lack of problem ownership.** "It's not my problem. Joe did it wrong; let him fix it." The lack of problem ownership causes many problems to stay with us when they could have been solved a long time ago.

3. **Lack of recognition.** "Sure, I could tell Joe that he is doing it wrong and show him how to do it right, but that doesn't give me any points with my boss. All it does is put me behind schedule and make Joe look better." Management needs to find ways to recognize people who go out of their way to help correct problems, who take the time to do the job right every time.

4. **Errors as a way of life.** "Mistakes are bound to happen; we're only human." This type of attitude is the beginning of the end for an organization. There are very few acceptable mistakes.

5. **Ignorance of the importance of the problem.** "It is just a little burr; it will fall off sometime." But what if that sometime occurs in a precision servo system that is used to navigate a plane and it jams the gears? Every job is important; if it isn't, it should be eliminated. An error that is repeated is unforgivable. To err is human; to forgive is divine. We have too many divine managers.

6. **Belief that no one can do anything about some problems.** "It cannot be solved or someone else would have solved it already." If everyone thought this way, no problems would be solved.

7. **Poor balance by upper management of schedule, cost, and quality.** "The boss wants it out now. You have spent all the time on it we can afford." If management places priority on quality, schedules and cost will take care of themselves. Remember that the bitterness of shipping poor quality lingers long after the sweetness of meeting schedules.

8. **People who try to protect themselves.** "That's not my fault. QC should find that kind of problem before it is shipped. Go talk to them." All too often, people are more interested in proving that they did not cause the problem than in solving the problem. When they realize that a problem is coming close to their front porch, they put it on a detour route so that it takes much longer to solve than it should have.

9. **Belief in "good enough."** "That's good enough. No, it's not perfect, but why waste any more time on it? I have other things to do." This is a cancerous condition that has spread throughout the country. It is the "I don't give a damn" complex or the "That's good enough for government work" complex. These are people who stop short of doing their very best. They have a negative impact on everyone they come in contact with and most of all themselves.

10. **Headhunting managers.** "Tell me who did it. I'll fire him." If management is more interested in placing blame than eliminating the problem, the error-prevention program is doomed.

The success of your war on waste rests in knocking down these roadblocks and creating a belief that eliminating waste will benefit the individual, the organization, and the customer.

Of course, as with any problem list, we should also identify the ingredients required to fix the problem and take advantage of the improvement opportunities as they occur. Listed below are the six ingredients needed to correct today's problems.

1. **Awareness.** Employees and management must be made aware of the importance of eliminating waste and of the cost of waste. In many organizations, eliminating waste could reduce costs by over 40 percent.

2. **Desire.** A desire to eliminate waste must be created. No one wants to be wrong; just give them a chance to do it right. No one wants to waste their time and efforts; let them help by preparing them so they can find a better way.

3. **Training in problem solving.** The individuals working to eliminate the problems need to be confident problem solvers. They need to do more than just present problems; they need to col-

lect cost and supporting data. They need to assemble a number of possible solutions and then select the very best one.

4. **Failure analysis.** A system is needed to translate symptoms into a precise understanding of what caused the problem (failure mode or root cause). Without this type of data, many problems can be solved only by trial-and-error methods that take too much time and cost too much.

5. **Follow-up system.** A system to track problems and action commitments is an essential part of the waste reduction system. It should also provide a means to evaluate the effectiveness of the improvement action.

6. **Liberal credit.** Credit and recognition should be liberally given to all who participate in solving problems.

Measurement Systems

The key to any important improvement process or waste-reduction activity is an effective measurement system that can identify improvement opportunities. Inaccurate measurement systems often cause valuable resources to be directed at non-existent problems. Inadequate measurement systems will cause important improvement opportunities to be overlooked. The starting point for any effective war on waste is a measurement system that can identify improvement opportunities and measure changes in performance.

When you can measure what you are speaking about and express it in numbers, you know something about it, and when you cannot measure it, when you cannot express it in numbers, your knowledge is of a meager and unsatisfactory kind. It may be the beginning of knowledge but you have scarcely in your thoughts advanced to the stage of a science.

—LORD KELVIN

One of the biggest sources of waste is poor and inadequate measurement systems. We can waste resources by:

▶ collecting data that are not used or needed
▶ using incorrect data
▶ not identifying negative trends until they become major problems
▶ collecting data that do not reveal the total problem
▶ highlighting non-existent problems
▶ presenting too much data

A good measurement system lets you know when you should react as well as when you should not react.

The following are some key definitions that will be used throughout the book:

This is a sample of the text for the definition, or these are more synonyms and usages that are commonly found in the English language.

Data—Factual information used as a basis for reasoning, planning, and action. The plural of datum.

Information—Knowledge acquired in any manner. It may or may not be true. (Typical sources of information are television, friends, teachers, books, magazines, newspapers, radio, and personal experience.)

Attributes data—Counted data that can be classified as either yes/no, accept/reject, black/white, go/no-go, etc. These data are usually easy to collect because they require only counting.

Variables data—Data that are always measured in units, such as inches, feet, volts, amps, ohms, centimeters, etc. Measured data, in contrast with attributes data, provide detailed knowledge of the system and allow for small samples to be taken

Item—Any output. Items include processes, products, services, equipment, and/or computer programs.

Process—Any activity or series that takes an input, adds value to it, and provides an output. A process can be as small as a single activity or it can include many activities.

What Are Data?

Data are objective information; that is, information on which everyone can agree. An objective measurement of a piece of string would be a ruler measure of its length. If all the rulers are alike, everyone measuring the string will come up with a very similar number. Measurability is important in collecting data. The more you use measurable data, the better your decision will be.

Attributes and Variables Data

Attributes data (often called "counted data") are simply a count of the number of items that are present or absent. Attributes data are generally answers to "How many?" or "How often?"questions. Examples of questions calling for attributes data include:

- ▶ How many of the final products are defective?
- ▶ How often are the machines repaired?
- ▶ How many people are ill each day?
- ▶ How many days did it rain last month?

Variables data (often called "measured data") are answers to such questions as "How long?" "What volume?" "How much time?" and "How far?" The key is that each datum is measured on some ruler, instrument, or device. Examples of questions calling for variables data include:

- ▶ How long is each item?
- ▶ At what rate is this job being done?
- ▶ How long does it take to complete this task?
- ▶ What is the volume of this substance?

Variables data are generally regarded as having more value than attributes data. Variables data are more precise and carry more information. For example, you would know much more about the climate of an area if you knew how much it rained each day rather than just how many days it rained.

Collecting variables data is sometimes difficult or expensive, so we may have to rely on attributes data. Some types of measurements can be evaluated only as attributes data. Take, for example, the problem of unpopped popcorn. If you counted the kernels of unpopped corn in each batch, you would be collecting attributes data. If you measured the maximum diameter of each unpopped kernel, you would be collecting variables data. If you understand what type of data your investigation requires, then you can collect and analyze the data better. (Measurement systems will be discussed in detail in Chapter 8.)

Location Data

A third type of data does not fit into either category. They are location data; they answer the simple question, "Where?"

Problem Definition

Understanding the problem is the most important step in solving a problem. Too often problems are not solved because the action taken did not address the real source of the problem.

Description of Problems

It has often been said, "A problem well-defined is half solved." Because we firmly believe that the problem-definition step is often implemented poorly, we will discuss this step in more detail. Defining the problem is one of the most important aspects of effective problem solving. In most teams not familiar with the problem-solving process, about 90% of wasted problem-solving time is spent:

► Solving the wrong problem
► Stating the problem so it can't be solved
► Stating the problem too generally
► Trying to get agreement on the solution before there is agreement on the problem

Thus, the first step in solving a problem is to define the problem precisely. There are two techniques described in this section that can be combined to help you develop good problem statements.

People use various levels of abstraction in defining problems. Some problem statements may be very specific (e.g., "It takes me too long to travel between home and work"), while others may be very abstract (e.g., "The United States is not a safe place to live"). The lowest level of abstraction might limit the creativity of potential solutions. The highest level of abstraction might result in impractical solution alternatives.

To generate a range of problem statements with varying abstraction levels so that a practical and meaningful problem statement can be selected, the "5 Whys" is a useful technique. It provides a broad range of new perspectives on a problem. It will help you better understand the nature of the problem and your goals and objectives. (The "5 Whys" is covered as a weapon in Chapter 4.)

Guidelines and Tips

Effective problem statements are:
  ▶ Specific
  ▶ Concise
  ▶ Objective
  ▶ Statements of a symptom
  ▶ Descriptions of observable conditions

And they describe undesirable or unacceptable:

  ▶ Circumstances
  ▶ Conditions
  ▶ Events
  ▶ Behaviors
  ▶ Results

Beware of and try to avoid:

- ► *Questions.* They are not problem statements.
- ► *Solutions masquerading as problems.* They are statements about what you'd like or what should be, not about what is.
- ► *"Lack of" statements.* They are, at best, statements about a possible cause of some condition. That condition is a problem.
- ► *Problems expressed in terms of "training."* Once again, "inadequate training" may be the cause, "proper training" may be the solution, but what is the problem? What is going wrong? The answer to that question is the problem statement.
- ► *Subjective statements about morale, motivation, and the like.* They are not particularly productive starting points. What are the undesirable circumstances, conditions, or behaviors?

Examples of Poor Problem Statements

Statement	Why It's a Poor Statement
Need for a computer	*Limits us to only one solution*
Machine set-ups	*Not descriptive enough*
Lack of training	*A possible cause—not the symptom*
Safety	*Too general—need more detail*
No commitment	*Too general—subjective statement*

Problem Statement Examples from Everyday Life

Don't State It This Way	Do State It This Way
The baby is hungry.	*The baby is crying.*
I don't get enough sleep.	*I am constantly tired.*
Lack of gasoline.	*The car will not start.*
Why can't you get to work on time?	*You're consistently late for work.*

Not having a clear problem statement will only add time to the problem-correction stage. A clear problem statement allows the team members to focus and provides an issue that they "can get their hands around."

A little time spent in proper problem identification will more than pay for itself in the end.

How This Book Is Organized

This book is divided into eight chapters:

- ▶ Chapter 1. Introduction to WOW (War on Waste)
- ▶ Chapter 2. Basic Battle Plans
- ▶ Chapter 3. Basic Data-Analysis Weapons
- ▶ Chapter 4. Basic Idea-Generation Weapons
- ▶ Chapter 5. Basic Decision-Making Weapons
- ▶ Chapter 6. Basic Action-Execution Weapons
- ▶ Chapter 7. Performance Improvement Teams
- ▶ Chapter 8. Measurement Systems

As mentioned in the Preface, 85 WOW weapons will be discussed in this book/CD-ROM combination. Each of the 85 WOW weapons is classified into one of the following categories:

Basic Weapons—WOW weapons that everyone in the organization should understand and be able to use when the weapon is needed. (This icon will be used throughout the book and CD-ROM to indicate Basic Weapons.)

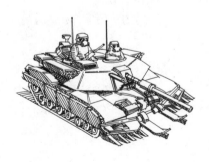

Specialized Weapons—WOW weapons that require special training for employees to be proficient. These weapons are normally not used by everyone in the organization. (This icon will be used throughout the book and CD-ROM to indicate Specialized Weapons.) The detailed discussion related to Specialized Weapons will be presented in the CD-ROM.

Mass-Destruction Weapons—Extremely powerful WOW weapons that require advanced special training. (This icon will be used throughout the book and CD-ROM to indicate Mass-Destruction Weapons.) The detailed discussion related to Mass-Destruction Weapons will be presented in the CD-ROM.

Strategic Weapons—Combinations of WOW weapons that have proven effective in taking advantage of complex improvement opportunities. (This icon will be used throughout the book and CD-ROM to indicate Strategic Weapons.) The detailed discussion related to Strategic Weapons will be presented in the CD-ROM.

Figure 1-1 shows how these 85 WOW weapons are classified in terms of type and usage.

Usage	Type of Weapons				
	Basic	Specialized	Mass Destruction	Strategic	**Total**
Battle Plans	7	7	6	5	**25**
Data Analysis	8	16	2	2	**28**
Idea Generation	6	5	1	0	**12**
Decision Making	5	2	1	0	**8**
Action/Execute	5	4	1	2	**12**
Total	31	34	11	9	**85**

FIGURE 1-1. The War-on-Waste weapons discussed in this book and CD-ROM

Overview of Weapons Classified as Battle Plans

Planning is key to eliminating waste.

The following is a list of the WOW weapons classified as Battle Plans. The definition for each weapon can be found in Appendix A.

Chapter 2—Basic Battle Plans

▶ Area Activity Analysis (AAA)
▶ Organizational Change Management (OCM)
▶ Performance Standards (PS)
▶ Shewhart Cycle (P-D-C-A)
▶ Six-Step Problem-Solving Cycle
▶ Six-Step Solution-Identification Cycle
▶ Visioning

CD-ROM, Section A—Specialized Battle Plans

▶ Fast Action Solution Technique (FAST)
▶ High-Impact Teams (HIT)
▶ Process Benchmarking
▶ Process Redesign
▶ Opportunity Cycle

▶ Reliability Management System

▶ Six-Step Error-Prevention Cycle

CD-ROM, Section B—Mass-Destruction Battle Plans

▶ Activity-Based Costing (ABC)

▶ Business Plans

▶ Just-in-Time (JIT)

▶ Performance Improvement Plan (PIP)

▶ Policy Deployment

▶ Process Reengineering

CD-ROM, Section C—Strategic Battle Plans

▶ Quality Management Systems—ISO 9000

▶ Six-Sigma System

▶ Total Cost Management (TCM)

▶ Total Productivity Management (TPM)

▶ Total Quality Management (TQM)

Overview of Weapons Classified as Data-Analysis Weapons

Take advantage of data analysis weapons.

The following is a list of THE WOW weapons classified as Data-Analysis Weapons. The definitions can be found in Appendix A.

Chapter 3—Basic Data-Analysis Weapons

- ▶ Checksheets
- ▶ Graphs
- ▶ Histograms
- ▶ Pareto Diagrams
- ▶ Root Cause Analysis
- ▶ Run Charts
- ▶ Scatter Diagrams
- ▶ Standard Deviation

CD-ROM, Section D—Specialized Data-Analysis Weapons

- ▶ Comparative Analysis
- ▶ Failure Mode and Effect Analysis
- ▶ Flowcharts
- ▶ Function Diagrams
- ▶ Interrelationship Diagrams
- ▶ Interviewing Techniques
- ▶ Matrix Data Analysis
- ▶ Process Decision Program Charts
- ▶ Spider Diagrams/Radar Charts
- ▶ Stratification
- ▶ Surveys
- ▶ Tree Diagrams
- ▶ Value-Added Analysis (VA)

CD-ROM, Section E—Mass-Destruction Data-Analysis Weapons

- ▶ Attributes Control Charts
- ▶ Design of Experiments
- ▶ Process Capability Studies
- ▶ Statistical Process Control (SPC)
- ▶ Variables Control Charts

CD-ROM, Section F—Strategic Data-Analysis Weapons

▶ Poor-Quality Costs (PQC)
▶ Simulation Modeling

Overview of Weapons Classified as Idea-Generation Weapons

Use idea-generation weapons to get creative in attacking waste.

The following is a list of the WOW weapons classified as Idea-Generation Weapons. The definition for each can be found in Appendix A.

Chapter 4—Basic Idea-Generation Weapons

▶ 5W's and 2H's Approach
▶ Ask "Why" 5 Times
▶ Brainstorming
▶ Cause-and-Effect Diagrams (Fishbone Diagrams)
▶ Force-Field Analysis
▶ Mind Maps

CD-ROM, Section G—Specialized Idea-Generation Weapons

▶ Affinity Diagrams
▶ Negative Analysis
▶ Nominal Group Technique
▶ Other Points of View (OPV)
▶ Storyboard

CD-ROM, Section H—Mass Destruction Idea-Generation Weapons

▶ Creative Thinking

Overview of Weapons Classified as Decision-Making Weapons

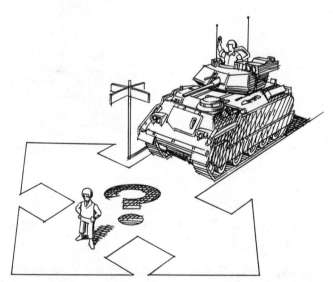

Learn to use the weapons that help you make sound decisions in the fight against waste.

The following is a list of the WOW weapons classified as Decision-Making Weapons. The definitions can be found in Appendix A.

Chapter 5—Basic Decision-Making Weapons

▶ Consensus
▶ Delphi Narrowing Technique
▶ Management Presentations
▶ Matrix Diagrams/Decision Matrices
▶ Plus-Minus-Interesting

CD-ROM, Section I—Specialized Decision-Making Weapons

▶ Assumption Evaluation
▶ Solution Analysis Diagrams

CD-ROM, Section J—Mass-Destruction Decision-Making Weapons

▶ Best-Value Future-State Solution (BVFS)

Overview of Weapons Classified as Action-Execution Weapons

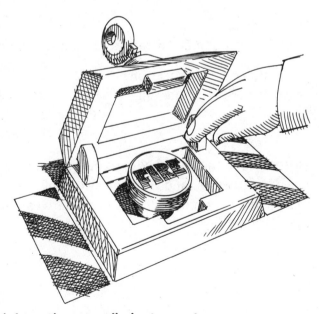

Take the right actions to eliminate waste.

The following is a list of WOW weapons classified as Action-Execution weapons. The definition for each can be found in Appendix A.

Chapter 6—Basic Action-Execution Weapons

- ► Cycle-Time Analysis and Reduction
- ► Executive Error-Rate Reduction (E^2R^2)
- ► Five S's
- ► Problem-Tracking Logs
- ► Process Simplification

CD-ROM, Section K—Specialized Action-Execution Weapons

- ► Arrow Diagrams/Activity Network Diagrams
- ► Bureaucracy Elimination Methods
- ► Error Proofing
- ► Project Management

CD-ROM, Section L—Mass-Destruction Action-Execution Weapons

- ► Quality Function Deployment (QFD)

CD-ROM, Section M—Strategic Action-Execution Weapons

- ► Process Qualification
- ► Reverse Engineering

Note: Due to the complexity of the weapons classified as Specialized, Mass-Destruction, and Strategic Weapons, and to keep the book at a reasonable length, the details of these weapons will be presented in the CD-ROM.

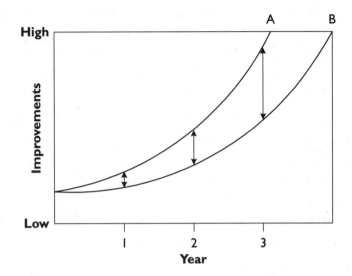

FIGURE 1-2. Two identical improvement curves offset by one year

Summary

Improvement efforts in many organizations around the world have failed not because the methods used were bad but because the organization selected the wrong approach for its particular set of conditions.

With over 1,001 WOW weapons available, an effective manager needs to be very careful to select the optimum configuration of weapons for the battle terrain (market segment).

You cannot look at the weapon your competitor is using and hope to win by building more of the same weapon, because by the time you have built the weapons and trained your team to use them, the war will be over and you will have been defeated.

Improvement is an expediential curve. (See Figure 1-2.) Curve A is the improvement curve for one company. Curve B is the improvement curve for a company that starts one year later and implements the same improvement concepts. Both curves are essentially the same, but the second curve is offset by one year. You will note that as both organizations progress with their improvement process, the difference between the two curves becomes greater and greater due to the expediential nature of the improvement curve. There is nothing we would like better than to have our competitors copy what we are doing, because by the time they have reached the point that we are at today, we will be far ahead of them, thereby ensuring that we always maintain market leadership.

You have just learned improvement rule #1: You cannot copy your competitors, for when you get to where you want to be, they will be far ahead of you. You must improve at a steeper rate than your competitors in order to be competitive.

Rule #2: Do not tell the world about all of your improvement secrets. Your competitors may listen to you.

You fight today's battles with the best combination of weapons you have today. You prepare to fight future battles by understanding the weaknesses you have today and designing a performance improvement plan that provides new weapons that will eliminate these weaknesses and provide you with a competitive advantage.

There's only one best combination of improvement weapons for your organization today. Without considering all of the options, you will never find that correct combination.

Additional Ammunition

Akao, Yoji, ed. *Hoshin Kanri: Policy Deployment for Successful TQM* (Portland, OR: Productivity Press, 1991).

Harrington, H. James. *Business Process Improvement: The Breakthrough Strategy for Total Quality, Producitivity, and Competitiveness* (New York: McGraw-Hill, 1991).

Ishikawa, Kaoru. *Guide to Quality Control* (Tokyo: Asian Productivity Organization, 1972).

2

Basic Battle Plans

Planning is an organization's best error-prevention weapon. Planning is an investment in the organization's future.

Chapter Preview

There's always a debate about what to do first: develop a plan, or collect and analyze data so that the plan can be based upon fact. If you collect data first, do you develop a plan so that you collect the right data? It's the old question, "Which came first, the chicken or the egg?" We agree that planning, data collection, and data analysis are iterative, interrelated processes (see Figure 2-1).

After much discussion, we decided to start our presentation of WOW weapons with a group of weapons we call "battle plans." These are combinations of weapons that define different ways to bring about performance improvement within the organization.

Here in Chapter 2 we will present the 25 battle plans that are used to direct the war on waste. The book contains 7 of them and the CD-ROM contains 18. Battle plans define what should be done and how.

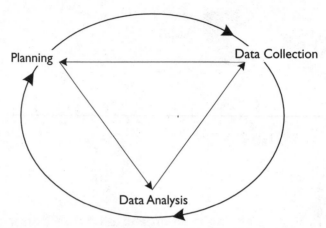

FIGURE **2-1. Performance improvement leadership cycle**

They do not provide direction on how to use the individual weapons that make up the battle plans. Parts II through V will provide this detailed information. The battle plans presented will range from the very simple to the very complex. They will be presented in the following order:

Chapter 2—Basic Battle Plans

- ▶ Area Activity Analysis (AAA)
- ▶ Organizational Change Management (OCM)
- ▶ Performance Standards (PS)
- ▶ Shewhart Cycle (P-D-C-A)
- ▶ Six-Step Problem-Solving Cycle
- ▶ Six-Step Solution-Identification Cycle
- ▶ Visioning

CD-ROM, Section A—Specialized Battle Plans

- ▶ Fast Action Solution Teams (FAST)
- ▶ High-Impact Teams (HIT)
- ▶ Process Benchmarking
- ▶ Process Redesign
- ▶ Opportunity Cycle
- ▶ Reliability Management System
- ▶ Six-Step Error-Prevention Cycle

CD-ROM, Section B—Mass-Destruction Battle Plans

- ▶ Activity-Based Costing (ABC)
- ▶ Business Plans
- ▶ Just-In-Time (JIT)
- ▶ Performance Improvement Plan (PIP)
- ▶ Policy Deployment (PD)
- ▶ Process Reengineering

CD-ROM, Section C—Strategic Battle Plans

- ▶ Quality Management Systems—ISO 9000
- ▶ Six-Sigma System
- ▶ Total Cost Management (TCM)
- ▶ Total Productivity Management (TPM)
- ▶ Total Quality Management (TQM)

Summary

Too many organizations pick individual WOW weapons to fight their war on waste but never step back to define how or even if they will impact the organization's bottom line. As a result these organizations drift from one weapon to another without internalizing any of them into the organization's personality. The proper approach is to select the battle plans that the organization will embrace, then collect and analyze data so that the present and future conditions are thoroughly understood and the terrain on which the battle will take place is well defined. The organization can then select the individual weapons to use and determine how to execute the battle plan (see Figure 2-2).

Spend more on planning; save much more on implementation.

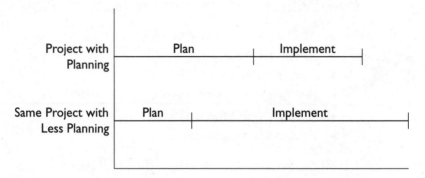

FIGURE 2-2. A time chart of the same project done two ways.

More battles are lost to poor planning than to poor soldiering.

Introduction

This chapter presents combinations of WOW weapons designed to bring about specific performance improvements within an organization. These are WOW weapons that should be used by all employees and should be part of all employees' basic training. The WOW weapons presented in this chapter are:

- ▶ **Area Activity Analysis**—This is a proven approach used by natural work teams (or "areas"). It helps them establish efficient and effective measurement systems, performance standards, improvement goals, and feedback systems that are aligned with the organization's objectives and understood by the employees involved.

- ▶ **Organizational Change Management (OCM)**—This is a methodology designed to lessen the stress and resistance of employees and managers to critical organizational changes.
- ▶ **Performance Standards (PS)**—This defines the acceptable level of error of each individual in the organization.
- ▶ **Shewhart Cycle (Plan-Do-Check-Act)**—This is a structured approach for improving services, products, and/or processes.
- ▶ **Six-Step Problem-Solving Cycle**—This is a basic procedure for understanding a problem, correcting the problem, and analyzing the results.
- ▶ **Six-Step Solution-Identification Cycle**—This is a procedure for defining how to solve a problem or take advantage of an opportunity.
- ▶ **Visioning**—This involves describing the desired future state of an organization, process, team, or activity.

Now let's look more closely at each of these WOW weapons.

WOW Weapon: Area Activity Analysis (AAA)

Definition: A proven approach used by each natural work team (area) to establish efficiency and effectiveness measurement systems, performance standards, improvement goals, and feedback systems that are aligned with the organization's objectives and understood by the employees involved.
Classification: Basic Battle Plan
Users: Natural Work Teams

Just the Facts

We believe that this is the most effective and efficient team-related weapon developed to date.

As viewed by the employees, the organization chart often looks like everyone above them exists just to generate work for them, and all management wants from them is their complete discipline.

Since the early 1960s, management has unsuccessfully chased after the elusive pot of gold at the end of the rainbow called "Internal Supplier/Customer Relationships." This concept is very sound and relatively simple, but extremely difficult to implement and maintain. Theoretically, treating the fellow employee who receives your output the same as you would treat an external customer is relatively straightforward. Unfortunately, people are less inclined to react to a person who is not paying for their output than to individuals who show the value they place on their output by paying directly for it.

To find an organization that has effectively implemented the internal customer concept is a lot like looking for the Holy Grail. You know it should exist, but no one has been able to find it. Area Activity Analysis (**AAA**) is a methodology developed to cement these internal customer relationships while also developing effective performance measurement systems that optimize the value-added content of each individual's activities.

Area Activity Analysis is a methodology designed to establish agreed-to, understandable efficiency and effectiveness measurement systems and communication links throughout the organization. The methodology consists of a seven-phase process. The last phase, Phase VII—Continuous Improvement, is a continuous process; the first six phases of the **AAA** process usually have fixed start and end points. These six phases are normally treated as a project and are included in the organization's strategic business plan. However, the measurements and the associated requirements that are developed should be updated on a regular basis.

We hear a great deal these days about the importance of developing the internal customer/supplier relationship within our organizations. No matter where you go, people profess to be concerned about satisfying their internal customers. Every quality training program teaches it, every book on quality preaches it, and clearly most people today truly believe that internal customer satisfaction is critical to business success. The truth of the matter is that it is very difficult for any organization to have good external customer satisfaction unless it has excellent internal customer satisfaction.

Natural Work Team (NWT) or Natural Work Group (NWG)— a group of people who are assigned to work together and report to the same manager or supervisor.

AAA will help you:

► Clarify your NWT's real purpose
► Identify those time-consuming activities that do and do not support your mission
► Align your NWT's mission and activities with the expectations of the internal and external customers
► Align your employees' activities with the NWT's priorities
► Identify which activities add real value and which can be minimized or eliminated
► Understand how to make the transition from finding and fixing problems to preventing them
► Clarify your requirements for your internal and external suppliers and measure their performance
► Define a comprehensive measurement system for the critical activities that take place within your NWT and set performance standards for each of them
► Put together an implementation plan to make it all happen

Many of us are frustrated with our inability to accurately put a finger on the source of the problems we are facing every day. We know we work hard, deliver quality output, and drive the people who work for us to do the same. The harder we work and the more we push, the more entrenched the problem seems to get and employees' morale seems to sink. It is indeed a vicious, negative cycle that can sap the energies of even the most dedicated manager or employee. Here again **AAA** can help.

- ► **AAA** is a simple but powerful tool that you can begin using immediately to provide clear direction for what may otherwise have become a confusing journey toward improving customer service.
- ► **AAA** can help you align your energy and resources with your organization's mission in a way that can result in greater effectiveness, efficiency, satisfaction, and teamwork.
- ► **AAA** serves as a compass to help you find your way through the jungle of overwork that threatens to overtake us all.
- ► **AAA** helps you sort out the vital few from the trivial many so that you can focus on delivering the value that you, and you alone, can add to your organization and your customers.

AAA was designed by busy managers who needed a way to analyze and organize their work areas to get better results from their current resources. As the weeks, months, and years go by, the organizations we manage inevitably take on more and more responsibilities and our jobs get more and more complex. We begin to feel like we're running on a treadmill while someone keeps turning up the speed.

AAA is unlike any other technique for improving processes, reducing costs, or decreasing turnover. It helps everyone clarify expectations and focus their efforts on the area's mission. **AAA** is the tool that should be used before other interventions such as continuous improvement, total quality management, or reengineering are put into operation.

AAA is an appropriate tool for new or existing areas or departments. It is a tool that will help to ensure that all employees understand their area's mission, customer expectations, what they need to do to succeed, and how to measure their performance.

AAA can be used by managers at any level of the organization to improve efficiency, effectiveness, and teamwork within their operations. It can be used by an individual unit or as part of a coordinated, organization-wide effort. It can also be used by an individual to improve his or her performance. It can and should be used by every person in the whole organization at every level, from the team of vice presidents who report directly to the president of the organization to the team of maintenance workers who report directly to the maintenance line manager.

We had problems naming this improvement tool. At first, in the 1980s, we called it Department Activity Analysis. But some managers didn't like that name because they used the term "department" for personnel, engineering, production control, and so forth, while other managers called them "functions." After using the term Department Activity Analysis for about five years, we eliminated the term "department" and the confusion it created, changing the name to Area Activity Analysis (**AAA**), so that it would relate to any organizational NWT at any level.

What Is Area Activity Analysis?

Area Activity Analysis (**AAA**) is the first performance improvement tool that a manager should use to help his or her area get started on a sound footing. **AAA** helps the organization accomplish the most basic of all management tasks, defining:

▶ The purpose of each area
▶ The activities that must be performed to fulfill the area's mission
▶ The requirements of the area's internal and external customers
▶ The ways to measure the area's performance
▶ The standards for acceptable performance

AAA is not another technique for improving processes, lowering cycle time, or reducing costs. Simply stated, it helps managers clarify what is expected of their groups, define key measurements, set performance standards, and focus employees' efforts like a laser beam on the organization's mission. It defines whether the area needs to improve and where the improvement opportunities exist. It helps the employees understand what is important for their customers and managers. It also helps the employees understand how they fit into the organization and contribute to the organization's goals. It is a people-building approach that helps them stand on their own feet with a high degree of self-confidence and helps them understand that they are doing something worthwhile.

Before we go any further, let's discuss what we mean by customer/supplier relationships as they relate to internal and external customers. Basically, a customer/supplier relationship can develop in two different ways.

1. An individual or organization can determine that it needs something that it does not want to create or produce for itself. As a result, it looks for some other source (supplier) that will supply the product or service at a quality level, cost, and delivery schedule that represents value to the individual or organization (customer).

2. An individual or organization develops an output that it believes will be of value to others. Then the individual or organization (supplier) looks for customers that will consider the supplier's output as being valuable to them.

Two key points need to be made:

▶ A customer/supplier relationship cannot exist unless both parties understand and agree to their requirements. Too often, customers expect input from suppliers without understanding their requirements and/or capabilities. Likewise, too many suppliers provide output without defining their potential customers' requirements and obtaining a common understanding and acceptance of both parties' requirements.

▶ Both the customer and the supplier have obligations to provide input to each other. The supplier is obligated to provide the product or service and define future performance improvements. The customer has an obligation to provide compensation to the supplier for its outputs and feedback on how well the outputs perform in the customer's environment.

The customer/supplier process has a domino effect. Usually, when a supplier is defined, that supplier requires input from other sources

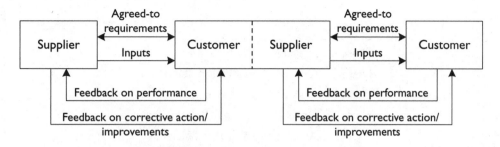

FIGURE 2-3. The cascading customer/supplier model

in order to generate the output for its customer. As a result, it becomes both a customer and a supplier (see Figure 2-3).

Although the procedures related to internal customer/supplier partnerships are less stringent and are simplified because the internal customer does not pay for the services that are provided, the concepts are equally valid. Too often, we set different standards for internal suppliers than for external suppliers. As a result, many of the internal suppliers provide outputs that are far less valuable than the costs of producing the outputs. This often results in runaway costs and added bureaucracy. With **AAA**, we will show you how to apply the customer/supplier model to the internal organization, thereby improving quality and reducing cost and cycle time of the services and products delivered both within and outside the organization.

Defining customer/supplier relationships is only one part of making an area function effectively. There are many other factors that also must be considered. For example:

► What is the area responsible for?
► How is the area measured?
► What is acceptable performance?
► How does the area fit into the total organization?
► How well do the area's employees understand their roles and the ways they can contribute?
► What are the important activities that the area performs from top management's standpoint?

Phase	Number of Steps
Phase I. Prepare for AAA	5
Phase II. Develop Area Mission Statement	6
Phase III. Define Area Activities	8
Phase IV. Develop Customer Relationships	7
Phase V. Analyze the Activity's Efficiency	6
Phase VI. Develop Supplier Partnerships	5
Phase VII. Performance Improvement	8
Total	45

FIGURE 2-4. The seven phases of the AAA methodology

It is important to note that all of these questions pivot around the activities that the area is involved in. It is for this reason that the **AAA** methodology broadened its perspective to go beyond the customer/supplier partnership concept to embrace a complete business view of the area.

The **AAA** methodology has been divided into seven phases (see Figure 2-4) to make it simple for the NWT to implement the concept. Each of these phases consists of a set of steps that will progressively lead the NWT through the methodology.

We will briefly describe each of the seven phases of **AAA**.

Phase I–Prepare for AAA

AAA is most effective when it precedes other initiatives such as continuous improvement, team problem solving, total quality management, reengineering, or new IT systems. It is also best to implement the **AAA** methodology throughout the organization. This does not mean that it will not work if other improvement activities are under way or if it is used by only one area within the organization. In the preparation phase, the good and bad considerations related to implementing **AAA** within an organization should be evaluated. A decision is made whether or not to use **AAA** within the organization. If the decision is made to use **AAA**, an implementation strategy is developed and approved by management.

Phase I—Preparation for **AAA** is divided into five steps:
Step 1—Analyze the Environment
Step 2—Form an **AAA** Project Team
Step 3—Define the Implementation Process
Step 4—Involve Upper Management
Step 5—Communicate **AAA** Objectives

Phase II–Develop Area Mission Statement

A mission statement is used to document the reasons for the organization's or area's existence. It is usually prepared before the organization or area is formed and it is seldom changed. Normally, it is changed only when the organization or area decides to pursue a different set of activities. For the **AAA** methodology, a mission statement is a short paragraph, no more than two or three sentences, that defines the area's role and its relationships with the rest of the organization and/or external customers.

Every area should have a mission statement that defines why it was created. It provides the area manager and the area employees with guidance in the activities on which the area should expend its resources. Standard good business practice calls for preparing an area's mission statement before forming that area. The mission statement should be reviewed each time there is a change in the organization's structure or a change in the area's responsibilities. It should also be reviewed about every four years, even if the organization's structure has remained unchanged, to be sure that the mission statement reflects the current activities that are performed within the area.

Also during Phase II, the area's service policy is developed. A service policy is a short statement that defines how the area will interface with its customers and supplier.

During Phase II, the **AAA** team will review and update the area's mission statement. If a mission statement does not exist, the **AAA** team will prepare a mission statement. In all cases, any change to the mission statement must be approved by upper management before it is finalized.

Phase II—Develop Area Mission Statement is divided into six steps:
Step 1—Obtain Present Mission Statement
Step 2—Develop Preliminary Area Mission Statement—NWT Manager
Step 3—Develop Preliminary Area Mission Statement—Each Employee
Step 4—Develop a Consensus Draft Area Mission Statement
Step 5—Finalize Area Mission Statement
Step 6—Develop the Area's Service Policy

Phase III–Define Area Activities

During this phase, the **AAA** team will define the activities that are performed within the area. For each major activity, the **AAA** team will define the activity's output(s) and the customers that receive the output(s).

Phase III—Define Area Activities is divided into eight steps:
Step 1—Identify Major Activities—Each Individual
Step 2—Combine into Broad Activity Categories
Step 3—Develop Percentage of Time Expended
Step 4—Identify Major Activities
Step 5—Compare List with Area Mission Statement
Step 6—Align Activities with Mission
Step 7—Approve the Area's Mission Statement and Major Activities
Step 8—Assign Activity Champions

Phase IV–Develop Customer Relationships

During this phase, the **AAA** team will meet with each of the customers that are receiving the outputs from the major activities conducted by the area to:

- Define the customer's requirements.
- Define the supplier's requirements.
- Develop ways to measure compliance with the requirements.
- Define acceptable performance levels (performance standards).
- Define the customer feedback process.

Phase IV—Develop Customer Relationships is divided into seven steps:

Step 1—Select Critical Activity

Step 2—Identify Customer(s) for Each Output

Step 3—Define Customer Requirements

Step 4—Define Measurements

Step 5—Review with Customer

Step 6—Define Feedback Procedure

Step 7—Reconcile Customer Requirements with Mission and Activities

Phase V—Analyze the Activity's Efficiency

For each major activity, the **AAA** team will define and understand the tasks that make up the activity. This is accomplished by analyzing each major activity for its value-added content. This can be done by flow-charting the activity and collecting efficiency information related to each task and the total activity. Typical information that would be collected is:

- Cycle time
- Processing time
- Cost
- Rework rates
- Items processed per time period

Using this information, the **AAA** team will establish efficiency measurements and performance targets for each efficiency measurement.

Phase V—Analyze the Activity's Efficiency is divided into six steps:

Step 1—Define Efficiency Measurements

Step 2—Understand the Current Activity

Step 3—Define Data-Reporting Systems
Step 4—Define Performance Requirements
Step 5—Approve Performance Standards
Step 6—Establish a Performance Bulletin Board

Phase VI–Develop Supplier Partnerships

Using the flowcharts generated in Phase V, the **AAA** team identifies the supplier that provides input into the major activities.

This phase uses the same approach discussed in Phase IV, but turns the customer/supplier relationship around. In Phase VI, the area is told to view itself in the role of the customer. The organizations that are providing the inputs to the NWT are called internal or external suppliers. The area then meets with its suppliers to develop and agree to requirements. As a result of these negotiations, a supplier specification is prepared that includes a measurement system, a performance standard, and a feedback system for each input. This completes the customer/supplier chain for the area, as shown in Figure 2-3.

Supplier—An organization that provides a product (input) to the customer (source: ISO 8402).

Internal Suppliers—Areas within an organizational structure that provide input into other areas within the same organizational structure.

External Suppliers—Suppliers that are not part of the customer's organizational structure.

Phase VI—Develop Supplier Partnerships is divided into five steps:
Step 1—Identify Supplier(s)
Step 2—Define Requirements
Step 3—Define Measurements and Performance Standards
Step 4—Define Feedback Procedure
Step 5—Supplier Agreement

Phase VII—Performance Improvement

This is the continuous improvement phase that should always come after an activity has been defined and the related measurements are put in place. It may be a full TQM effort or just a reengineering activity. It could be a minimum program of error correction and cost reduction or a full-blown Total Improvement Management project.

During Phase VII, the NWT will enter into the problem-solving and error-prevention mode of operation. The measurement system should now be used to set challenge improvement targets. The NWT should now be trained to solve problems and take advantage of improvement opportunities. The individual efficiency and effectiveness measurements will be combined into a single performance index for the area. Typically, the area's key measurement graphs will be posted and updated regularly.

During Phase VII, management should show its appreciation to the NWTs and individuals who expended exceptional effort during the AAA project or who implemented major improvements.

Phase VII—Performance Improvement is divided into eight steps:
Step 1—Set Up the Reporting Systems
Step 2—Identify the Activities to Be Improved
Step 3—Install Temporary Protection if Needed
Step 4—Identify Measurements or Task to Be Improved
Step 5—Find Best-Value Solutions
Step 6—Implement Solutions
Step 7—Remove Temporary Protection if Installed
Step 8—Prevent Problem from Recurring

Examples

Area Mission Statement and Major Activities		
Function Name: Insurance Department		
Area Name: Insurance Policy Processing Dept.	**Area No. 351**	
Area Mission Statement		
Our mission is to efficiently and effectively process insurance policies that conform to the individual requirements defined by our agents.		
List major activities of area and % of time for each		
1. Processing new policies	34%	
2. Researching data for salesperson before sale	20%	
3. Updating policies	15%	
4. Preparing financial reports	15%	
5. Personal activities	10%	
6.	%	
7.	%	
8.	%	
9.	%	
Misc.	6 %	
Coordinated by Bob Wilson	**Date** 1/1/00	
Approved by (Upper Management)	**Date** 1/1/00	
Understood by (NWT Members)		
		Revision Date

FIGURE 2-5. Area mission statement and activities filled-in form

Customer Partnership Agreement

Area Name and Number: _____

Activity: _____

Output: _____

Output Performance Standard: _____
_____

- Customers:
  1. _____
  2. _____
  3. _____
- Requirement: ____: _____
  - Performance Standard: _____
  - Performance as of _____ / _____ / _____ : _____
  - Measured: _____ Estimated: _____
  - Meets standard: _____Yes _____No
  - Customer feedback process: _____
    _____

- Requirement ____: _____
  - Performance Standard: _____
  - Performance as of _____ / _____ / _____ : _____
  - Measured: _____ Estimated: _____
  - Meets standard: _____Yes _____No
  - Customer feedback process: _____
    _____

- Requirement ____: _____
  - Performance Standard: _____
  - Performance as of _____ / _____ / _____ : _____
  - Measured: _____ Estimated: _____
  - Meets standard: _____Yes _____No
  - Customer feedback process: _____
    _____

Prepared by: _____ Date: _____

Supplier Approval: _____ Date: _____

Customer Approval:
  Agent Manager _____ Date: _____

  _____ Date: _____

  _____ Date: _____

FIGURE 2-6. Customer partnership agreement form

Efficiency Performance Analysis			
Area Name and Number: Customer Service Support Department/107			
Activity: Answering service support phone calls			
Measurement: Percent real-value-added phone time			
• Performance Standard: 90%			
• Present Value: 95%			
(Measured ___X___		Estimated _____)	
Met Requirements on ___9/1/99___	Yes ___X___		No _____
Measurement: Call duration in minutes			
• Performance Standard: 3.3 minutes			
• Present Value: 8.2 minutes			
(Measured ___X___		Estimated _____)	
Met Requirements on ___9/1/99___	Yes _____		No ___X___
Measurement: Cost per question answered			
• Performance Standard: $23.17			
• Present Value: $32.00			
(Measured _____		Estimated ___X___)	
Met Requirements on ___9/1/99___	Yes _____		No ___X___
Prepared by: NWT		Date 9/1/99	
Approved by: Second-level manager		Date 10/1/99	
Third-level manager		Date 10/1/99	
_____		Date _____	

FIGURE 2-7. Filled-in efficiency performance analysis form for answering service support phone calls

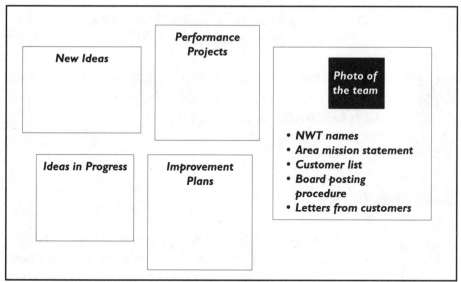

FIGURE 2-8. Performance bulletin board

Additional Ammunition

Akao, Yoji, ed. *Hoshin Kanri—Policy Deployment for Successful TQM* (Portland, OR: Productivity Press, 1991)

Harrington, H. James. *The Improvement Process: How America's Leading Companies Improve Quality* (New York: McGraw-Hill, 1987)

Harrington, H. James, Glen D. Hoffherr, and Robert P. Reid, Jr. *Area Activity Analysis: Aligning Work Activities and Measurements to Enhance Business Performance* (New York: McGraw-Hill, 1998)

Harrington, H. James, and James S. Harrington. *Total Improvement Management: The Next Generation in Performance Improvement* (New York: McGraw-Hill, 1995)

WOW WEAPON: ORGANIZATIONAL CHANGE MANAGEMENT (OCM)

Definition: A methodology designed to lessen the stress and resistance of employees and management to individual critical changes.
Classification: Basic Battle Plan
Users: Groups and Teams

Just the Facts

You can improve your creativity by learning about and using tools that help you see and understand the world from new perspectives.

Organizations today are in a continuous state of change. In the past, individuals were called upon once in a while to adjust and change their work patterns and then had time to master this new process. Today things are changing so fast we seldom become comfortable with one change in the way we do business before it changes again. In all organizations there are hundreds of change activities going on at the same time and many individuals are impacted by a number of processes that are changing simultaneously.

We like to think that the people in our organization are resilient and can handle this rapidly changing environment without additional help. The truth of the matter is that everyone is for change—as long it does not impact him or her. But when the change becomes personal, everyone suffers from disruptions of the four C's.

- ▶ **Comfort:** Their comfort level has been destroyed.
- ▶ **Confidence:** They lose confidence in their ability to meet the requirements in the future-state solution.
- ▶ **Competence:** They are not sure if they will have the skills required to perform. They are no longer the individuals who know the most about the job.
- ▶ **Control:** They have lost control over their own destiny. Someone else is defining what they will do and how they will do it.

As a result of the disruption of the four C's, the individuals and groups within the organization suffer some severe emotional changes.

The stress level within the organization goes way up as people worry about the future. Productivity declines because people spend excessive amounts of time discussing what's going to happen to them and how it's going to impact them. Anxiety levels rise as the future state remains uncertain and the individuals begin to fear loss of security. This results in a great increase in conflict between groups and individuals. An attitude develops of "What's wrong with the future-state solution?" rather than "How can we help to implement the future-state solution?" Everyone is most comfortable and happiest with the current state (status quo). Human beings are extremely control-oriented. We feel the most competent, confident, and comfortable when our expectations of control, stability, and predictability are being met.

Change—A condition in which your expectations based upon past performance are not met. A condition in which you can no longer rely upon your past experience.

We resist change because we don't know if we will be able to prosper or even survive in the new environment. Organizational Change Management (OCM) is a methodology designed to successfully manage the change process. Today, managers at all levels of the organization must be able and willing to deal with the tough issues associated with implementing major change. They must be capable of guiding their organization safely through the change process. This involves convincing people to leave the comfort of the current state and move through the turbulence of the transition state to arrive at what may be an unclear, distant future state. (See Figure 2-9.) Specifically, these three states are defined as:

Current State—The status quo, the established pattern of expectations, the normal routine an organization follows. You know and understand what will happen.

Present State—Your expectations are being met. You may not like the current state, but you have learned how to survive in it and you know what to expect.

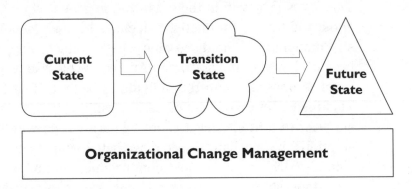

FIGURE 2-9. The change process

Transition State—The point in the change process where people break away from the status quo. They no longer behave as they have in the past, yet they have not thoroughly established a new way of operating.

Future State—The point at which change initiatives are implemented and integrated with the behavioral patterns that are required by the change.

The focus of the OCM methodology is on the transformation from the current state to the future state. The journey can be long and perilous and, if not properly managed with appropriate strategies and tactics, it can be disastrous.

There are hundreds of changes going on within your organization all the time and the OCM methodology should not be applied to all of them. You need to look very carefully at the changes and select the ones that should be managed. Typical changes that should have the OCM methodology applied to them are:

▶ When the change is a major change
▶ When there is a high risk that certain human factors would result in implementation failure

In most organizations there are critical, major, and minor changes. Certainly this methodology should be used in all of the critical changes as well as most major changes. Few of the minor changes will require the discipline involved in the OCM methodology.

The organizational change management methodology consists of the following seven phases.

Phase I—Defining Current-State Pain

The individuals involved in the change need to feel enough heat related to their present situation to make them want to leave the security of the status quo and move into the uncertainty in the transformation phase (transition state) of the change management process. Management may reason that the employees have an excellent understanding of the pain related to the status quo and that is probably true, but they have little understanding of the lost opportunities that will impact them and the organization if the change does not take place. As a result, management needs to surface the pain related to lost opportunities.

The pain related to the current state must be great enough to get the employees to consider leaving the safety of the current state platform and move on to the transformation phase. The highlighting of pain is called "establishing the burning platform."

The term comes from an oil rig that was on fire in the North Sea. The platform got so hot that the workers jumped off the rig into the sea, because they realized that their chances of survival were better in the cold North Sea than on the burning oil rig platform.

Phase II—Establishing a Clear Vision of the Future-State Solution

Employees are going to weigh the pain related to the present situation against the pain they will undergo during the transformation and the pain related to the future-state solution. (Note: Your employees are smart enough to realize that there will always be some pain in even the very best future-state solution.) As a result, management needs to provide the employees with an excellent vision of the future-state solution and its impact upon them so they can compare the pain of the current state with the combined pain of the transition state and future state. If the pain related to the current state is not greater, in their view, than the pains related to the transition state and the future state combined, the change can be implemented only over the objections of the employees. In that case, there is a high degree of probability that it will not be successfully implemented. The vision has to crisply define:

▸ Why is the change necessary?
▸ What's in it for me?
▸ Why is it important to the organization?

Phases I and II are often called "pain management."

Phase III–Defining Change Roles

The roles of the individuals involved in the change must be clearly defined. These roles are divided into five general categories:

This is a sample of the text for the definition, or these are more synonyms and usages that are commonly found in the English language.

Initiating Sponsor—Individual/group that has the power to initiate and legitimize the change for all of the affected individuals.

Sustaining Sponsor—Individual/group that has the necessary political, logistical, and economic proximity to the targets to influence their behavior.

Change Agent—Individual/group that is responsible for implementing the change management aspects of the project.

Change Target (sometimes called a "Changee")—Individual/ group that must actually change.

Advocate—An individual/group that wants to achieve change but does not have sufficient sponsorship.

Each person needs to be trained in his or her duties related to his or her change management role.

FIGURE 2-10. Typical role map diagram

Phase IV—Mapping Change Roles

A change role map should be prepared identifying each individual's role related to the change. (Note: This is a concept developed by Daryl Conner of ODR.) This map generates a visual picture of the individuals, groups, and relationships that must be orchestrated to achieve the change. It is important to note that one individual can serve many roles. For example, every sustaining sponsor is first a target or changee before he or she can accept the role as a sustaining sponsor (see Figure 2-10).

Phase V—Defining the Degree of Change Required

The communications system and the change management plan must be designed to achieve the proper degree of acceptance of the change initiative. There is a great deal of difficulty and effort required to have a change internalized, in comparison with just having it adopted. For example, there is much less change management required to standardize a new computer program for use throughout the organization than to have the individuals accept that software as being the very best alternative. Typically, degrees of acceptance can be broken down into:

- ▶ **Adoption** The change has been fully implemented, the new practice is being followed consistently, and its objectives are being met. "We are doing it this way."
- ▶ **Institutionalization** The change has not only been adopted, but is formalized in written policies, practices, and procedures. The organizational infrastructure (hiring, training, performance measures, rewards, etc.) is aligned to support continued conformance to the new practice. "We always do it this way."
- ▶ **Internalization** The new practice is understood to be fully aligned with individual and organizational beliefs, values, and norms of behavior and, as such, commitment to sustain the practice comes from within. "Of course we always do it this way. I believe in doing it this way, and to do otherwise would be inconsistent with the way we like to do things here!"

Phase VI—Developing the Organizational Change Management Plan

Any planning activity involves thinking out in advance the sequence of actions required to achieve a pre-defined objective. A change management plan is now prepared to ensure the degree of acceptance that is required to support the project.

Now the change management plan needs to be integrated into the project management plan. This normally is a timeline chart that reflects the movement throughout the change management process. (See Figure 2-11 under Examples at the end of this section.) The change management plan should also include any risk related to internal or external events such as the following:

- ▶ Competing initiatives
- ▶ Too many initiatives
- ▶ Loss of sponsorship
- ▶ Economic trends in the business
- ▶ Industry trends

Phase VII–Implementing the Change Management Plan

The OCM plan is now implemented in conjunction with the project plan. Usually a number of surveys are conducted to help refine the OCM plan. Typical surveys or evaluations that could be conducted are:

- ▶ Implementation Architecture Assessment
- ▶ Internal/External Event Assessment
- ▶ Vision Clarity Assessment
- ▶ Commitment vs. Compliance Needs Analysis
- ▶ Strategy Analysis
- ▶ Predicting the Impact of the Change
- ▶ Organizational Effectiveness
- ▶ Business Imperative Analysis
- ▶ Sponsor Evaluation
- ▶ Implementation History Assessment
- ▶ X-Factor Change Readiness Assessment

Examples

Change Management Activities	Phase I Assess	Phase II Plan	Phase III Redesign	Phase IV Implement	Phase V Audit	Phase VI Improve
Identify, document, and communicate cost of the status quo (business imperative)	████	████	████	████		
Create and communicate the future-state vision (people, process, and technology)	████					
Clarify the change and obtain initiating sponsor understanding and commitment	████					
Create needed infrastructure and implementation architecture	████					
Conduct a high-level QMS-wide change risk assessment (the 8 risk factors)		████	████			
Create a high-level QMS-wide organizational change plan		████	████			
Create role maps to identify all personnel having key change roles		████	████	████		
Conduct tier-level change risk assessments (the 8 risk factors)		████	████			
Conduct change readiness assessments		████	████			
Assess organizational alignment (structure, compensation, rewards, etc.)		████	████			
Assess enablers and barriers		████	████			
Develop tier-level transition management plans		████	████			
Develop a communication plan		████	████			
Develop cascading sponsorship (communications, training, performance management)			████	████	████	
Implement the communication plan			████	████		
Provide change management training for sponsors, change agents, and others			████	████		
Form change agent, sponsor, and advocate teams			████	████		
Provide training for targets (those affected by the change)				████		
Implement organizational alignment enablers				████		
Analyze effectiveness of communications and training strategies				████		
Monitor commitment levels of sponsors, change agents, advocates, and targets				████		
Monitor and measure implementation effectiveness and schedule adherence					████	
Modify transition management plans as needed to ensure effectiveness					████	
Track and report planned versus actual activities and results					████	
Identify opportunities for continuous improvement of the change process						████

It is evident from this chart that a number of change management activities are iterative and not confined to the QMS phase.

FIGURE 2-11. Typical Change Management Plan for ISO 9000

FIGURE 2-12. To win the game today, you need to get the most out of every player on the board

Additional Ammunition

Beckhard, Richard, and Wendy Pritchard. *Changing the Essence: The Art of Creating and Leading Fundamental Change in Organizations* (San Francisco: Jossey-Bass, 1992)

Bouldin, Barbara M. *Agents of Change: Managing the Introduction of Automated Tools* (New York: Yourdon Press, 1988)

Conner, Daryl R. *Leading at the Edge of Chaos: How to Create the Nimble Organization* (New York: John Wiley & Sons Inc., 1998)

Conner, Daryl R. *Managing at the Speed of Change: How Resilient Managers Succeed and Prosper Where Others Fail* (New York: Villard Books, 1993)

Conner, Daryl R., H. James Harrington, and Richard Horney. *Project Change Management: Applying Change Management to Improvement Projects* (New York: McGraw-Hill, 1999)

Harrington, H. James, and James S. Harrington. *Total Improvement Management: The Next Generation in Performance Improvement* (New York: McGraw-Hill, 1995)

Huse, Edgar F., and Thomas G. Cummings. *Organization Development and Change.* 3rd edition (St. Paul, MN: West Publishing Company, 1985)

Hutton, David W. *The Change Agent's Handbook: A Survival Guide for Quality Improvement Champions* (Milwaukee, WI: ASQ Quality Press, 1994)

Kanter, Rosabeth Moss. *Rosabeth Moss Kanter on the Frontiers of Management* (Cambridge, MA: Harvard Business School Press, 1997)

Smith, Douglas K. *Taking Charge of Change: 10 Principles for Managing People and Performance* (Reading, MA: Addison-Wesley Publishing Co., 1996)

WOW WEAPON: PERFORMANCE STANDARDS (PS)

Definition: Defines the acceptable error level of each individual in the organization.
Classification: Basic Battle Plan
Users: Groups, Teams, and Individuals

Just the Facts

One of management's major jobs is to set the performance standards for the organization. In the 1980s, a new, "error-free" performance standard gained favor throughout the world. AOQs (Average Outgoing Quality) and AOQLs (Average Outgoing Quality Limit) lost favor and began to be viewed as a way of allowing shabby products to reach the customer. One supplier, when delivering an order for 1,000 parts at an AOQL of 2%, sent two boxes, one containing 980 parts marked "to specification," and another containing 20 parts marked "not manufactured to specification." The two boxes were accompanied by a note saying, "We had to readjust our equipment specifically to make the 20 bad parts, and would you mind if the next time we sent all good parts? It will cost less."

The concept of 95%, 99%, or even 99.9% being good enough is being discarded around the world. Just take a look at what it would mean if we were right only 99.9% of the time:

▶ At least 10,000 incorrect drug prescriptions each year
▶ 50 newborn babies dropped at birth by doctors or nurses each day
▶ 43 minutes of unsafe drinking water each month
▶ No electricity, water, or heat for 8.6 hours each year
▶ No telephone service or television transmission for nearly 10 minutes each week
▶ 2 short or long landings at O'Hare Airport each day (also at John F. Kennedy, LA International, Atlanta Hartsfield, and so on)
▶ Nearly 500 incorrect surgical operations per week
▶ 2,000 lost articles of mail per hour
▶ 22,000 checks deducted from the wrong account each hour
▶ Your heart fails to beat 32,000 times each year

There is no problem so small that you cannot lose a customer over it, so how can any manager tell his or her employees how many errors are acceptable? Could you possibly tell your son or daughter that it is all right to drive through the back wall of the garage once every 1,000 times he or she borrows the car? Motorola uses a six sigma program to set acceptable performance standards. The company is trying to reduce errors to 3.4 errors per million units of output. But is that good enough? The answer is no. Consider the truck driver who has 10,000 opportunities for a head-on collision every day. Certainly six sigma is not an acceptable performance standard in that case. What we need is a performance standard that communicates to our employees that they should continuously strive to improve until they have eliminated errors. We suggest that the only acceptable performance standard is error-free optimum performance.

Let's dissect this statement. The term "error" was used in place of "defect," because everyone makes errors, while only the production floor makes defects. The performance standard must apply to everyone. The word "optimum" was chosen because in most decision-making situations, there are a number of options available, all of which will provide error-free performance, but only one will provide the best results. "Optimum" indicates that the activity is only correct when the very best alternative is selected.

Everyone is an error-free performer today. What differs between individuals and processes is the length of time between errors. In one individual circumstance, a person/process combination could average one error every two hours. Is that good enough? Using the error-free optimum performance standard, the answer is obviously no. So, if he or she sets an improvement goal of a certain duration between errors of two days and succeeds at meeting this goal, is that good enough? No. After reaching that goal, he or she needs to set another goal. For example, it could be to extend the duration between errors to seven days, then to two weeks, then to two months, etc.

Even that is not good enough today. Doing things right every time is high-quality performance, but to be world-class you need to go beyond that. You need to do the right thing right every time. Error-free optimum performance is selecting the best option every time and then executing it as effectively as it can be done. You are not performing error-free if you do a perfect job in ten hours and someone else can do the same job perfectly in three hours.

Everyone needs to strive to be better, and we will never reach a good enough performance level until every decision is perfect all the time. To excel is to fulfill a basic human need.

Some of the major advantages of using an error-free optimum performance standard are:

- ▶ It applies to everyone from the boardroom to the boiler room.
- ▶ It adjusts to the complexity of the individual assignment.
- ▶ It can be measured by the individual.
- ▶ It focuses on performance, not just quality.
- ▶ It is easy for everyone to understand.
- ▶ It supports the continuous improvement concept.

Examples

To explain the error-free optimum performance standard concept to a group, we like to conduct this simple experiment.

1. The instructor asks the participants to write their names in the air using their index fingers. They should write their first name, middle initial, and last name. When they complete the assignment, they should raise their hand.
2. The instructor says, "Go" and times the group to see how long it takes. For example, a typical cycle time would be 22 seconds.
3. The instructor then samples the class, asking, "Were you able to do the assignment error-free?" Of course, all the participants should have been able to write their names without making an error.
4. The instructor then goes on to explain: "Sure, everyone did it error-free because management provided them with the four T's that must be provided to all employees in order for them to do error-free work:

   ▶ T1: Technology—The process was well-defined and communicated before the group was required to perform the task.

   ▶ T2: Training—The participants were well-trained in how to write their names prior to being required to perform the task. Just think back to when you were 3 years old and you wrote the letters in your name backwards and you often spelled it incorrectly.

   ▶ T3: Tools—Everybody had an index finger and all the air they wanted for writing. Many of the participants used more than three feet to write their names. If the standard set by management were two inches, everyone would have failed.

   ▶ T4: Time—Everyone had all the time they needed to write their name. If the standard were eight seconds, everyone would have failed because no one had a hand up at eight seconds. Management needs to provide adequate time for all employees to do their job.

"There is a fifth T required to do error-free work—a 'team' to support each individual, but that could not be demonstrated in this particular experiment.

"Now what you have done is performed error-free for 22 seconds. The challenge to the group is to go back and work in their offices for 22 minutes, error free. When they are able to work error-free for 22 minutes, they should get up, go out and find a friend, and have that friend pat them on the back. Then, they should turn around and go back to work with the objective to work for 22 hours, error-free.

"Everyone is an error-free worker. We just have different lengths of error-free performance. What we want to do is continuously extend the period between errors from 22 seconds to 22 minutes to 22 hours to 22 days to 22 weeks to 22 months and so forth. Each time we meet a personal performance objective, we've reached the point where a new target should be defined."

Additional Ammunition

Harrington, H. James. *The Improvement Process: How America's Leading Companies Improve Quality* (New York: McGraw-Hill, 1987)

Harrington, H. James, and James S. Harrington. *Total Improvement Management: The Next Generation in Performance Improvement* (New York: McGraw-Hill, 1995)

Harrington, H. James, Glen D. Hoffherr, and Robert P. Reid. *Area Activity Analysis: Aligning Work Activities and Measurements to Enhance Business Performance* (New York: McGraw-Hill, 1998)

WOW WEAPON: SHEWHART CYCLE (PLAN-DO-CHECK-ACT)

Definition: A structured approach for the improvement of services, products, and/or processes.
Classification: Basic Battle Plan
Users: Groups, Teams, and Individuals

Just the Facts

The Plan-Do-Check-Act (P-D-C-A) Cycle is a very simple approach to project management that can be used effectively on non-complex programs and for implementing corrective action. Often incorrectly called "The Deming Cycle," it was actually designed by Walter A. Shewhart and was first published in his book, *Statistical Method from the Viewpoint of Quality Control.*

Although Deming always referred to this activity as the "Shewhart Cycle," the Japanese called it the "Deming Cycle." This was because it was Deming who introduced this process to Japan in 1950. Deming stated:

The Shewhart Cycle was on the blackboard for top management for every conference beginning in 1950 in Japan. I taught it to engineers—hundreds of them—that first hot summer. More the next summer, six months later, and more six months from that. And the year after that, again and again.

We can safely say that, while Shewhart invented the weapon, Deming became its salesman.

Most people today associate the P-D-C-A activity with four key steps shown in Figure 2-13.

Actually there are five steps required to complete the cycle. Let's take a look at all five. The first part of each step comes from Shewhart's book.

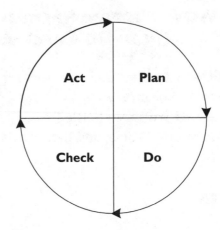

FIGURE **2-13. The Shewhart Cycle**

Step 1. Plan: *What could be the most important accomplishments of this team? What changes might be desirable? What data are available? Are new observations needed? If yes, plan a change or test. Decide how to use the observations.*

Begin by studying an organization's current situation. Before any improvement plans are made, ensure that the current best known methods are documented and standardized. It is imperative to start from a stable base so the effectiveness of actions can be evaluated later.

Next, gather data to identify and define the problem(s) and to help formulate a plan. Only then can planning be initiated for the desired accomplishments over a given period of time and for systematically measuring the effect of the planned actions. The plan should include specific actions, changes, or tests that are the outgrowth of a systematic study of the probable causes of the problem(s) or effect(s) in question, using statistical methods and problem-solving tools.

Step 2. Do: *Carry out the change or test decided upon, preferably on a small scale. (Also, search for all available data, which may assist in answering the questions in Step 1.)*

Implement the plan. If possible, try it out on a small scale first. Insist that all relevant changes be recorded during implementation and any changes from the planned measures be documented. Ensure that data are collected systematically and in a way that facilitates evaluation (e.g., use checksheets).

Step 3. Check: *Observe the effects of the change or test.*

Evaluate the data collected during implementation to see if the desired objectives were met. Check the results to see if there is a good fit between the original goals and what was actually achieved.

Step 4. Act: *Study the results. What did we learn? (Also, what can we predict?)*

Depending on the results of the previous evaluation, take further actions. If successful, adopt the changes. That is, institutionalize the changes made by documenting the new procedures, communicating them to all personnel in the process, and training people to the new standards. The new methods, procedures, and specifications then can be replicated in all areas with similar processes.

If unsuccessful, abandon the changes.

Step 5. *With the knowledge accumulated, repeat Steps 1 through 4.*

To Summarize

Organizational improvement will last only if it is a continuous process. Standards and processes, both manufacturing and business, must be constantly reviewed, improved or reengineered, measured, and monitored. Continuously passing them through Shewhart's P-D-C-A Cycle is an effective way of driving the continuous improvement process.

Example

The Shewhart Cycle has been used in many ways. The environmental group that designed ISO 14001 built it around the Shewhart Cycle (see Figure 2-14.).

While the original Shewhart Cycle begins with the planning phase, the ISO 14001 pattern begins by setting directions to the organizations,

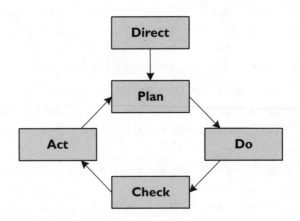

FIGURE **2-14. ISO 140001 Pattern**

then progresses through the rest of the P-C-D-A Cycle. The following is a list of all the ISO 14001 clauses that apply to each of the five categories.

Direct
4.1.0 General
4.2.0 Environmental Policy

Plan
4.3.0 Planning
4.3.1 Environmental Aspects
4.3.2 Legal and Other Requirements
4.4.3 Objectives and Targets
4.3.4 Environmental Management Programs

Do
4.4.0 Implementation and Operation
4.4.1 Structure and Responsibility
4.4.2 Training, Awareness, and Competence
4.4.3 Communication
4.4.4 Environmental Management System Documentation
4.4.5 Document Control
4.4.6 Operational Control
4.4.7 Emergency Preparedness and Response

Check

4.5.0 Checking and Corrective Action

4.5.1 Monitoring and Measurement

4.5.2 Nonconformance and Corrective and Preventive Action

4.5.3 Records

4.5.4 Environmental Management System Audit

Act

4.6.0 Management Review

Additional Ammunition

The Ernst & Young Quality Improvement Consulting Group. *Total Quality: An Executive's Guide for the 1990s* (Homewood, IL: Dow Jones-Irwin, 1990)

Ishikawa, Kaoru. *Guide to Quality Control* (Milwaukee, WI: ASQ Quality Press, 1986)

Larson, Carl E., and Frank M.J. LaFasto. *Teamwork: What Must Go Right, What Can Go Wrong* (Newbury Park, CA: Sage Publications, 1989)

Lynch, Robert F., and Werner, Thomas J. *Continuous Improvement Teams and Tools: A Guide for Action* (Milwaukee, WI: ASQC Quality Press, 1991)

Scherkenbach, William W. *Deming's Road to Continual Improvement* (Knoxville, TN: SPC Press, Inc. 1991)

Shewhart, Walter A. *Statistical Method from the Viewpoint of Quality Control* (Washington, D.C.:Graduate School, Department of Agriculture, 1939; New York: Dover, 1986), p. 45

Walton, Mary. *The Deming Management Method* (New York: Putnam, Perigee Books, 1986)

WOW WEAPON: SIX-STEP PROBLEM-SOLVING CYCLE

Definition: A basic procedure for understanding a problem, correcting the problem, and analyzing the results.
Classification: Basic Battle Plan
Users: Groups, Teams, and Individuals

Just the Facts

You can improve your creativity by learning about and using tools that help you see and understand the world from new perspectives.

The most basic problem-solving approach is the ShewhartCycle—Plan-Do-Check-Act. The Six-Step Problem-Solving Cycle is the next simplest approach. As its name indicates, it consists of six steps:

> ► Step 1. Identify and classify the problems
> ► Step 2. Define the problem
> ► Step 3. Investigate the problem
> ► Step 4. Analyze the problem
> ► Step 5. Solve the problem
> ► Step 6. Confirm the results

Step 1. Identify and Classify the Problem

Before any issue can be addressed, it must be brought into the open. An issue may be brought to the team's attention by the manager or team members, who can be asked to make known the problems they perceive to be present. Either of these methods can present a significant problem for solution, and both can stimulate active team participation. It is often very beneficial, if not necessary, for the team to work together to determine which problems are most urgent and thus should be addressed first.

One further point will assist you in problem identification: knowing the differences among problems, causes, and solutions. Effective, creative solutions are much more likely if those differences are understood. Precise language helps us focus on an issue, as the following illustrates.

A team has been asked to identify some problems to address:

First Person: "I would say that our main problem is the lack of another service representative."

Second Person: "The number of people requiring our help is the major problem. There are just too many people for us to handle."

Third Person: "I think that the problem is our not getting back to people who call us. We are trying, but the response time is not good."

These people all seem to be talking about the same thing. However, a careful look at the statements will indicate that only one person has actually identified a problem.

The first suggestion, "lack of another service representative," is a solution posing as a problem. This person has not stated what the problems are or what may be causing them, but thinks that an added representative will solve the problem. To start by suggesting a solution is to skip most of the problem-solving process.

The second contribution is a cause instead of a problem. The number of people seeking help is not a problem, but it may well be causing problems for the team. This cause could be having an effect on the service given to customers; it should be remembered when causes are discussed.

We are then left with the third offering: delayed response to calls. This is a problem affecting the quality of service provided. The person who identified it may have some ideas as to causes for the delays, and even some notion of potential solutions. The time will come for these ideas to be expressed.

The first thing that needs to happen is the identification of the problems that concern the manager and other members of the team.

Classifying Problems

There is a system of categorizing problems to help clarify which problems are best for a team to tackle. Here are the three general classes.

Type I: The problem can be identified, analyzed, and solved without involving outside people. These are the easiest problems to solve because they relate directly to the work the team does, involve no one else, and do not require fund allocations for solution. The team has or can get all of the necessary data and has the authority to act.

The group has complete control of the problem and

- ▶ can identify and define the problem
- ▶ has control of data collection, including specialists' inputs
- ▶ has expertise to analyze the problem and find solutions
- ▶ has authority to implement solutions

Type II: The team may have to go outside its own area to get information and may have to get authorization to implement a solution. Type II problems usually require a presentation to higher management or authorization from another manager before the solutions can be implemented. They are larger problems, with more complicated and thorough analysis required.

The group has limited control of the problem, but

- ▶ can identify and define the problem
- ▶ has control of data collection, including specialists' inputs
- ▶ may lack experience to analyze the problem or find solutions
- ▶ may lack authority to implement solutions
- ▶ can reach and influence the ultimate decision maker

Type III: The team either does not have access to all of the relevant information on the problem or does not have access to the authority to implement the solution. Typically, Type III problems are outside the scope of the team and may have an impact on the entire organization. These problems should be passed on to the person or team that can solve them.

The group has no control of the problem, but

- ▶ can identify and define the problem
- ▶ may be able to collect data
- ▶ lacks expertise to analyze the problem and find solutions
- ▶ lacks authority to implement solutions
- ▶ cannot reach or influence the ultimate decision maker

If the members of the team and all others in the organization understand the differences among these three classes of problems, the likelihood of team success will be greatly enhanced.

Step 2. Define the Problem

The issue being addressed must be clearly understood by the entire team. The statement of the problem should be as specific as possible; vague definitions result in wandering discussions. The specifics of the situation as it exists must be identified. This may require some effort to collect data on the status of the problem. Initial statements of broad problems may have to be broken down into smaller issues for a focused effort toward solution. A clear definition and current data can also assist in prioritizing problems for consideration.

Step 3. Investigate the Problem

Some preliminary investigation may already have taken place in your efforts to define the problem. What is required here is an in-depth investigation that will provide objective and accurate data. (It should be noted that such data might already be available.) There is need for clarity on what the situation is, if the efforts to determine why it is a problem and what might be done to improve it are to be successful.

Step 4. Analyze the Problem

This step focuses on determining the causes of the problem being addressed. Several of the cause-analysis techniques will assist this effort. Once all possible causes have been identified, there is need to separate real causes from apparent ones and then determine which of the true causes are of major significance.

Step 5. Solve the Problem

When the principal causes have been identified, the team decides how best to eliminate them. Alternative solutions will be considered and every effort will be made to reach consensus. Agreement on the solution and the plan for implementing it will make ownership on the part of each member of the team possible.

Step 6. Confirm the Results

The effectiveness of the solution implemented must be measured and confirmed. Is the problem solved? Does more need to be done? If success is achieved, who should be informed?

The six steps of the problem-solving cycle are not always clearly distinguishable. For example, can one investigate without some analysis? Yet, the process indicated here can serve as a general strategy to help us stay on track. Specifically, it can prevent us from seeking solutions prematurely.

Steps and Appropriate Techniques

The use of the problem-solving techniques will vary according to the nature and scope of the problem to be solved. What follows is a list of those techniques that can assist you at each step of the problem-solving process.

Steps 1 and 2: Identify and Define the Problem

- ▶ Brainstorming
- ▶ Pareto Principle

Steps 3 and 4: Investigate and Analyze the Problem

- ▶ Brainstorming
- ▶ Cause-and-Effect Diagrams
- ▶ Force-Field Analysis
- ▶ Checksheets, Graphs, Histograms

Step 5: Solve the Problem

- ► Brainstorming
- ► Solution-Analysis Diagram
- ► Force-Field Analysis
- ► Nominal Group Technique
- ► Graphs, Management Presentations

Step 6: Confirm the Results

- ► Pareto Diagrams, Graphs, Histograms

Combining the techniques with a systematic approach to problem solving will enhance your efforts to achieve consensus and truly effective solutions to problems. Participation in a proven method of problem solving will usually lead to ownership of changes designed to improve the way team members do their jobs.

Examples

Let's look at a very simplified example that takes us through each step of this six-step process. We will use the problem we identified in Step 1.

Step 1. Identify the Problem

A group in customer service goes to their manager and states, "Our main problem is the lack of another service representative."

One of the first steps the manager will take is to decide if he or she can solve this alone or if a team should be considered. Also, what type of problem is this—Type I, II, or III?

The manager decides on the team approach. The team determines that this is at least a Type II problem, and possibly a Type I. This is an issue the department will try to correct itself.

Step 2. Define the Problem

We already know that "lack of" statements are not very good problem statements. The only possible solution to this type of statement is to correct the "lack of" issue. In the case of this example, the solution would be to hire another customer service representative. But would this necessarily solve the issue? Probably not. Let's try to better define the problem.

"The number of people requiring our help is the major problem. There are just too many people for us to handle."

Obviously a better statement, but we are not quite there yet. We must think, "What is the real issue here?" Our third response gets us really close to the correct problem issue.

"I think that the problem is our not getting back to people who call us. We are trying, but the response time is not good."

Now our task is to take this problem issue and turn it into a problem statement that the team can understand and fix. The final problem statement that the team actually works on might look like this:

"Our office is not responding to customer calls in a timely manner, resulting in reduction of our quality service."

Now the team has a problem statement that can be solved. Let's move on to Step 3.

Step 3. Investigate the Problem

A good tool to start with in investigating the problem is brainstorming. The people who work in this customer service department will have many different ideas about why their office is unable to respond to customer calls in a timely manner. They might also interview key customers to get their opinions. The key here is to better understand the issue and gather information as to what may be causing the problem.

Let's assume our investigative tactics produced the following possible causes after brainstorming and narrowing:

- ▶ Not enough service reps
- ▶ Not enough incoming phone lines

- ► Improper training
- ► No training
- ► Too many customers
- ► Too many complaints
- ► Not enough hours in the day
- ► Poor response time
- ► Using part-time reps
- ► Computer program outdated
- ► Incorrect information given out
- ► Can't hire good people
- ► Supervision is poor
- ► Management doesn't care

If the team feels this investigation is adequate, it can then move to the next step.

Step 4. Analyze the Problem

There are many ways to conduct cause analysis, but one of the most useful is to use a fishbone diagram. Let's take the information from our brainstorming and narrowing session and put it in diagram form (Figure 2-15).

You may note that after proper review our team has identified three key causes for the effect:

- ► Using part-time customer service representatives
- ► Improper training of customer service representatives
- ► Poor or inadequate supervision

Upon further review the team decided that in order to maintain this as a Type I problem (one the team could fix with little outside assistance) it would not attempt to resolve the "Poor or inadequate supervision." That issue would be passed to the customer service management team for review and resolution.

Our team's focus will be on a new problem statement—"The use of part-time customer service representatives and overall customer service training."

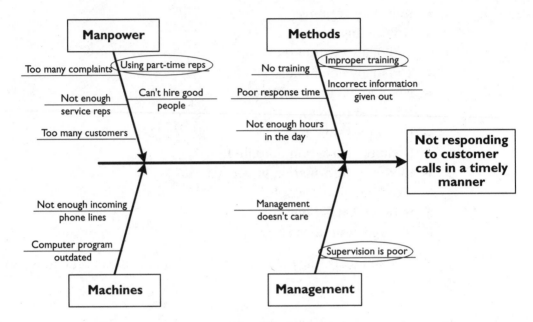

FIGURE 2-15. Example of fishbone diagram

Step 5. Solve the Problem

Now that the principal two causes have been identified, the team will look at a number of different ways to correct them. Remember: we really don't solve problems—we eliminate the things that cause the problem.

To keep our example simple, let's assume that, after proper analysis and research, the team has made the following recommendation: *Place 50% of the current part-time customer sales representatives on full-time status and provide them with the full customer service training program. For all remaining part-time customer service representatives, provide an additional four hours of training in the computer software and how to handle difficult complaints.*

For our simple problem there was a simple solution. This is not always the case, but it happens more often than not. We tend to make the problems more complex than they need to be.

Now, how do we know we actually solved the problem?

Step 6. Confirm the Results

One activity the team must design into its process is measurement. Obviously one key measure is "Are we now responding to more customer issues than we were before?" Another measure might be "Is the number of customer complaints about our customer service decreasing?"

The key here is to confirm that we are actually doing what we set out to accomplish. If yes, our solution was correct. If no, we have to go back to the problem-solving process and look at our causes or proposed solution.

As you can see, if we had attempted to solve the first suggested problem, "Our main problem is the lack of another customer service representative," we would have missed the key issues. If problem solving is approached as a process, the effort becomes much more efficient and effective.

Additional Ammunition

Cartin, Thomas J. *Principles and Practices of TQM* (Milwaukee, WI: ASQ Quality Press 1993)

Ernst & Young LLP. *Tools and Techniques Resource Guide* (Cleveland, OH: The Quality and Productivity Group, 1992)

Ernst & Young Quality Improvement Consulting Group. *Systematic Participative Management: Team Member Manual* (San Jose, CA: Ernst & Young LLP, 1991)

Harrington, H. James. *The Improvement Process: How America's Leading Companies Improve Quality* (New York: McGraw-Hill 1987)

Lynch, Robert F., and Thomas J. Werner. *Continuous Improvement Teams and Tools: A Guide for Action* (Milwaukee, WI: ASQ Quality Press, 1991)

WOW Weapon: Six-Step Solution-Identification Cycle

Definition: A procedure for defining how to solve a problem or take advantage of an opportunity.
Classification: Basic Battle Plan
Users: Groups, Teams, or Individuals

Just the Facts

For some teams, identifying the problem is relatively simple—or at least they say it is. However, you will almost never hear a team say, "We had no trouble identifying a solution." This is because there is rarely only one solution to any properly identified problem.

If problem solving dictates a designated process, then it stands to reason that identifying a solution will also require a designated process. Listed below are six solution-identification steps you may find useful.

Step 1. Brainstorm

As a team, brainstorm all possible solutions. Follow good brainstorming guidelines and do not allow for discussion during this activity.

Step 2. Add Creatively

After the initial brainstorming exercise, take the time to add creatively to the list of solution ideas. Try to come up with analogies. Think about "What if anything is possible?" and you have all the resources necessary for the "perfect" solution.

Step 3. Narrow

Using a narrowing technique (the Delphi Narrowing Technique works well here) with clear criteria, narrow the list to three or four potentially workable solutions.

Step 4. Make Initial Selection

Using a decision matrix, make a tentative decision on one solution to go forward with. The decision matrix should be designed with realistic criteria.

Step 5. Test

Test or verify the selected solution using a solution-analysis diagram. Often a "test pilot" is desirable prior to taking the solution organization-wide. Evaluate the solution against the desired future state and/or any targets management may have established.

Step 6. Validate

One of the problems with identifying the "right" solution is we forget that there may be more than one. Any solution should be monitored closely with a measurement process that will quickly catch planning or implementation errors.

Following these six steps won't guarantee a perfect solution, but it will get you much closer than solution intuition. Listed below are several examples of idea-generating questions to ask when trying to develop innovative solutions.

Idea-Generating Questions for Solutions

How else could this be done?

Can we: Use a different approach? Another process? A new system? Another mode? Some other device or tool?

Example: Handwriting analysis instead of "personality tests." Closing surgical incisions with staples. Statistical analysis/manage by facts instead of intuition.

Where else could we use this approach?

Could we: Use it in another place? Use it under different circumstances?

Example: Worms to process garbage and sewage? How about aluminum as house siding? Could we use it in other divisions/departments?

Is there an existing approach we can adapt to this situation?

Can we borrow a solution from another problem to fit this one?

Example: Laser device for detecting objects ahead fitted into a cane for the blind. The idea for the stapler came from the riveter.

Does expanding or enlarging add value?

Can we: Use more? Design a larger size? Exaggerate the idea? Make it stronger, more concentrated, heavier? Allow more time? Increase the speed? Do it more often? Multiply it? Use several? Do two or more at once?

Examples:
Make larger: giant plastic sausages have been used as barges.
Exaggerate: rubber swimming fins are used to "enlarge" our feet.
Multiply: condominiums, cluster packaging, triple-decker sandwiches, planes with four engines.

Does reducing, condensing, or separating really add value?

Can we: Compress? Use less, a smaller size? Miniaturize? Split up? Do it in installments? Divide into sections? Make lighter? Thin out? Have fewer steps? Have fewer parts? Do less often? Slow the action?

Examples:
Compress: car pool, sofa bed
Reduce size: microprocessor, compact cars, miniature collectibles
Less time: microwave ovens, rapid transit

Can we add something to change the result?

Can we: Add another function, another procedure, another component, another ingredient, an additional dimension, a new feature? Include other attachments? Add spare parts?

Examples: Electronic filters added to heating and air-conditioning systems purify air. Low-level electric stimulation fuses broken bones that won't mend.

Can we remove something to change the result?

Can we: Omit a step, a function, a procedure, a component? Leave out an ingredient? Remove non-essentials?

Examples: Tubeless tires eliminated inner tubes. Living hinges eliminated hinge pins.

Can we substitute something to change the result?

Can we: Use a different ingredient, a different material, other tools, other equipment? Have some one else do it? Do it in some other place?

Example: Saccharin for sugar, umbilical cords as grafts for arteries, "voiceprints" instead of fingerprints.

What happens if we modify it?

Can we: Change the shape, form, dimension, proportions, density, weight, color, texture, motion, procedure?

Examples: Adhesive on 3M's Post-It notes, speed limit change, adding color to create traffic lights, adding sound/color to movies.

Will rearranging change the result?

Can we: Change sequence? Switch places? Change positions? Regroup? Change locations? Revise the schedule?

Examples: Daylight saving time, separate parking areas for smaller vehicles, moving holidays to combine with the weekend, flextime for workers, four-day work week, ten-hour work day.

Will reversing change the result?

Can we: Go backwards? Turn it upside down, inside out? Flip-flop? Reverse the order, direction, approach?

Examples: Front-wheel drive, test before teaching, office at home.

Will combining change the result?

Can we: Do two steps in one? Add two or more functions? Do a joint effort? Pack or bundle items together? Form clusters? Make an assortment, a blend, an alloy?

Examples: Four-color pens, watches with built-in calculators, pens that also are pointers, computers with built-in fax, CD, etc.

Implementing the Solution

Designing the Activity Plan

Whew! Now that we have finished our team task and have identified the perfect solution, our job is done, right? Wrong! Very often the team assigned to take an issue from problem identification to a workable solution will also be assigned the task of developing a plan to implement the solution. This is a most critical part of the problem-solving process and requires the synergy of the entire team.

The activity plan (see Figure 2-16) is a simple chart that lists implementation activities in sequence. It identifies the individual responsible for a particular activity and the projected timing of that activity. The activity plan chart should be as simple as possible. Detail is not necessary. You can back up the chart with a written document that explains the necessary detail.

One of the key initial activities in the action plan is to identify "key stakeholders" or individuals who have a stake in the overall success or failure of the process. Identifying the stakeholders and developing a stakeholder analysis plan (see Figure 2-17) will enhance the overall opportunity for ultimate plan success.

Completing the plan is much easier than it looks. The most important part is to take the time to identify all the key players. The five basic steps are listed below:

No.	Activity	Time Required	Person(s) Responsible
1	Assign responsibility	6/1-6/1	Dorothy P.
2	Identify key stakeholders	6/1-6/2	John J.
3	Stakeholder analysis	6/2-6/3	John J./Team
4	Commitment action plan	6/3-6/5	John/Team
5	Measurement plan	6/5-6/7	John/Team
6			
7			
8			
9			

FIGURE 2-16. Example of an implementation plan

Name	Negative	Nothing	Let	Help	Make	Comments

FIGURE 2-17. Stakeholder analysis plan example

1. Identify all the key individuals or stakeholders whose commitment and support are critical to successful implementation. List

them in the "Name" column.

2. Determine the level of involvement, support, or commitment needed from each. Place a "0" in the appropriate column.

3. Identify the current status of key individuals or stakeholders. Are they trying to make it happen, help it happen, let it happen? Are they doing nothing? Are they negative to the implementation idea? Place an "X" in the appropriate column.

4. Now draw an arrow from the "X" to the "0."

5. In the "Comments" column, note possible actions that may be taken to get the stakeholder on board with the solution or out of the way.

Figure 2-18 shows the completed stakeholder analysis plan.

You may note that in this example some individuals need to be moved from feeling negative about the issue to helping with the implementation or even making the implementation a reality.

Name	Negative	Nothing	Let	Help	Make	Comments
Bob Jones		X ——————→			O	Need plan to bring Bob on board with the solution
Terrie Smith			O ◄— X			No action needed
Allie Dixon				X —►O		No action needed
Daryl Axon	X ———————————→			O		Need plan to bring Daryl on board with the plan and help buy in
Earl Chang			O ◄— X			No action needed
Darla White		O ◄————————————			X	Need to convince Darla that she doesn't need to be a part of the plan
Jack Erickson		X ————→		O		Need plan to bring Jack on board with the solution
Vicki Terrile			X ————————→		O	Need plan to bring Vicki on board with the solution

FIGURE 2-18. Example of a completed stakeholder analysis plan

Also, there are normally individuals who may feel they have a stake or role in the implementation when they really don't. While you do not want to do anything to alienate these individuals (you may need their assistance some time in the future), you need to create a plan to move them out of the picture.

If an individual needs to be moved only one block, either way, it is not normally necessary to create a plan for that person. However, for the rest of the folks, you will need to create a "commitment action plan" that takes them from where they are to where you need them to be.

This plan should be very detailed and could include things such as making a presentation to them on the proposed solution or making them a part of the implementation plan, team, etc.

Additional elements of the implementation plan should include appropriate detail, particularly when talking about cost, resources, and measurements.

Examples

 The examples are included in the text.

Additional Ammunition

Lomax, Kenneth. *The Six-Step Solution Cycle* (Abilene, TX: Lomax Consulting Group, 1996)

WOW WEAPON: VISIONING

Definition: A vision describes the desired future state of an organization, process, team, or activity.
Classification: Basic Battle Plan
Users: Organizations, Groups, or Teams

Just the Facts

Father Theodore Hesburgh, former president of Notre Dame University, stated:

"The very essence of leadership is that you have to have a vision. It's got to be a vision that you articulate clearly and forcefully on every occasion. You cannot blow an uncertain trumpet."

Today, almost every manager in the world has had the advantages of having vision statements explained to him or her at least once. As a result, most organizations have developed vision statements that define how the organization will look when it "grows up." Vision statements for organizations are usually prepared by top management and are directed at what the organization's output will look like and/or how it will be used 10 to 30 years in the future.

The vision statement can be as simple as "An affordable, easy-to-use personal computer on everyone's desk" or "News available immediately from anyplace in the world." But typically, organizational vision statements have taken on a completely different form. Too often, the organizational vision statement requires that the organization become the biggest, most profitable, best quality, most advanced, with the highest level of customer satisfaction of any organization in the industry.

What these statements do not do is require that the transformation to meet the vision ever take place. Grandiose vision statements like these, although inspirational, set the organization up for failure and provide little guidance for management or the employees. It is difficult to stay the best. For example, of the top 100 companies in *Fortune* magazine's 1956 top companies list, only 29 remain in the top 1000 companies today.

We believe that all vision statements should paint a picture of how the organization will look at some specific point in time. What a vision statement should do is provide the organization with insight and guidance that will help lead the organization from its current, as-is state to an improved future state.

When you consider developing a time-directed vision statement, there are four factors that need to be considered (see Figure 2-19):

1. By what time should the organization develop to the point that it is in compliance with its vision statement?
2. How will the organization change under its normal momentum (normal future state)?
3. What is the ideal future state?
4. What is the best-value future state that would be realistic, based upon outside pressures and internal constraints?

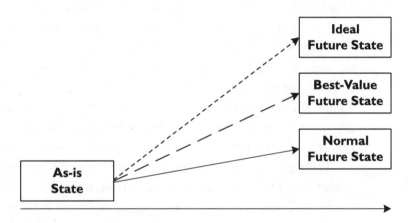

FIGURE 2-19. The four key considerations in developing a vision statement

We believe that best-value future state solutions are the best way to go. They set challenging, but not unrealistic expectations for your stakeholders.

"Can you tell me what I must do to achieve my goal?" asked Page.
"It depends on what your goal is," replied Princess."I don't know," Page said, "And I don't care what it is."
"Then it matters little what it is you do," Princess said.
—LEWIS CARROLL, FROM *ALICE IN WONDERLAND*

A grand overall vision statement is less useful and less effective in bringing about change than a more specific group of vision statements.

We like to develop a series of vision statements that defines how the organization wants to change its internal environment to meet its business objectives. Here are several examples of typical performance drivers that are good focus points for developing vision statements:

- ▶ Leadership and support
- ▶ Customer partnerships
- ▶ Measurement system

Employees, management, and customers feel much more comfortable with and committed to a group of performance-driver vision statements that relate to the way they behave and the situation that they are encountering every day, than with one grand, overall vision statement. If the organization has just one vision statement, it often is so large in scope that most employees do not relate to it and/or feel that it is unrealistic. What needs to be done is to prepare a group of vision statements that can support the overall corporate or organizational vision statement by defining the way the internal performance drivers will change over the next five years (see Figure 2-20).

Typically, the performance-driver vision statements paint a picture of the best-value future state three to five years in advance. They represent a commitment from management to provide the resources required making the transformation from the as-is state to the best-value future state. In all cases, management should involve the appro-

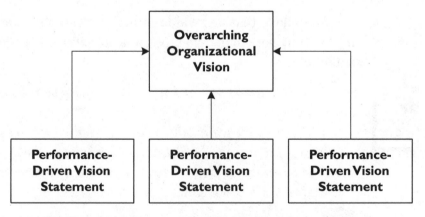

FIGURE 2-20. Typical performance-driver vision statement

priate affected stakeholders in creating the vision statements so that all stakeholders support and agree with the final vision statement.

Once the organization has painted its performance-driver landscape, it can then start its improvement processes. Starting any trip prior to defining a destination may provide the illusion of movement, but it results in a great deal of wasted effort and often leads to failure. It has been estimated that TQM initiatives fail from 40% to 90% of the time. You can argue over the exact percentage, but even if it's 5%, it is too much. We personally believe the reason most TQM initiatives fail is because management did not paint a picture of the best-value future state and communicate it to the organization before the organization started to select the TQM improvement tools.

Figure 2-21 shows the correct process flow in creating an organizational vision.

Prior to developing the vision, the organization should take some action to identify "where it is" in relation with "where it wants to be." In other words, to move forward to the future state, we must first identify the present state.

The first step in taking a trip is not in knowing where you are going—it's in knowing where you are starting. Conducting an organizational assessment will assist you in this. If your organization is new to continuous improvement, you will also want to have the management team trained in basic change management principles.

The next thing the executive team needs to do is define what type of business the organization will be in 10 to 30 years. To accomplish

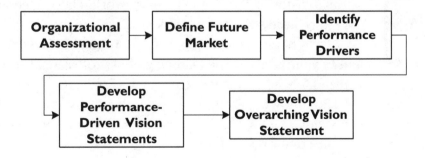

FIGURE 2-21. Vision statement processflow

this, the executive team reviews the mission statement and projects how the market will change over time. Here's a quick example. For a quality consulting firm in the 1970s, team and SPC consulting was the "in thing." In the 1990s, Business Process Improvement (process reengineering, redesign, and benchmarking) was the "in thing." In the 2000s, performance improvement and reliability may drive the market. The very best team-training consulting firm will not grow if the market is not there to support it.

Once management understands the organization's future market, it's time to identify the performance drivers that will form the focus for individual vision statements. The management team should brainstorm ideas about major performance-driven categories. A simple cause-and-effect diagram (shown in Figure 2-22) will help accomplish this. After brainstorming, the group should evaluate all ideas and consolidate its thinking to no more than six to 10 categories. These performance drivers will be the basis for developing vision statements.

Once each of these performance drivers has generated a vision statement, the management team can start developing the overarching organizational vision statement. Remember: all the performance-driven vision statements must align and support the overarching statement. They must never be in conflict, but only in support.

Examples

Sprint's vision statement: "To be a world-class telecommunications company—the standard by which others are measured."

A very personal example, Ernst & Young LLP's "Global Vision/2000 and Beyond": "To be the leading global professional services firm recognized for delivering value to clients."

The following are typical examples of five-year performance-driven vision statements for Management Support and Leadership from five different organizations we have worked with.

1. Leadership exists at all levels, creating an open and trusting environment. Decisions are made by the people responsible for

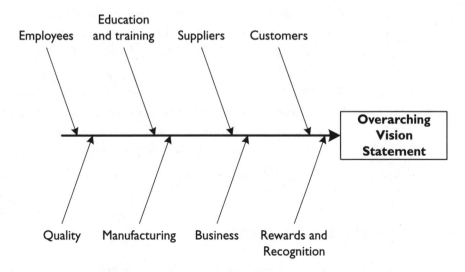

FIGURE 2-22. Cause-and-effect diagram

getting the job done. Performance and continuous improvements are recognized and rewarded.

2. Managers are leaders who inspire confidence through communication of a clear understanding of the company's goals and objectives and empower all employees to be leaders in accomplishing the desired result.

Leaders lead by example. They facilitate, motivate, coach, and mentor, providing the tools.

3. Management fosters an environment of open communication where opinions and suggestions are encouraged and valued; visions, plans, and priorities are shared throughout the organization.

Management provides the necessary time, tools, and training for employees which enable everyone to contribute their personal best towards the mission of the organization.

Teamwork is stressed; decision making is accomplished at the lowest appropriate level. Bi-directional feedback occurs on an ongoing basis to measure results and provide input for a continuous improvement process.

4. Management provides leadership to foster individual and team participation. Managers facilitate and support continuous improvement of the organization by providing training, resources, information, review, and recognition.

5. All managers provide groups and individuals with conditions that allow them to achieve continuous improvement and self-achievement. Recognition and rewards clearly flow to those who are using the improvement process. Decisions are made at the lowest level possible.

Additional Ammunition

Harrington, H. James, and James S. Harrington. *Total Improvement Management: The Next Generation in Performance Improvement* (New York: McGraw-Hill, 1996)

Lewis, C. Patrick. *Building a Shared Vision: A Leader's Guide to Aligning the Organization* (Portland, OR: Productivity Press, 1996)

Lomax, Kenneth. *Vision and Long-Range Strategic Planning* (Abilene, TX: Lomax Consulting Group, 1998)

Thompson, John L. *Lead with Vision: Manage the Strategic Challenge* (Milwaukee, WI: ASQ Quality Press, 1997)

Visions that are communicated to everyone get everyone fighting the same battle.

CHAPTER | **3**

Basic Data-Analysis Weapons

There can be a big difference between data and facts. All facts are data, but all data are not facts. When you are provided with inputs, be sure you know if these inputs are information data or factual data.

Chapter Preview

Dd

This is a sample of the text for the definition, or these are more synonyms and usages that are commonly found in the English language.

Fact—Something that actually exists, reality, truth. A truth known by actual experience or observation; something known to be the truth.

Information—Knowledge gained through study, communication, research, instruction, etc.

Knowledge—Acquaintance or familiarity gained by sight, experience, or report. The perception of fact or truth. (It may or may not be fact.)

You can improve your creativity by learning about and using tools that help you see and understand the world from new perspectives.

We are all bombarded with mountains of data every day. We are drowning in it. There is so much data available that there is no way that we can review the onslaught of information that comes at us every day. Even if we read, surf the Internet, attend conferences, and watch television 24 hours a day, we will have just scratched the surface of the data that are available.

In addition, we need to have time to analyze the data, to separate fact from fiction, and to determine how we are going to use inputs. It is a waste of time and effort to collect data that are not used. Some people collect information for the self-satisfaction of being knowledgeable. This is great if you're going to earn your living as a game show contestant. For those of us in business, we need to be selective about the information that we spend our valuable time understanding.

In addition, we need to have ways that will take individual pieces of information that are available to us and organize them so that we obtain a total understanding of the entity rather than just a microscopic view of the situation. For example, if you look at one donut and it doesn't have a hole in its center, then the only logical conclusion is that donuts do not have holes in them. But when you sample all the trays of donuts in the bakery, you discover that it is only the filled donuts that do not have holes in them. As obvious as this example is, many executives are making very important business decisions based upon a small sample taken from a non-random part of the total population that does not truly represent the situation.

In this chapter, we will provide you with a number of ways designed to help you look at information to determine if it is factual data and gain a better understanding of what it means in a minimum amount of time. This chapter also provides weapons that minimize the risk related to drawing the wrong conclusion from your analysis of the data.

The data analysis weapons presented in this chapter range all the way from the very simple to the very complex. The book contains eight of the data-analysis weapons and the CD-ROM contains 20. The data-analysis weapons will be presented in the following order:

Chapter 3—Basic Data-Analysis Weapons

- ▶ Checksheets
- ▶ Graphs
- ▶ Histograms
- ▶ Pareto Diagrams
- ▶ Root Cause Analysis
- ▶ Run Charts

▶ Scatter Diagrams
▶ Standard Deviation

CD-ROM, Section D—Specialized Data-Analysis Weapons

▶ Comparative Analysis
▶ Failure Mode and Effect Analysis (FMEA)
▶ Flowcharts
▶ Function Diagrams

▶ Interrelationship Diagrams
▶ Interviewing Techniques
▶ Matrix Data Analysis
▶ Process Decision Program Charts
▶ Spider Diagrams/Radar Charts
▶ Stratification
▶ Surveys
▶ Tree Diagrams
▶ Value-Added Analysis (VA)

CD-ROM, Section E—Mass Destruction Data-Analysis Weapons

▶ Attributes Control Charts
▶ Design of Experiments
▶ Process Capability Studies

▶ Statistical Process Control (SPC)
▶ Variables Control Charts

CD-ROM, Section F—Strategic Data-Analysis Weapons

▶ Poor-Quality Costs (PQC)
▶ Simulation Modeling

Summary

We will present 28 data-analysis weapons—only a small portion of those WOW weapons available. It is important to remember that you should be collecting data and analyzing data for a specific purpose. Too many organizations ask themselves, "We have all these data. How are we going to analyze and use these data?" That is the wrong approach. Always define how you want to use the data first, then you can define what data should be collected and how the data should be analyzed.

Your data-collection and data-analysis systems should be based upon your measurement system. In truth, measurements are one of the most important weapons that we have against waste. Because of the importance of this WOW weapon, we have dedicated Part VIII to the subject of measurements.

Remember the old saying, "What gets measured gets done."

Introduction

This chapter presents WOW weapons used to organize data so that they are simpler to analyze and use. These weapons are easy to use and should be well understood and used by all the employees. The only mathematics required to use them is arithmetic. Training in these WOW weapons should be part of basic training for everyone.

The WOW weapons that are presented in this chapter are:

Dd

This is a sample of the text for the definition, or these are more synonyms and usages that are commonly found in the English language.

- ▶ **Checksheets** Simple forms on which data are recorded in a uniform manner. The forms are used to minimize the risk of errors and to facilitate the organized collection and analysis of data.

- ▶ **Graphs** Visual displays of quantitative data. They visually summarize a set of numbers or statistics.

- ▶ **Histograms** A visual representation of the spread or distribution. It is represented by a series of rectangles ("bars") of equal sizes or widths. The height of the bars indicates the relative number of data points in each class.

- ▶ **Pareto Diagrams** A type of chart in which the bars are arranged in descending order from the left to the right. It is a way to highlight "the vital few" in contrast to "the trivial many."

- ▶ **Root Cause Analysis** The process of identifying the various causes affecting particular problems, processes, or issues and determining the real reasons that caused the condition.

- ▶ **Run Charts** A graphic display of data used to assess the stability of a process over time or over a sequence of events (such as the number of batches produced). The run chart is the simplest form of control chart.

- ▶ **Scatter Diagrams** A graphic tool used to study the relationship between two variables. The scatter diagram is used to test for possible cause-and-effect relationships. It does not prove that one variable causes the other, but it does show whether a relationship exists and reveals the character of that relationship.

▶ **Standard Deviation** An estimate of the spread (dispersion) of the total population based upon a sample of the population. The Greek letter Sigma (σ) is used to designate the estimated standard deviation.

WOW WEAPON: CHECKSHEETS

Definition: Checksheets, sometimes called data tables, are basic but important tools for collecting and organizing facts and data. They are the foundation on which all of the more advanced data analysis techniques are built.
Classification: Basic Data-Analysis Weapon
Users: Groups, Teams, and Individuals

Just the Facts

A key to successful problem solving is the use of facts and data rather than opinion and guesswork. By collecting data, individuals and teams can identify problems more accurately and can effectively analyze causes and effects, thereby making better decisions, solving problems faster, and gaining management support for those solutions.

Data are objective information; that is, information on which everyone can agree. An objective measurement of a piece of string could use a ruler as a tool to determine its length. If all their rulers are alike, the people measuring the string should have no difficulty agreeing on its length.

Types of Data

There are three primary types of data: counted, measured, and location data.

Counted data (sometimes called attributes data) are noted as simply being present or absent. Counted data generally answer the questions "How many?" or "How often?" Examples include:

▶ How many of the final products are defective?
▶ How often are the machines repaired?
▶ How many people are absent each day?
▶ How many days did it rain last month?

Measured data (sometimes called variables data) answer questions such as "How long?" and "What volume?" and "How much time?" and "How far?" The key is that each datum is measured in some way by an instrument or device. Examples include:

▶ How long is each rod?
▶ How long does it take to complete this task?
▶ What is the weight of this material?
▶ What is the pH of this solution?

Measured data are generally regarded as being more useful than counted data, as they are more precise and carry more information. For example, you would probably have more useful information about the climate of an area if you knew how much it rained there each day rather than just how many days it rained. However, collecting measured data is frequently more time-consuming and expensive, so it is important to be very clear about the purpose of the data to be collected, to choose the right type of data, and to provide the right checksheet with which to collect and organize it.

Location data, the third type covered here, answer the simple question "Where?" Examples include:

▶ Where are accidents occurring?
▶ What parts of the body are being injured?
▶ On what part of the product are defects occurring?

Types, Construction, and Uses of Checksheets

Two primary types of checksheets will be described here, *recording checksheets* for collecting counted or measured data, and *location checksheets* for collecting location data. A brief description of the third type, *checklist checksheets*, which serve as memory aids to ensure that all necessary tasks are accomplished, will conclude this chapter.

In preparing to construct a checksheet, begin by considering the type of data to be collected. What data will best meet your needs—counted, measured, or location? How much data do you need to collect? How long do you need to collect data in order to learn what you need to know from the data? Do you need to record who collected the data? Where it came from? When it was collected? What about attributes, such as size or color? What about variables, such as weight, length, and time period? When you have considered these questions, you are ready to design and construct the checksheet best suited to your data-collection needs.

Recording Checksheets

Let's begin our look at some examples with a simple recording checksheet for counted (attributes) data about the frequency of defects on a production line (Figure 3-1).

Problem	Place a mark each time it occurs
Missing Component	〃 〃 ///
Wrong Component	〃 〃 /
Scratches	〃 〃 〃 〃 〃 //
Chips	〃 ////
Failed Test	〃 /

FIGURE 3-1. A recording checksheet—counted data

Notice that the addition of data regarding defects by shift (Figure 3-2) provides even more useful information.

Adding data regarding defects by day of the week (Figure 3-3) sheds even more light on possible causes deserving further investigation.

Defect	Shift 1	Shift 2	Total
Missing Component	卌	卌 ///	卌 卌 ///
Wrong Component	卌 卌	/	卌卌 /
Scratches	卌 卌 卌	卌 卌 //	卌 卌 卌 卌 卌 //
Chips	卌	////	卌 ////
Failed Test	卌 /		卌 /

FIGURE 3-2. A recording checksheet—counted data by shift

Defects	Shift 1					Shift 2				
	M	T	W	T	F	M	T	W	T	F
Missing Component	//	//	/	//	卌/	///	//	/		//
Wrong Component	///	//		/	///	/				
Scratches	////	///	///	//	///	///	//	/	//	///
Chips	//		/		//	/		/		//
Failed Test	//	/		/	//					

FIGURE 3-3. A recording checksheet—counted data by shift and day of week

When using a recording checksheet to document measured data, choose the data carefully and be sure to provide sufficient room to enter the data. An example of a measured data recording checksheet is shown in Figure 3-4.

Solution X Test Results	8:00	9:00	10:00	11:00	12:00	1:00	2:00	3:00	4:00	5:00
High pH	4.6	4.9	5.1	5.2	4.4	4.7	4.9	5.0	5.4	5.5
Low pH	3.9	4.0	4.1	4.4	3.9	3.9	4.0	4.1	4.1	4.1
Salinity	27.0	27.0	26.5	27.0	27.7	27.9	27.2	27.0	26.8	27.1
Specific Gravity	46	52	56	59	45	49	53	60	62	67
Density	12%	14%	14%	15%	14%	15%	16%	15%	15%	16%

FIGURE 3-4. A recording checksheet—measured data

Location Checksheets

The second type of checksheet is the *location checksheet*, used to depict the location of problems or defects. These checksheets are pictures, illustrations, or maps on which the data are entered, rather than data tables. Entering data in this way often simplifies the collection process and helps us visualize the problem more clearly. Here are some examples of location checksheets:

Defects on a part are checked off on a picture of that part, so that corrective or preventive action can be taken (Figure 3-5).

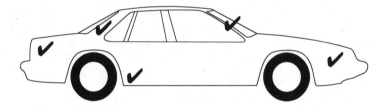

FIGURE 3-5. Defect location checksheet

Injury location checksheets are often posted so that employees can see where injuries are likely to occur or what protective equipment is necessary (Figure 3-6).

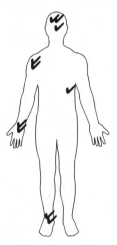

FIGURE 3-6. Injury location checksheet

Accident location checksheets can help in the analysis of risk areas or accident causes. Employees might then help make an area safer (Figure 3-7).

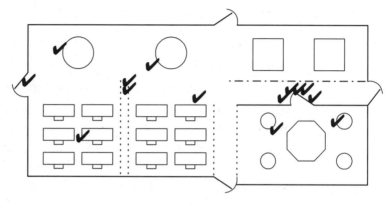

FIGURE 3-7. Accident location checksheet

Checklist Checksheets

The third type of checksheet is the *checklist checksheet*. When we have a number of tasks to do, complex tasks or critical tasks that must be done just right, we sometimes start by making a list. We can use the list as a memory aid and then also check off each task as it is completed so we can be sure that nothing has been missed.

Excellent examples of checklists for critical tasks are those used by pilots or astronauts before takeoff. At home, grocery lists are more common examples of checklists. On the job, checklists can be very useful for inspecting machinery or merchandise or when setting up complex or delicate equipment. Supervisors frequently use checklists to be sure they have checked the entire area. Workers can just as easily design their own checklists to ensure thorough operations or inspections.

Checksheet Preparation: A Checklist

Now that you have studied some of the types and uses of checksheets, you are ready to prepare your own checksheet. To help you get started, you can use this checklist of points to consider:

- ❏ Are the data historical or new?
- ❏ How much data will be involved? A hundred points? A thousand? A million?
- ❏ What checksheet format should be used: recording, location, or checklist?
- ❏ Will an existing form do the job?
- ❏ Who will be responsible for coordinating the data collection?
- ❏ How can the tabulation best be done to avoid error?
- ❏ If the tabulation is interrupted, can it be restarted without errors?
- ❏ Is there an advantage to having several operators tabulate for short time, as opposed to one operator for a long time?
- ❏ What labels will be needed on the checksheet?
- ❏ Should copies be distributed? To whom?
- ❏ Is any training required?

Examples

The examples are included in the text.

Additional Ammunition

Harrington, H. James. *The Improvement Process: How America's Leading Companies Improve Quality* (New York: McGraw-Hill, 1987)

Harrington, Hurd & Rieker, Inc. *Systematic Participative Management: Team Member Manual* (Los Gatos, CA: Harrington, Hurd & Rieker, 1986)

Lynch, Robert F., and Thomas J. Werner. *Continuous Improvement Teams and Tools: A Guide for Action* (Milwaukee, WI: ASQ Quality Press, 1992)

WOW WEAPON: GRAPHS (CHARTS)

Definition: Visual displays of quantitative data. They visually summarize a set of numbers or statistics.
Classification: Basic Data-Analysis Weapon
Users: Groups, Teams, or Individuals

Just the Facts

Graphs (the term "charts" is often used interchangeably) should present data as simply and clearly as possible. The comprehension and interpretation that graphs normally enhance are not ends in themselves. Grasping the data is one aspect; our reaction to how the data are presented is another. Graphs tell us what is, and they may point out significant problems, causes of problems, or areas of potential difficulty. But graphs remain, finally, tools to assist us in making decisions based on their data.

Uses for Graphs

Graphs are most often used to show trends, comparisons, progress, and controls. The following are typical applications:

- ▶ Rate of change in temperature, pressure, size, volume, weight, and other measurements
- ▶ Quality performance trends
- ▶ Process, procedure, operating efficiency
- ▶ Distinguishing major and minor factors for setting priorities (Pareto diagrams)
- ▶ Distribution of variations in measurements of the same thing (histograms)
- ▶ Cost trends
- ▶ Records of attendance, turnover, training, safety, etc.

There are many graphic ways to display facts and statistical data. The type of data and the ideas to be presented determine the most suitable method. Line graphs, bar and column graphs, area graphs, milestone/planning graphs, and pictorial graphs will all prove to be valuable tools.

Value of Well-Prepared Graphs

The more significant values of well-prepared graphs are listed below:

- ▶ In comparison with other types of presentations, properly designed graphs are more effective in creating interest and in attracting the attention of the reader.
- ▶ Visual relationships, as portrayed by charts and graphs, are clearly grasped and easily remembered.
- ▶ The use of graphs and charts saves time, since the essential meaning of large masses of statistical data can be understood at a glance.
- ▶ Graphs and charts provide a comprehensive picture of a problem that makes possible a more thorough and better understanding than could be derived from tabular or textual forms of presentation.
- ▶ Graphs and charts bring out hidden facts and relationships, and can stimulate and aid analytical thinking and investigation.

Characteristics of Graphs

A well-made graph has these characteristics:

- ▶ summarizes data
- ▶ guides problem solving
- ▶ demonstrates a point
- ▶ does not mislead
- ▶ is visually interesting

These characteristics are ensured if the graph is not cluttered with too much information. The point must be clearly perceived.

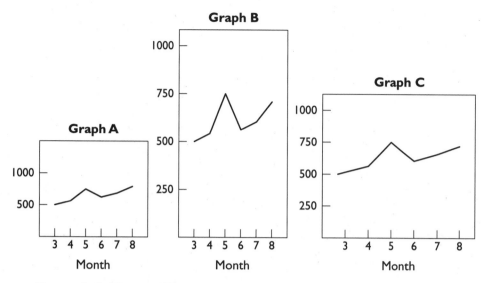

FIGURE **3-8. Three different graphs showing the same data**

One necessity for ease of interpretation is a legend. The legend records what the graph covers, when and where the data were obtained, and who collected the data. It also explains any special symbols used. These factors are relatively straightforward, requiring no more than accurately transcribing correct data onto the graph.

The choice of numerical increments for the graph may require careful thinking. Different numerical increments will create different impressions, and these can lead to misinterpretation of the data. Figure 3-8 shows three graphs displaying the same data on three different scales. It is clear that a particular choice of scale can distort and thus misrepresent the data.

It should also be noted that, for the sake of clarity, fractional increments should be avoided whenever possible. It is easier to read and interpret 2-4-6-8 than 2.5-5-7.5-9.

Use of Multiple Graphs

In analyzing problems and certainly in presenting details about problems and possible solutions, a combination of graphs is normally used. For example, data obtained from research into the major causes of a

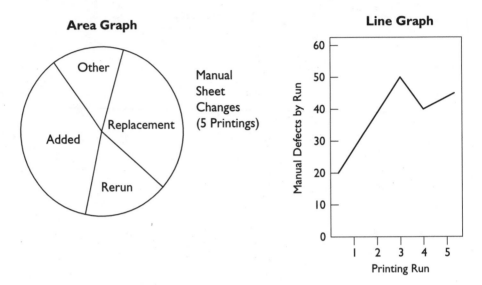

FIGURE **3-9. Different types of graphs**

single problem can result in a cause-and-effect diagram, a Pareto diagram, and the checksheet used to gather the data. Two Pareto diagrams can be used to show dollar cost comparisons and also to show the frequency of occurrences. A line graph can be made to depict different aspects of the same problem or summarize some of the changes occurring over a period of time. The point is that a number and variety of graphs and charts are frequently used to clarify the data when analyzing a problem or determining and presenting its solution. Different aspects of the same problem are shown in the two types of graphs in Figure 3-9.

Comprehension and interpretation of many facts, especially statistical data, are often best attained by analyzing graphs. Our own experience tells us that lengthy tabulations of data are the most difficult to understand. Summaries of tabulations are a step toward easier comprehension, but graphic presentation does the most to simplify interpretation. In fact, numbers and data are often meaningless without graphic forms to depict them. It is best summarized by the age-old axiom, "A picture is worth a thousand words" or, to paraphrase, "worth a listing of a thousand figures."

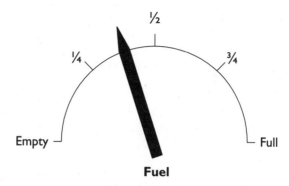

Fuel

FIGURE 3-10. One-dimensional graph

A graph that shows a single set of numbers is termed "one-dimensional." This is a common graph, one that we view each time we look at the fuel gauge in our cars (Figure 3-10) or the temperature gauge on a machine.

Our interest is in multi-dimensional graphs. These allow us to depict the relationship between two or more sets of data. In almost all of the graphs to be explained here, the starting point of the graphic representation is the construction of the X and Y axes.

X-Y Axes Graphs

An X-Y axes graph is a pictorial presentation of data on sets of horizontal and vertical lines, called a grid. The data are plotted on the horizontal and vertical lines, which have been assigned specific numerical values corresponding to the data.

X axis is the name given to the *horizontal* line in a two-dimensional graph. The *vertical* line is called the Y axis (Figure 3-11).

The point where the two lines meet is called the zero point, point of origin, or simply origin. When numbers are used, their value is increased along both axes as they move away from the origin.

The X axis (horizontal) is most frequently used to record the *time-frame* or *cause* of data being plotted. Because of the fixed nature of the time frame or cause, this is also termed the *independent variable*.

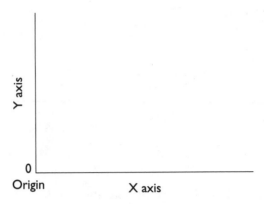

FIGURE 3-11. Axes of graphs

The *effect* of the cause or the effect over a period of time is almost always plotted on the Y axis (vertical). This is termed the *dependent variable,* as the values vary in relationship to the independent variable or the X axis (Figure 3-12).

If two variables depend on each other or if both are affected by some other factor, they can be arbitrarily placed on either axis.

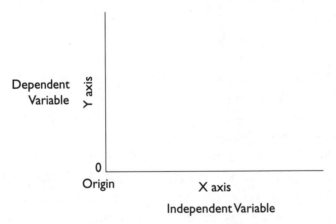

FIGURE 3-12. Dependent and independent variable axes

Types of Multi-Dimensional Graphs

Line Graphs

The simplest graph to prepare and use is the line graph. It shows the relationship of one measurement to another over a period of time. Often this graph is continually created as measurement occurs. This procedure may allow the line graph to serve as a basis for projecting future relationships of the variables being measured (Figure 3-13).

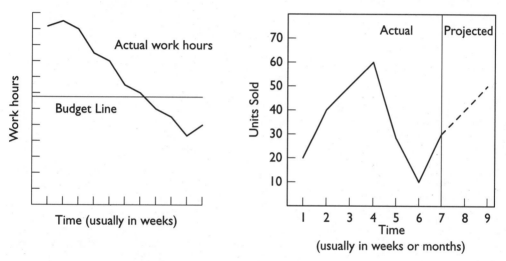

FIGURE 3-13. Basic line graphs

Multiple-line Graphs

Multiple-line graphs are prepared to show on the same axes the relationships of more than two sets of measurements (Figure 3-14).

Area Graphs

Area graphs are convenient methods of showing how 100% of something is apportioned (Figure 3-15). The most commonly used area graph is the pie chart.

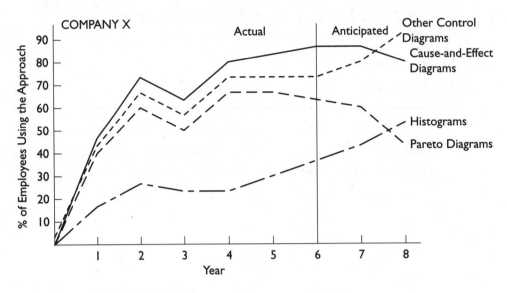

FIGURE **3-14. Multiple-line graph**

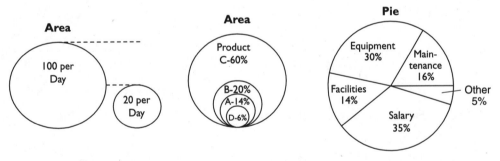

FIGURE **3-15. Area graphs**

Bar and Column Graphs

Bar graphs have bands positioned horizontally (bars) or vertically (columns) which, by their length or height, show variations in the magnitude of several measurements. The bars and columns may be multiple to show two or more related measurements in several situations.

Bar graphs have the bars originating from the Y-axis. As a consequence, the normal location of dependent and independent variables is reversed (Figure 3-16).

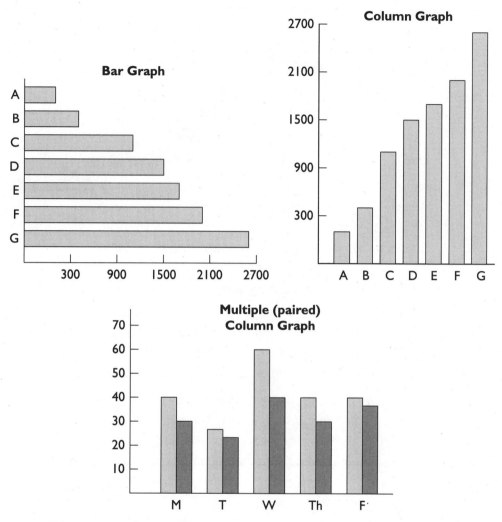

FIGURE 3-16. Bar graphs

Milestone or Planning Graphs

A milestone or planning graph shows the goals or target to be achieved by depicting the projected schedule of the process. A primary purpose is to help organize projects and to coordinate activities (Figure 3-17).

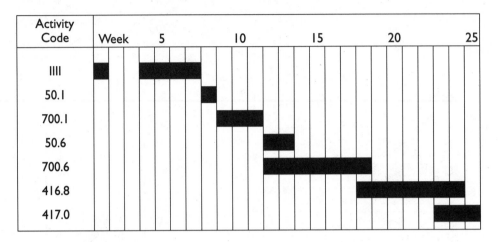

FIGURE 3-17. Milestone or planning graph

Pictorial Graphs and Pictograms

Pictorial graphs use pictures or drawings to represent data. Pictograms are a type of pictorial graph in which a symbol is used to represent a specific quantity of the item being plotted. The pictogram is constructed and used like bar and column graphs (Figure 3-18).

Many of the graphs represented in the previous figures are what we call "X-Y graphs," because they have an X axis and a Y axis. Although that's rather elementary, many of us have forgotten the basics when creating these graphs. Let's do a brief refresher.

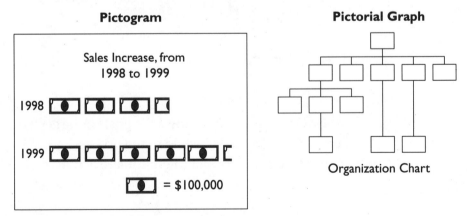

FIGURE 3-18. Pictograms and pictorial graphs

Creating an X-Y Axes Graph

The creation of an X-Y axes graph is easy if the following process is used.

1. Collect and List Data

No graph is possible without the collection of accurate data. Precise data demand that uniform types of data be gathered in uniform time periods. When these are listed on some form of worksheet (data-analysis table, as in Figure 3-19), it is best to arrange the data in sequence from smallest to largest or, in terms of time, from earliest to latest. The information is thus organized to facilitate transfer onto the graph.

X Days	Y Units
1	12
2	9
3	8
4	11
5	10
6	11
7	7
8	6
9	11
10	14
11	12
12	10

Data collection days are independent variable on X axis. Units sold per day are dependent variable on the Y axis.

FIGURE 3-19. Data-analysis table

2. Convert and Round Off Data

Raw data come in a variety of forms. One source may list a fraction (2 1/2 hours), while another may use decimals (2.5 hours). A uniform system of measurement is necessary. Some data may have to be converted to achieve that uniformity.

When numerical data appear in decimal form, you need use only the level of accuracy necessary to make your point clear. Usually hundredths and thousandths can be rounded to tenths; sometimes tenths can be rounded to whole numbers.

Note: *How to Round Numbers*

Certain circumstances will demand an accuracy that requires a more systematic process of rounding. There are several methods available. The most common follows this rule:

1.1, 1.2, 1.3, and 1.4 round down to 1

1.5, 1.6, 1.7, 1.8, and 1.9 round up to 2

This method results in a number rounding down four times out of the nine (.1, .2, .3, and .4) and up five times (.5, .6, .7, .8, and .9), thus introducing a statistical bias.

A preferred rule eliminates this bias by rounding .5 down half the time and up half the time. When an odd number precedes the .5, it rounds upward; when an even number precedes the .5, it rounds downward:

0.5 rounds down to 0

1.5 rounds up to 2

2.5 rounds down to 2

3.5 rounds up to 4

Since the number preceding the .5 has an equal chance of being odd or even, no statistical bias is introduced. This method can be used in rounding decimals of any length. For example, 8.075 becomes 8.08 and 14.3945 becomes 14.394.

3. Select and Scale the Grid

The next step is to determine the range of your data range for both axes. Examine the listed data, appropriately converted and/or rounded. You will easily see the time span or number of causes, and the smallest and largest numbers. You are now able to determine the major divisions necessary for a graph that will demonstrate your data clearly (Figure 3-20).

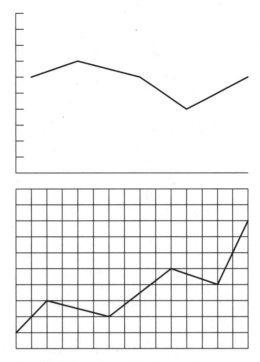

Fɪɢᴜʀᴇ 3-20. Types of grids

Then you need to choose the type of graph that will be most appropriate for your data. Will a line graph or column graph best show the data and your intent in using this information? Do the data require single or multiple lines or columns?

A question of basic format must also be answered. Will your completed graph show a two-dimensional grid or will the line or columns appear on a blank background within the X-Y axes?

A two-dimensional grid is made by drawing perpendicular lines from the X and Y axes to create a series of squares or rectangles. These lines are called divisions or scale lines. The lines must be uniformly scaled on an axis, but the mathematical progression need not be the same on both axes. If the data require, accent lines can be added. For example, the X axis may have a series of divisions marking months, with bolder accent lines indicating years.

The choice between grid or blank background may be determined by which of the two formats makes the data easier to read and under-

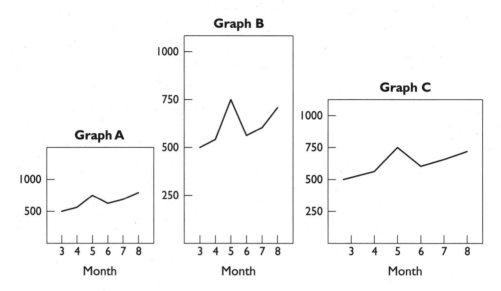

FIGURE 3-21. Production charts—each of these charts shows the same data

stand. Sometimes the choice may be just a matter of preference. Ultimately, clarity is the key concern.

Scaling

Scaling the grid is important because you want to avoid visual distortion of the data's message, as we mentioned in our opening comments about graphs (Figure 3-21).

The distortions in Figure 3-21 are clear; unfortunately, there is no firm rule to follow to avoid such misrepresentation. The general practice is to place the lowest point on the Y axis within the bottom 20% of the graph and the highest point within the top 20%. A further aid to accurate representation is to use a square or rectangular proportion for the graph. The ratio between the sides should not exceed 7 to 10, that is, neither side should be less than 70% or more than 140% of the length of the other side.

Multiple Scales

More than one scale will be needed on either the X or the Y axis when you plot on the same graph multiple sets of data that use different

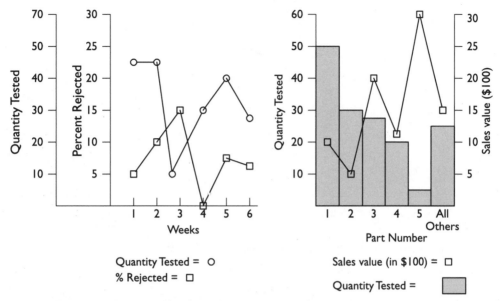

FIGURE 3-22. Multiple scales on a graph

units of measurement. Place the additional scales on either the same side or opposite sides of the graph, drawing an additional vertical line when necessary.

Multiple scales will always be used in creating a Pareto diagram, one for the percentage increments and the other to show frequency or cost. Other uses of multiple scales include such information as dollar sales and unit codes, or days, weeks, and months (Figure 3-22).

Break in the Axis

Sometimes it is necessary to highlight small changes in data of large magnitude. These changes can be accented by interrupting the axis and showing only the top portion of the data on a more refined scale.

It should be remembered that such a break distorts the amount of change because the graph will not give a true picture of the relation of the emphasized data to the base. It is best to extend the break across the entire graph, to make it easy to see (Figure 3-23).

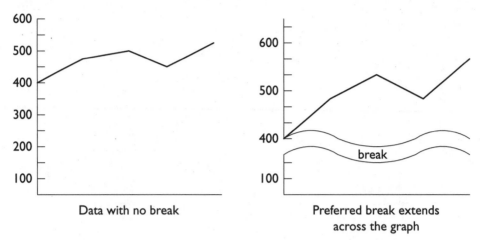

Data with no break

Preferred break extends
across the graph

FIGURE **3-23. Typical use of a break in the axis of a graph**

4. Label Axes and Title Graph

Every graph should have a full title. The title can be placed at the top or bottom of the graph, or it may be boxed within the graph. A title is easier to read if it is parallel to the X axis.

Each axis should be clearly labeled with its numerical values or categories and with appropriate descriptions. Horizontal labels are easiest to read, but vertical or even top-to-bottom labels are acceptable.

A graph should also contain a legend indicating the source of data, who collected the data, and the dates the data were gathered.

5. Plot, Connect, and Identify Data Points

Now that you have the framework to display your data, you are ready to plot those data on the graph. Each data point is plotted at its X and Y coordinates. It is always wise to double-check your points with the data to make sure there are no plotting errors. Keep in mind that when the X axis represents time, your data point is to be located in line with the mark or number that represents the end of the time period (Figure 3-24).

The process of connecting the plotted points will obviously vary according to whether you are making a line graph or a bar graph. In

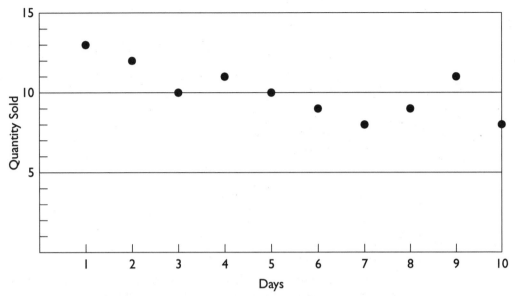

FIGURE 3-24. Typical points on a graph

the latter case, you construct the horizontal or vertical bars by drawing horizontal and vertical lines to depict the proper height and width.

On a line graph, data points are usually connected by drawing straight lines between the points. One may also use a "French curve."

French curve—A flat drafting instrument, usually made of plastic or celluloid, with curved edges and scroll-shaped cutouts, used as a guide in connecting a set of individual points with a smooth curved line. (Note: A line connecting plotted points is referred to as a curve even if it is a straight line. See Figure 3-25.)

Note: Normally, either the straight line or the French curve is used on a single graph, not both.

If more than one line is to be drawn on a graph, you can avoid confusion by plotting and connecting all the points of one line before moving along to the next. It is necessary that different forms of lines be used in this case. For example:

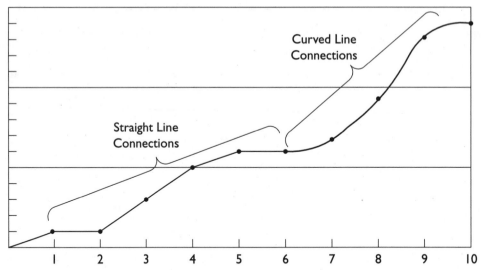

Data points may be connnected with straight lines or a French curve. (Normally, either the straight line or the French curve approach is used on a single graph.)

FIGURE 3-25. **Line graph**

Primary Data ——————

Secondary Data ------------------

Tertiary Data ----------------

If more than three sets of data are presented, use combinations of these three types or clearly darker or lighter versions of them. For example, instead of one solid line (as used for the primary data), use a double solid line. The same applies for dotted and dashed lines.

In all cases where data are represented by a graph, the graph should have a legend that clearly identifies the types of data represented.

Identifying the value of each plotted point can often be a means of making a graph easier to read. When this is done, the value should be written in a place where it does not interfere with the line.

On occasion you may want to show the range of the data that occurred in a period prior to that which the graph depicts. To do so, use a vertical bar inside the Y axis and label it.

There are a number of ways to smooth out a graph. One of the most frequently used methods is a three-period average. In this

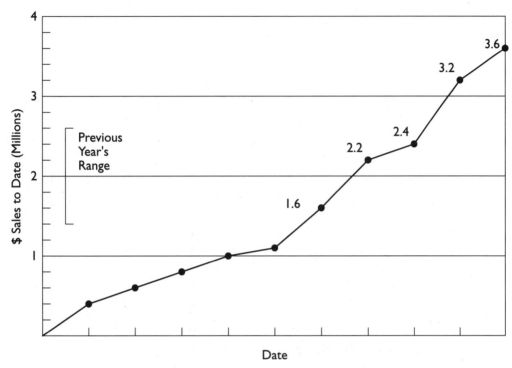

FIGURE 3-26. Connecting data points on a graph

approach, three points are added together and divided by three to get the plot point. The rolling three-point average is plotted on the graph (Figure 3-27).

Another approach is plotting a best-fit cover between the points on the graph (Figure 3-28).

Sometimes bar graphs and line graphs are plotted together. The Pareto diagram uses this approach (Figure 3-29).

Examples

No examples are shown here because 22 examples were included in the text. You will also find many examples of graphs throughout this book.

**Addi-
tional**

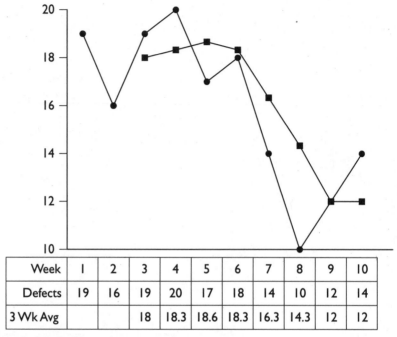

Week	1	2	3	4	5	6	7	8	9	10
Defects	19	16	19	20	17	18	14	10	12	14
3 Wk Avg			18	18.3	18.6	18.3	16.3	14.3	12	12

FIGURE 3-27. Rolling three-week average

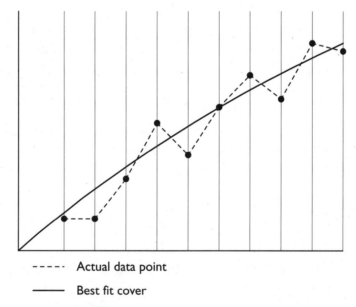

- - - - - Actual data point

——— Best fit cover

FIGURE 3-28. Best fit cover

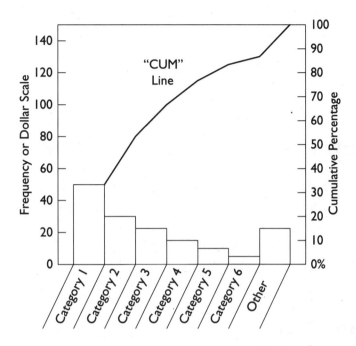

FIGURE 3-29. Pareto diagram

Ammunition

Brassard, Michael. *The Memory Jogger Plus* (Milwaukee, WI: ASQC Quality Press, 1989)

Cleveland, William S. *The Elements of Graphing Data* (Monterey, CA: Wadsworth Advanced Books and Software, 1985)

Harrington, H. James. *The Improvement Process: How America's Leading Companies Improve Quality* (New York: McGraw-Hill, 1987)

Ishikawa, Kaoru. *Guide to Quality Control* (Milwaukee, WI: ASQ Quality Press, 1986)

Lynch, Robert F., and Thomas J. Werner. *Continuous Improvement Teams and Tools: A Guide for Action* (Milwaukee, WI: ASQ Quality Press, 1991)

Tague, Nancy R. *The Quality Toolbox* (Milwaukee, WI: ASQC Quality Press, 1995)

Tufte, Edward R. *The Visual Display of Quantitative Information* (Cheshire, CT: Graphics Press, 1983)

Zelazny, Gene. *Say It With Charts*, 3rd edition (New York: McGraw-Hill, 1998)

WOW Weapon: Histograms (Frequency Distribution)

Definition: A visual representation of a spread or distribution, using a series of rectangles or bars of equal sizes or widths. The height of the bars indicates the relative number of data points in each class.
Classification: Basic Data-Analysis Weapon
Users: Groups, Teams, and Individuals

Just the Facts

You can improve your creativity by learning about and using tools that help you see and understand the world from new perspectives.

Data gathered about any set of events, series of occurrences, or problem will show variation. If the data are measurable, the numbers will be found to vary. The reason for this is that no two or more of the same item are identical. Absenteeism rates, sales figures, number of letters mailed, items or units produced, or any set of numbers will show variation. These fluctuations are caused by any number of differences, both large and small, in the item or process being observed.

If these data are tabulated and arranged according to size, the result is called a frequency distribution. The frequency distribution will indicate where most of the data are grouped and will show how much variation there is. The frequency distribution is a statistical tool for presenting numerous facts in a form that makes clear the dispersion of the data along a scale of measurement.

Description of a Histogram

A histogram is a column graph depicting the frequency distribution of data collected on a given variable. It visualizes for us how the actual measurements vary around an average value. The frequency of occurrence for each given measurement is portrayed by the height of the columns on a graph.

The shape or curve formed by the tops of the columns has a special meaning. This curve can be associated with statistical distributions that in turn can be analyzed with mathematical tools. The various shapes that can occur are given names, such as normal, bimodal (or multi-peaked), or skewed. A special significance can sometimes be attached to the causes of these shapes. A normal distribution causes the distribution to have a "bell" shape and is often referred to as a "bell-shaped curve." It looks like Figure 3-30.

Normal distribution means that the frequency distribution is symmetrical about its mean or average. To be technically correct, the bell-shaped curve would pass through the center point at the top of each of the bars. We have plotted it at the outside corner to make the histogram look less complicated.

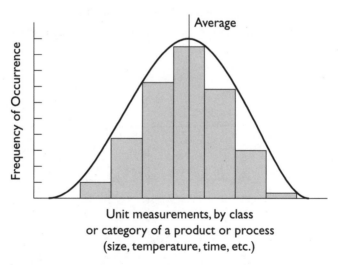

FIGURE 3-30. **Bell-shaped histogram**

Uses of Histograms

Histograms are effective tools because they show the presence or absence of normal distribution. Absence of normal distribution is an indication of some abnormality about the variable being measured. Something other than "chance" causes are affecting the variable and thus the population being measured is not under "statistical control." When any process is not under statistical control, its conformance to any desired standard is not predictable and action needs to be taken. A histogram is also useful in comparing actual measurements of a population against the desired standard or specification. These standards can be indicated by dotted, vertical lines imposed over the histogram (Figure 3-31).

Figure 3-31 indicates that even though all the parts that were sampled met the specification requirements, all of the parts will need to be screened or a high percentage of defective product will be accepted.

Consequently, histograms enable us to do three things:

► Spot abnormalities in a product or process
► Compare actual measurements with required standards
► Identify sources of variation

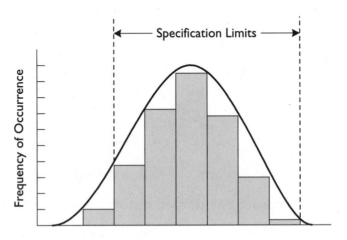

Figure 3-31. Histogram with specification limits added

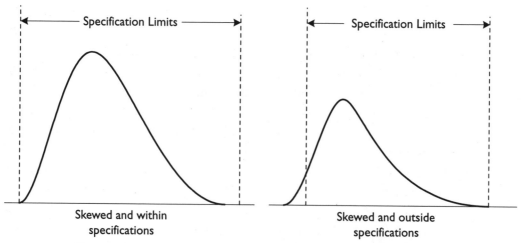

FIGURE 3-32. Abnormal distributions: skewed

Abnormalities are indicated when the data do not result in a bell-shaped curve; i.e., when there is not a normal distribution (Figure 3-32).

Even when all samples fall within the specifications, a skewed histogram (as in Figure 3-32) can serve as a warning that the process is being affected by other than normal variations and is susceptible to drifting outside the standards. This has happened in Figure 3-33.

The second way to use histograms is to determine whether the process is producing units that fall within the established specifications or desired standards and, if not, to detect clues as to what is needed to fix the situation.

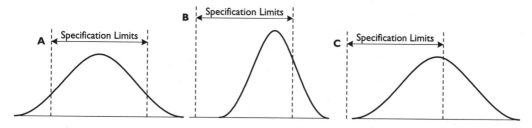

FIGURE 3-33. Outside established specifications

In Figure 3-33, the histogram labeled "A" shows an excessive spread, exceeding both lower and upper limits. This would indicate that, although the process is under control, action needs to be taken that will "tighten up" its range of variability. The histogram labeled "B" shows a process also under control but whose average value is too far to the right-hand side of the specifications. Action is needed to cause a leftward shift of the population. The histogram labeled "C" has two problems. The spread is too wide, as the spread in histogram A, and is biased to the right, as is the spread in histogram B. Both kinds of corrective actions are required, to tighten up and shift the spread.

The third use of histograms is to reveal the presence of more than one source of variation in the population of the histogram. This is shown when the measurements of the data form a multi-peaked curve. Figure 3-34 illustrates the bimodal curve formed by data measurements from two varying sources.

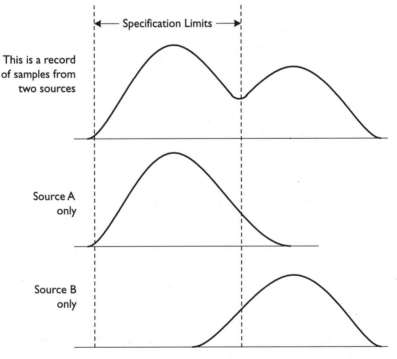

FIGURE 3-34. Bimodal curve modeled from data from two different sources

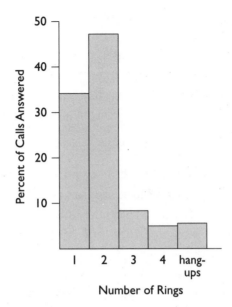

FIGURE 3-35. Distorted histogram

A histogram can be very distorted (Figure 3-35). This type of distribution usually occurs when there is a natural barrier at one end of the measurement.

A good example would be the following data from a phone call center:

34% of calls are answered on the first ring.

47% of calls are answered on the second ring.

8% of calls are answered on the third ring.

5% of calls are answered on the fourth ring or later.

6% of calls end in hangups.

The natural barrier in this case is the expectation that the call center staff will answer the phone as soon as it rings. There could be a natural barrier at the other end as well, if the company installed a system that would transfer to voice mail all calls that remained unanswered after a certain number of rings.

Constructing a Histogram

The foregoing examples of histograms illustrate most of the different types. The following example is used to demonstrate the steps to be taken in constructing a histogram, using for our data the variations in time required to complete a single method, Method A.

Step 1. Collect and Organize Data

To construct a histogram, you need data. The more data you have, the more accurate your histogram will be. A minimum acceptable number of data is from 30 to 50 measurements; there is no maximum number.

You need a certain type of data to properly construct a histogram. All of the measures must be of the same item or process and measurements should be taken in the same way. The measure could be how much time it takes to do a certain thing, measured each of the 50 times it is done on a certain day. Another measure could be how many units were processed in an hour, with a simple count being taken for each hour in a 40-hour week. The measurements are of items or processes that should be about the same.

Construct a data table to collect and record data (Figure 3-36). Find the range by subtracting the smallest measurement (15) from the

Method A Length of Processing Time n = 50				
25	23	25.5	24	29
24	25	33	27	22.5
31	29	20.5	37	25.9
20	17	21	28.1	32.5
19	25.5	30.2	15	25
34	25	24	23.5	30
22	22.1	17.4	24.2	31
19.4	22	23	27	28
26.5	26	18	21.9	19.5
28.5	22	27.9	27.5	24

37 - 15 = 22 = Range
22 ÷ 10 = 2.2 = Width of each column

FIGURE 3-36. Data table

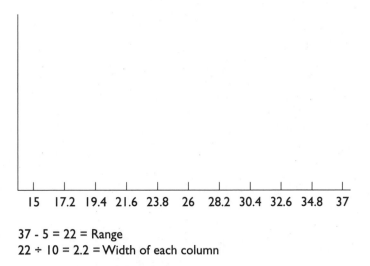

15   17.2 19.4 21.6 23.8 26   28.2 30.4 32.6 34.8 37

37 - 5 = 22 = Range
22 ÷ 10 = 2.2 = Width of each column

Figure 3-37. Setting histogram interval limits

largest measurement (37). In the example, the range is 22. Divide the range by 10. This tells you the width of the intervals (columns) to be plotted on the X (horizontal) axis of the histogram.

Step 2. Set Histogram Interval Limits

Put 11 marks along the X axis at equal intervals. Take the largest measurement on the data table (37) and record it on the right end of the horizontal axis (Figure 3-37). Put the smallest measurement (15) on the left end of the horizontal axis. Then add to the smallest measurement the figure you got when you divided the range by 10 (2.2) and place this new figure (17.2) by the first interval on the horizontal scale. Continue moving to the right so that each interval point is increased the same amount over the adjacent interval on the left.

The more data you have, the larger the number by which you should divide to determine the interval. Use the following as a guide.

Number of Measurements	Divide by
50-100	6-10
100-250	7-12
over 250	10-20

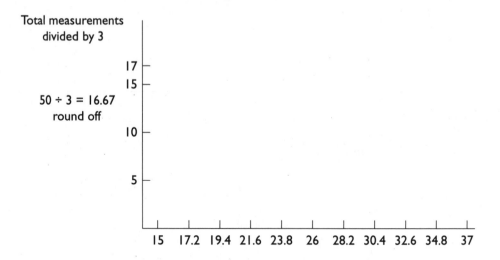

FIGURE 3-38. Setting the scale for the vertical (Y) axis

Step 3. Set the Scale for the Y Axis

Count the total number of measurements and divide this number by 3. You may round off this answer. The number 3 is used as a general practice, related to the probability that the highest frequency for any one interval is not likely to be more than 30% of the total measurements you have taken. This number—in our example, 50 (3 = 16.67, rounded off to 17)—is plotted at the top of the Y (vertical) axis of the histogram (Figure 3-38).

Step 4. Plotting Data

Count the measurements that fall between the first two numbers on the horizontal axis. Make a mark at the appropriate height. Do this for the remaining intervals along the horizontal line. In counting the number of measurements for each interval, a number that falls on the line between intervals is included in the column that begins with that number. For example, if you were plotting data on Figure 3-38 and the value of a specific measurement was 17.2, it would be plotted in the interval that is marked as 17.2 to 19.4. Then, draw and fill in the columns.

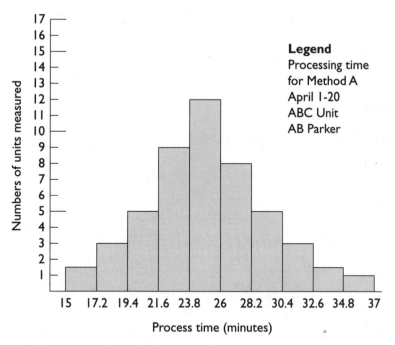

FIGURE **3-39. A completed histogram**

Step 5. Label the Histogram

Add a legend telling what the data represent and where, when, and by whom they were collected (Figure 3-39).

Histograms are extremely valuable in presenting a picture of how well a product is being made or how well a process is working. This is not something that can be readily detected by a mere tabulation of data. The simplicity of their construction and interpretation make histograms effective tools for the analysis of data. Perhaps most important, histograms speak a language all can understand. They tell whether a process is under "statistical control" and whether the process is designed to meet its expected standard or specification.

The width of the histogram total population can be defined by calculating the standard deviation (SD) of the data. Standard deviation is an estimate of the spread of the total population based upon a sample of the population. Sigma (σ) is the Greek letter used to designate the estimated standard deviation. (Note: standard deviation is presented later in this chapter.)

Examples

See the examples at the end of the Standard Deviation part of this chapter.

Additional Ammunition

Brassard, Michael. *The Memory Jogger Plus* (Milwaukee, WI: ASQ Quality Press, 1989)

Harrington, H. James. *The Improvement Process: How America's Leading Companies Improve Quality* (New York: McGraw-Hill, 1987)

Lynch, Robert F., and Thomas J. Werner. *Continuous Improvement Team and Tools: A Guide for Action* (Milwaukee, WI: ASQ Quality Press, 1992)

WOW Weapon: Pareto Diagrams

Definition: A type of chart in which the bars are arranged in descending order from the left to the right. It is a way to highlight "the vital few" in contrast to "the trivial many."
Classification: Basic Data-Analysis Weapon
Users: Groups, Teams, and Individuals

Just the Facts

A Pareto diagram is a specialized type of column graph. Data are presented in a manner that allows comparison of a number of problems or a number of causes. The comparison is necessary to set priorities. The Pareto diagram facilitates the process by graphically distinguishing the few significant problems or causes from the less significant many. This diagram is the graphic representation of the "Pareto principle."

The Pareto Principle

The *Pareto principle* states as a "universal," applicable to many fields, the phenomenon of the vital few and the trivial many. In our context, this means that a few significant problems or causes will be most important to our decision-making process.

This principle derives its name from Vilfredo Pareto, a 19th century economist who applied the concept to income distribution. His observations led him to state that 80% of wealth is controlled by 20% of the people. (Hence, the principle is often referred to as the "80-20" principle.) The name "Pareto" and the universal applicability of the concept are credited to Dr. Joseph M. Juran, who applied the Lorenz curve to graphically depict the universal.

The Pareto Diagram

The *Pareto diagram* (Figure 3-40) is distinguished from other column graphs in that the columns representing each category are always ordered from the highest on the left to the lowest on the right. The one exception to this rule is the "Other" column, a collection of the less important factors. When it is used, it is always the last column on the right. With this arrangement it is possible to make a cumulative or "cum" line (the Lorenz curve), which rises by steps according to the height of the columns to show the total of the percentages, the cumulative percentage. With the "cum" line, the Pareto diagram becomes a combined column and line graph.

Uses of Pareto Diagrams

Like other graphic representations, Pareto diagrams visualize data to assist investigation and analysis. They are employed to:

1. *Establish Priorities*
   By a comparison of related data; major categories of problems and causes are identified.
2. *Show Percentage of Impact*

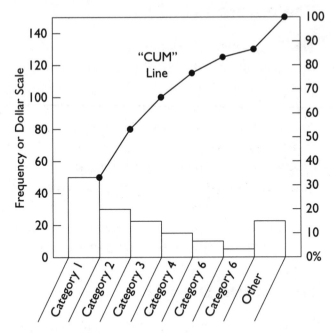

FIGURE **3-40. Pareto diagram form**

The "cum" line defines the proportionate importance of combined categories and thus indicates the likely impact of dealing with all of the categories up to that point in the diagram.

3. *Show Change over Time*

Two or more diagrams can be used to demonstrate the result of decisions and actions by showing "before" and "after" data (Figure 3-41).

4. *Aid Communication*

The diagram is an accepted form of communication, readily understood.

5. *Demonstrate Use of Data*

This can be particularly helpful in management presentations to show that activities are solidly rooted in facts, not just opinions.

Classifications of Data

The data collected for transfer to a Pareto diagram are of three major types:

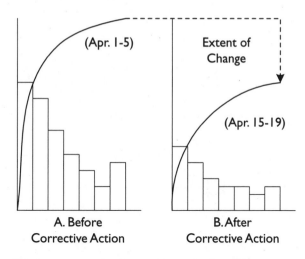

FIGURE **3-41.** Performance before (A) and after (B) corrective action

Problems: including errors, defects, locations, processes, procedures
Causes: including materials, machines, equipment, employees, customers, operations, standards
Cost: of each category of data

The purpose of using a Pareto diagram is to:

- ▶ establish the biggest problems and rank the rest
- ▶ establish the most important causes and rank the rest

"Biggest" and "most important" need to be measured not solely in terms of frequency but also in terms of cost. The number of occurrences may not be as significant as the cost of particular occurrences. Consequently, it is usually important to construct a Pareto diagram using cost data. Mere frequency can be misleading in judging significance.

Constructing a Pareto Diagram

Before a Pareto diagram can be constructed, it is necessary to collect data according to the classifications or categories judged most suitable. With these data the diagram is constructed as follows:

Problems with Overseas Shipments	Number	% of Total	"Cum" %
Containers Opened	112	40	40%
Containers Broken	68	24	64%
Items Missing	30	11	75%
No Shipping Forms	28	10	85%
Wrong Shipping Forms	18	6	91%
Other	24	9	100%
Total	280	100%	–

FIGURE **3-42. Data table**

Step 1. Summarize the data on a worksheet.

 a. Arrange the data in order, from largest to smallest, and total them (Figure 3-42, "Number" column).
 b. Calculate percentages (Figure 3-42, "% of Total" column).
 c. Calculate the cumulative percentages (Figure 3-42, "Cum" % column).

Step 2. Draw the horizontal and two vertical axes.

 a. Divide the horizontal axis into equal segments, one for each category (Figure 3-43).
 b. Scale the left-hand vertical axis so that the top figure on the axis is the total of all the occurrences in the categories.
 c. Scale the right-hand vertical axis so that 100 % is directly opposite the total on the left-hand axis. The percent scale is normally in increments of 10%.

Step 3. Plot the data.

Construct a series of columns, putting the tallest column on the extreme left, then the next tallest, and so on. If several minor cate-

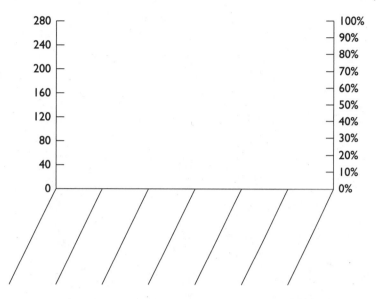

FIGURE 3-43. Vertical scales and horizontal segments for a Pareto diagram

gories are consolidated into an "Other" column, it is plotted on the extreme right, regardless of its height (Figure 3-44).

Step 4. Plot the cumulative line.

a. Place a dot in line with the right side of each column, at a height corresponding to the number in the cumulative percentage column on the worksheet. In our example, the points would be plotted at 40%, 64%, 75%, 85%, and 91%.

b. Beginning with the lower left corner of the diagram (the zero point of origin), connect the dots up to the 100% point on the right vertical axis (Figure 3-45).

Step 5. Add labels and the legend.

a. Label each axis.

b. Add the legend. It should include the source of the data, date prepared, where collected, who collected them, period covered, and any other pertinent information (Figure 3-46).

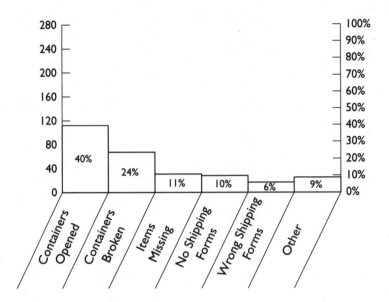

FIGURE 3-44. Plotted Pareto diagram without cumulative line

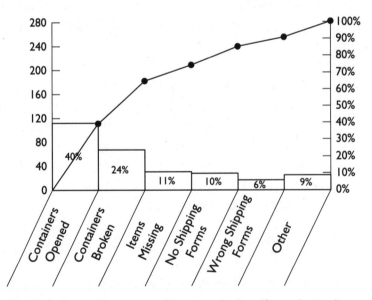

FIGURE 3-45. Pareto diagram with cumulative line plotted

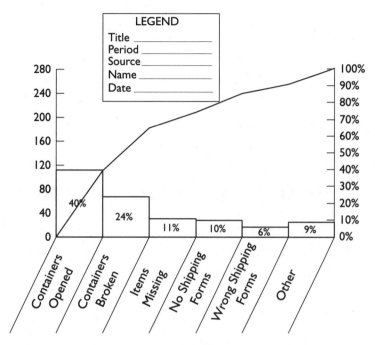

FIGURE 3-46. Completed Pareto diagram

Example

No examples are shown here because examples were included in the text.

Additional Ammunition

Harrington, H. James. *The Improvement Process: How America's Leading Companies Improve Quality* (New York: McGraw-Hill, 1987)

Juran, Joseph M. *Managerial Breakthrough,* revised edition (New York: McGraw-Hill, 1994)

Lefevre, Henry L. *Quality Service Pays: Six Keys to Success!* (Milwaukee, WI: ASQ Quality Press, 1989)

Lynch, Robert F., and Thomas J. Werner. *Continuous Improvement Team and Tools: A Guide for Action* (Milwaukee, WI: ASQ Quality Press, 1992)

Miller, George L., and LaRue L. Krumm. *The Whats, Whys, and Hows of Quality Improvement* (Milwaukee, WI: ASQ Quality Press, 1992)

Pitt, Hy. *SPC for the Rest of Us: A Personal Path to Statistical Process Control* (Reading, MA: Addison-Wesley, 1994)

WOW WEAPON: ROOT CAUSE ANALYSIS

Definition: The process of identifying the various causes affecting a particular problem, process, or issue and determining the real reasons that caused the condition.
Classification: Basic Data-Analysis Weapon
Users: Groups, Teams, and Individuals

Just The Facts

You can improve your creativity by learning about and using tools that help you see and understand the world from new perspectives.

Everyone talks about industrial problem solving and some books explain how to do it. These books typically provide precise methods for selecting the problem to work on and ways to protect customers from receiving defective products. They all advise you not to treat the symptoms, but to define the root cause so that the real problem can be corrected. It sounds so simple. All you have to do is define the root cause—but most books never tell you how.

Why do they avoid giving details about this crucial activity? The reason is simple. Defining the root cause is often very difficult and complex; there is no one right way that works all the time. The practitioner must be skilled at selecting the most effective approach.

There are a number of ways to get to the root of a problem. A good failure analysis laboratory can provide the insight necessary to understand how a failure such as a broken bolt occurred. Duplicating the failure under laboratory conditions also has proved to be an effective way to define the root cause of problems. You know you have found the root cause when you can cause the problem to occur and go away at will. Either of these approaches works well, but they require expensive laboratories and highly trained personnel.

Excessive variation is at the heart of most problems, at least the difficult ones. Variation is part of life. No two items or acts are exactly identical. Even identical twins have very different fingerprints, voice patterns, and personal values. No two screws made on the same machine are exactly the same. Equipment may not be sensitive enough to measure the variation, but it exists. Some variation is good. It keeps our lives from being monotonous. No one would like steak, mashed potatoes, and peas three times a day, every day of the week. They are good once in a while, but would get old and boring if eaten at every meal.

Some variation, within specific limits, has little or no effect on output. In other cases, variation can cause an entire plant to come to a halt. The variation we're concerned about here is the variation that causes problems resulting in waste. There is no such thing as a random problem, just problems whose occurrence is more or less infrequent, meaning that the combination of specific variables occurs more or less infrequently. The art of defining the root cause is the art of variables analysis and isolation.

The root cause of a problem has been found when the key variables that caused the problem have been isolated. Over the years, there have been many methods developed to isolate key variables. Designed experiments and Taguchi methods are popular today. But the difficulties and effort required to prepare and conduct these studies cause them to be used on only a small fraction of the problems. Engineers, managers, production employees, and sales personnel solve most of their problems by brute force and a lot of luck. Even then, most of the time the answer that is implemented is not the best solution to the problem.

While this part of our book covers root cause analysis, not statistical process control, we need to understand that by studying different types of variation, the source of the variation can be identified. Then the problem solver can quickly and effectively reduce the many potential sources to a critical few and often to a single factor, thereby great-ly simplifying the problem-evaluation cycle and reducing the amount of data for collection. The results can be profound:

▶ Problems can be solved faster.
▶ Fewer samples are required.
▶ Less-skilled people can solve very complex problems.
▶ Preventive and corrective action plans can be evaluated quickly.
▶ Nontechnical people can easily understand the results of a tech-nical evaluation.

How to Do a Root Cause Analysis in Six Steps

Step 1. Identify the potential root causes for the problem.

The most effective method of root cause analysis is to determine how the root cause will be identified or what tool will be used. One of the most frequently used tools for identifying root cause is the cause-and-effect or "fishbone" diagram. This tool is explained in detail in Chapter 4. Its pri-mary function is to provide the user with a visual picture of all the pos-sible causes of a specific problem or condition (Figure 3-47).

Step 2. Gather data on the frequency of the problem.

Use checksheets or other tools to track occurrences of problems and to identify the causes. Figure 3-48 shows how a checksheet can be used for several problems that may result from one or more of sever-al causes.

Step 3. Determine the impact of the problem.

Use a scatter diagram (Figure 3-49) or similar tool. (Scatter dia-grams will be explained a little later in this chapter.)

Step 4. Summarize all major root causes and relate them back to the major opportunity areas.

The purpose of this is to:

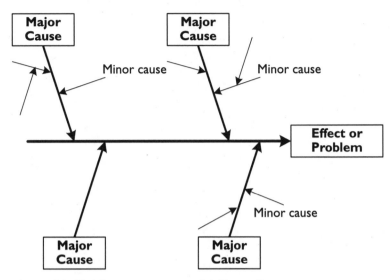

FIGURE 3-47. Model for a cause-and-effect diagram

Checksheet for Defective Copies				
Machine No. Operator's Name: Date:				
	Missing Pages	Muddy Copies	Show-Through	Pages Out of Sequence	Total
Machine Jams	///			////	7
Paper Weight	//		////		6
Humidity		//		/	3
Toner		////			4
Condition of Original	////	////	//	////	14
Other (specify)					
				Total	34
Comments				

FIGURE 3-48. Example of a checksheet

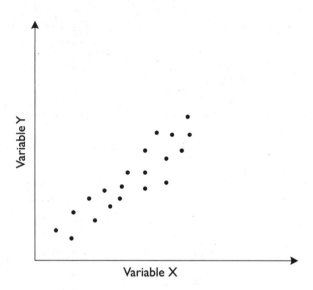

FIGURE **3-49. Example of a scatter diagram**

- ▶ Identify root causes that impact several problems.
- ▶ Ensure that the major root causes are identified in all opportunity areas.
- ▶ Aid in selection of the key root cause to eliminate.

Step 5. Prioritize the root causes.

Use a prioritization matrix (see Figure 3-50). This procedure consists of the following four steps:

- ▶ List the criteria to be used to evaluate the causes.
- ▶ Weight each criterion according to its relative importance. Put the weight for each criterion in that column heading.
- ▶ Using one criterion at a time, rank order all of the causes—with 1 being the least important. Enter the ranking in the column under the criterion in question.
- ▶ Multiply each rank order figure for each cause by the weight of each of the criteria, to arrive at a total for each cause. Enter these totals in the final column of each row.

Criteria / Root Causes	Criterion 1	Criterion 2	Criterion 3	Criterion 4	Totals
Root Cause 1					
Root Cause 2					
Root Cause 3					
Root Cause 4					
Root Cause 5					
Root Cause 6					
Root Cause 7					
Root Cause 8					

FIGURE 3-50. Example of prioritization matrix

Step 6. Select the key root cause to eliminate.

This decision should be based on the analysis of all available data. If you use a prioritization matrix, you may simply decide according to the totals in the final column.

Example

The fault-tree analysis (Figure 3-51) is another alternative and sometimes is more effective than the approach just described. We like to think of it as the "What could cause this?" approach.

This is an example of the "What could cause this?" approach in use.

Symptom: TV will not turn on.

What could cause this? (Level 1)

► TV defective
► Electrical power out

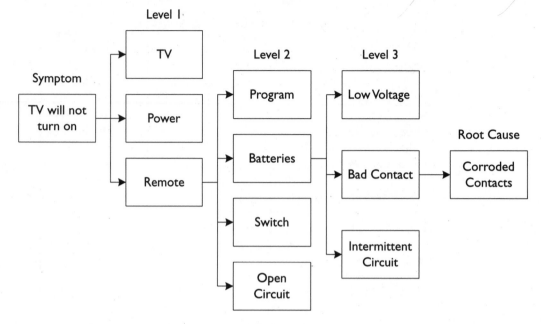

Figure 3-51. Fault-tree analysis

▶ Remote control defective

Investigation: TV turns on when the "on" button on the TV is pushed, but not when the "on" button on the remote control is pushed. What could cause this? (Level 2)

▶ Not programmed to the TV
▶ Discharged batteries
▶ Defective "on" switch
▶ Open circuit

Investigation: Replaced batteries. Remote control now turns on the TV. Put the old batteries back in and the remote turns on the TV. What could cause this? (Level 3)

▶ Batteries' voltage low so remote control works intermittently
▶ Bad contact
▶ Intermittent circuit

Investigation: Inspected battery terminals and found that they were corroded. Cleaned terminals. Checked the age of the batteries. They were less than two months old. Checked the voltage and current of the batteries. They checked out well. Put the old batteries in the remote control and it turned on the TV at a distance of two times normal usage.

Root cause of failure: corroded terminals.

Additional Ammunition

Anderson, Gaylord F., Larry D. Dell, and Paul F. Wilson. *Root Cause Analysis: A Tool for Total Quality Management* (Milwaukee, WI: ASQ Quality Press, 1993)

Das, A.K. *Metallurgy of Failure Analysis* (New York: McGraw-Hill, 1998)

Harrington, H. James. *Excellence—The IBM Way* (Milwaukee, WI: ASQC Quality Press, 1988)

Lynch, Robert F., and Thomas J. Werner. *Continuous Improvement Teams and Tools: A Guide for Action* (Milwaukee, WI: ASQC Quality Press, 1992)

Nikkan Kogyo Shimbun, Ltd. *Poka-Yoke: Improving Product Quality by Preventing Defects* (Portland, OR: Productivity Press, 1989)

Stamatis, D.H. *Failure Mode and Effect Analysis: FMEA from Theory to Execution* (Milwaukee: ASQC Quality Press, 1995)

WOW WEAPON: RUN CHARTS

Definition: A way of visualizing data to show a trend over a time period.
Classification: Basic Data-Analysis Weapon
Users: Groups, Teams, and Individuals

Just the Facts

You can improve your creativity by learning about and using tools that help you see and understand the world from new perspectives.

Run charts are graphic displays of data that are used to assess the stability of a process over time or over a sequence of events (such as the number of batches produced). The run chart is the simplest form of a control chart. It does not include the statistically determined upper and lower control limits or the range. It is a simpler tool, intended only to determine if there are changes in a process over time.

Run charts can be plotted for either attributes data or variables data. Runs—plot points that occur consecutively on one side or the other of a center line—are a phenomenon that provides a simple method for detecting whether a process is experiencing a shift or change in its pattern of output.

To understand the concept of runs and the probability of their occurrence, think of a coin tossed for heads or tails a number of times. On the average, 50% of the time the coin will turn up heads and 50% of the time it will turn up tails. The probability that there will be a run of the same outcome two times in a row (twice heads or twice tails) is calculated as .50 x .50 or .25. The probability of a run of six heads or tails in a row is therefore .50 x .50 x .50 x .50 x .50 x .50. This means there's a 1.5% chance (very unlikely) that this run will occur.

The upper and lower halves of a control chart can be compared to the sides of a coin. The likelihood of six consecutive plots on one side or the other of the center line is very small. Therefore, when this occurs you can be reasonably certain that something different is happening in the process.

With this principle, a run chart can be created to monitor process output for abnormal change without having to resort to computing standard deviations and control limit lines. A run chart can also be used in situations where variables data are hard to obtain or only attributes data are available.

Steps to Prepare a Run Chart

1. Determine what data are to be captured.
2. Decide on the sample and/or frequency of measurement. Also decide on the time frame over which data are to be captured.
3. To create a run chart, simply start out the same as for any control chart and plot 20 points. Then calculate the median and use that figure to draw a center line.
4. Begin to monitor the process for runs of six or more, that is, when there are six or more points in sequence on one side or the other of the center line (Figure 3-52). When such a sequence occurs, investigate to determine the cause of the change. If the direction of the change represents deterioration, attempt to correct the problem in order to bring the process back to the better condition. If the change represents an improvement, adopt the improvement as a new standard: plot 20 points and compute a new centerline as the basis for monitoring for future runs..
5. Analyze the run chart on an ongoing basis to determine possible changes in the process.

Guidelines and Tips

Some of the same guidelines and tips as for checksheets apply here. They are basically good rules of thumb in any data collection. The most important thing is to know what information you are trying to get out of the data. What question are you trying to answer? It is also important to keep the data collection simple.

A danger in using the run chart is that there is a natural tendency to overreact to variations displayed on the chart. Use the following

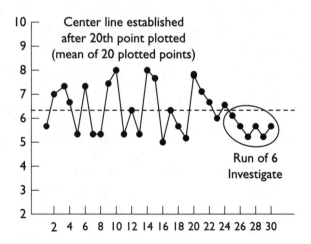

FIGURE 3-52. Example of a run chart

guidelines to determine if observed patterns are statistically significant, that is, if the patterns are likely to indicate a change in the process:

- ▶ When six consecutive data points fall on one side or the other of the centerline.
- ▶ When six consecutive points increase or when six consecutive points decrease, suggesting a trend.

Example

See Figure 3-52, an example of a typical run chart.

Additional Ammunition

Brassard, Michael. *The Memory Jogger Plus* (Milwaukee, WI: ASQC Quality Press, 1989)

Harrington, H. James. *The Improvement Process: How America's Leading Companies Improve Quality* (New York: McGraw-Hill, 1987)

Ishikawa, Kaoru. *Guide to Quality Control* (Milwaukee, WI: ASQC Quality Press, 1986)

Lynch, Robert F., and Werner, Thomas J. *Continuous Improvement Teams and Tools: A Guide for Action* (Milwaukee, WI: ASQC Quality Press 1992)

Zelazny, Gene. *Say It With Charts*, 3rd edition (New York: McGraw-Hill, 1998)

WOW Weapon: Scatter Diagrams

Definition: A graphic tool used to study the relationship between two variables.
Classification: Basic Data-Analysis Weapon
Users: Groups, Teams, and Individuals

Just the Facts

The scatter diagram is used to test for possible cause-and-effect relationships. It does not prove that one variable causes the other, but it does show whether a relationship exists and reveals the character of that relationship.

The relationship between the two sets of variables can be evaluated by analyzing the cluster patterns that appear on the graph when the two sets of data are plotted with each axis being used for one of the sets of data. The direction and tightness of the cluster give an indication of the relationship between the two variables.

Steps to Prepare a Scatter Diagram

1. Collect samples of data.
2. Construct the horizontal and vertical axes of the diagram. The vertical axis is usually used for the variable on which we are to predicting or measuring the possible effect. The horizontal axis

is used for the variable that is being investigated as the possible cause of that effect.

3. Plot the data on the diagram. Circle data points that are repeated.

4. Analyze the cluster pattern that appears.

Guidelines and Tips

Though a scatter diagram is completed to study cause-and-effect relationships between two variables, you should be cautious about the statement that "Variable 1 causes Variable 2." There might be other reasons why two variables appear to be related, such as a third variable not represented in the plot, but related to both of the other variables.

Keep in mind that the full range over which Variable 1 varies is sometimes key in detecting a correlation between two variables. For example, experimental studies are often done over a wider range than normal production.

Also keep in mind that correlations do not have to be linear. Notice the last example, showing two variables that are correlated, but not in a linear fashion. Look for patterns that might indicate a relationship between two variables.

Example

See Figure 3-53.

Additional Ammunition

Brassard, Michael. *The Memory Jogger Plus* (Milwaukee, WI: ASQ Quality Press, 1989)

Harrington, H. James. *The Improvement Process: How America's Leading Companies Improve Quality* (New York: McGraw-Hill, 1987)

Lynch, Robert F., and Thomas J. Werner. *Continuous Improvement Team and Tools: A Guide for Action* (Milwaukee, WI: ASQC Quality Press, 1992)

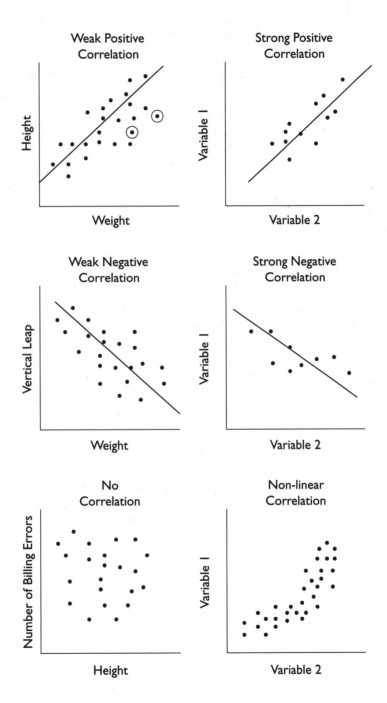

FIGURE 3-53. Sample scatter diagrams

WOW Weapon: Standard Deviation (SD) (Sigma)

Definition: An estimate of the spread (dispersion) of the total population based upon a sample of the population. Sigma (σ) is the Greek letter used to designate the estimated standard deviation.
Classification: Basic Data-Analysis Weapon
Users: Groups, Teams, and Individuals

Just the Facts

You should read the section of this book on histograms before reading this section unless you already have a good understanding of histograms.

Discussion of standard deviation focuses on distances between data points. So, we first need to understand how central tendency is used related to histograms and then the concept of dispersion.

Central Tendency—A measure of the center of the distribution.

Measures of Central Tendency

There are three measures of central tendency:

- ► Average or arithmetic mean
- ► Median
- ► Mode

The average or mean is easy to calculate because it is simply the sum of the numbers divided by the number of values involved. In Figure 3-54, 17 divided by 3, or 5.67, is the average. Symbolically, this is usually shown as the sum of Xs (ΣX) divided by n to get $\overline{X}$ (X bar).

The median is the value that divides a series of numbers into two equal parts. In the series 3, 7, 10, 12, and 16 (see Figure 3-55, example 1), 10 is the median because there are two numbers above it and two

---

Average (arithmetic mean)

Example:
3 + 8 + 6 = 17 ÷ 3 = 5.67 (avg)

$X1 + X2 + X3 = {}^{\Sigma X}/n = \overline{X}$ (X bar)

FIGURE 3-54. Average calculations

below it. If the series contains an even number of values, such as in the second example, then the median is a number halfway between the two middle numbers. Here, 11 is halfway between 9 and 13.

Median

3, 7, 10, 12, 16
10 is median

4, 8, 9, 13, 17, 19
11 is median

FIGURE 3-55. Median calculations

The mode is the number that occurs most frequently in a series of numbers (Figure 3-56). In a frequency distribution it would be the value that makes the tallest peak of the curve.

Mode

1, 2, 2, 3, 3, 3, 3, 4, 4, 5, 5, 6

3 is mode

FIGURE 3-56. Mode calculations

How are these measures used? The average or mean is the one used most often. It is used to report average size, average yield, average percent defective, and so on. The median is usually used only in some special situations, such as for data that can be ranked but not easily measured—for example, the shades of colors, softness of material, or the smoothness of a surface. The mode is used with skewed distributions. It removes the influence of extreme values.

Those are the essentials of central tendency. Now that we know several ways to measure the central tendency of a data sample, we can move on to discussing how to measure how far individual data points are dispersed or distributed away from the central tendency.

Measures of Dispersion

There are four measures of dispersion:

- ▶ range
- ▶ average deviation
- ▶ variance
- ▶ standard deviation

We can look at each one separately.

The simplest measure is the *range*. The range is the difference between the largest and the smallest values in a series (Figure 3-57). Sometimes there is occasion to use an average of the ranges of several series. In that case, it is called $\bar{R}$ (R bar).

Range

Example:
11, 13, 16, 9, 7, 17
Range is: 17 - 7 = 10
Symbolically
$X_{high} - X_{low} = R$

FIGURE 3-57. Range calculation

Another simple measure of dispersion is the *average deviation*. It is the average amount that the values vary from the mean (X). In the example in Figure 3-58, the mean of the series 7, 10, 12, 17, and 19 is 13 (first column). Each of those five numbers varies from 13 by the amount shown in the second column. If we total the variations (deviations) in that column, then divide the total (20) by the number of figures (5), we have the average deviation—5.

Average Deviation	
Values of X	**Deviation from $\overline{X}$**
	6
7	3
10	1
12	4
17	6
19	Total 20
Total 65	Avg Deviation = 4
Mean = 13 ($\overline{X}$)	

FIGURE 3-58. Average deviation calculation

The next and slightly more complicated measure of dispersion is called the *variance*. To arrive at the variance, first square each number in the deviation column, then add these squared numbers and divide the total by the number of items minus 1. The result is the variance. In our example (Figure 3-59), the variance is 24.5.

The most important and most useful of all of the measures of dispersion is the standard deviation. In dealing with a frequency distribution, you will usually be calculating the standard deviation. It is simply the square root of the variance (Figure 3-60). In our example, 24.5 is the variance, so the standard deviation is the square root of 24.5, or 4.94. This is expressed symbolically by the lower-case Greek letter sigma (σ).

Because standard deviation is so important to the measurement of frequency distributions, let's review the steps.

Variance

Values of X	Deviation from $\overline{X}$	Squared Deviation
	6	
7	3	36 (6x6)
10	1	9 (3x3)
12	4	1 (1x1)
17	6	16 (4x4)
19	Total 20	36 (6x6)
Total 65	Avg Deviation = 4	98
Mean = 13 ($\overline{X}$)		Variance = 24.5

FIGURE 3-59. Variance calculation

Standard Deviation

Variance = 9.5

Square root = 4.95
the standard deviation

FIGURE 3-60. Standard deviation calculation

Step 1. Compute the average (mean or $\overline{X}$) of the total distribution.
Step 2. Find the difference between each number and the average—the deviation.
Step 3. Square each deviation, add those squares, and then divide by the number of deviations minus 1 to get the variance.
Step 4. Find the square root of the variance. This is the standard deviation.

The standard deviation is, by far, the most valuable and used measure of a frequency distribution. It expresses dispersion in a single number and a very important relationship exists between the standard deviation and a normal curve.

Figure 3-61 illustrates that relationship. 68.27% of all the readings will fall within ±1 standard deviation from the mean. 95.45% of all

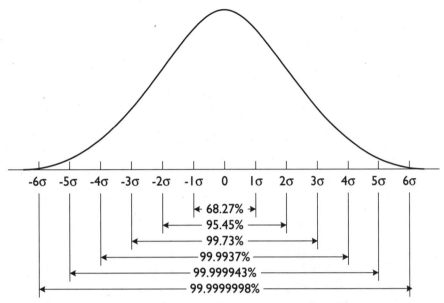

FIGURE 3-61. Normal distribution histogram and standard deviation

readings will fall within ±2 standard deviations. 99.73% will fall within ±3 standard deviations. With the standard deviation, it is possible to predict the percentage of values that will fall between any two readings on the curve, and to know the amount of total variation in the process that will occur. (3σ=99.73% of all values).

Examples

Example 1

We want to calculate the standard deviation for the following seven numbers:

130, 120, 110, 121, 125, 108, 105

We will first calculate $\overline{X}$ (average or mean).

$130+120+110+121+125+108+105 = 819 \div 7 = 177 = \overline{\overline{X}}$

Now we will subtract $\overline{X}$ from each of the seven values, square the results, and get the sum of the squares.

(X - $\bar{X}$)	(X - $\bar{X}$)^2
130 - 117 = 13	13^2 = 169
120 - 117 = 3	3^2 = 9
110 - 117 = -7	-7^2 = 49
121 - 117 = 4	4^2 = 16
125 - 117 = 8	8^2 = 64
108 - 117 = -9	-9^2 = 81
105 - 117 = -12	-12^2 = 144
	532

The sum of the squares (532) is then divided by the number of values (7) minus 1 (n – 1), to get the variance.

532 ÷ (7-1) = 88.67

The standard deviation is the square root of this number.

Standard deviation (σ) = square root of 88.67 = 9.42σ

Example 2

We looked at the height of male soldiers in the United States Army. The average height of men in the army was 67.7 inches, but heights of individual soldiers varied all the way from 60 to 76 inches. 68% were between 65.1 and 70.3 inches tall. 95% measured between 62.5 and 72.9 inches. You would seldom see a soldier over 75.5 inches tall and the army did not want men under 60 inches in height.

Do you suppose that we got all those figures from a list of data? Well, not exactly: Figure 3-62 is the reference table we used. It tells us only two things about each height measurement. Using $\bar{X}$, we are able to ascertain that the average height is 67.7 inches. That is the mean or middle of the curve. It is the height of the largest percentage of men.

The second thing the table tells us is variation in human proportions. The measurement of variation is called the standard deviation. If you want to get technical, it is the distance from the center to the place where the curve begins spreading out more than dropping down.

	Men		Women	
Measurement	**X̄**	**6**	**X̄**	**6**
Height (standing)	67.7	2.6	62.5	2.4
Height (sitting)	36.0	1.3	33.9	1.2
Length of foot	10.1	1.0	8.2	0.8
Arm span	69.9	3.1	62.4	2.7

FIGURE 3-62. Data table of human proportions for men and women

If you know enough about mathematics, you can use σ and $\overline{X}$ in the formula for the normal curve and compute the number of men between any two heights you might specify (Figure 3-63).

For most purposes, however, we are interested only in the points at one, two, and three standard deviations, measured from the center or target. If we measure a standard deviation on each side of the center of this curve, we have $X \pm 1\sigma$, or 68% of the area between the lines

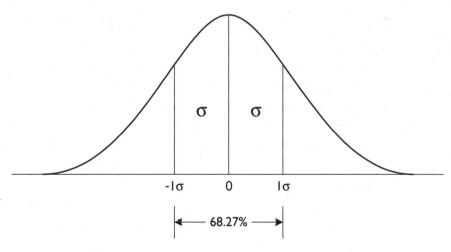

FIGURE 3-63. Plus or minus 1 sigma value

drawn through these points. In other words, 68% of all of the data falls within the mean plus or minus one standard deviation. We will teach you how to use σ by simply adding, subtracting, multiplying, and dividing. It is not hard and, once you understand the operation, you can use a calculator or a computer to do the arithmetic for you.

The table of human proportions tells us that the standard deviation for men's height is 2.6 inches. By using simple subtraction and addition, we determine that 68% of the men are between 65.1 (67.7 − 2.6) and 70.3 (67.7 + 2.6) inches tall.

Two standard deviations would be 5.2 inches. Once again, using simple subtraction and addition, we know that 95% of the men are between 62.5 (67.7 − 5.2) and 72.9 (67.7 + 5.2) inches tall.

Three standard deviations would be 7.8 inches. This table shows that 99.73% of the area of the normal curve is between -3σ and +3σ. We can say that practically all of the men will be between 59.9 (67.7 − 7.8) inches and 75.5 (67.7 + 7.8) inches tall.

There certainly are some men taller than 75.5 inches, but only 15 in 10,000. There is about the same proportion of men under 59.9 inches.

What have all these calculations to do with providing good service or making nuts and bolts or Jeeps or aspirin tablets (except, you say, that we are giving you a headache)? Now, be patient. Pretend that you are still in the army and are staying there until you learn something about probability. Suppose we could go down the street and measure the height of the next male soldier who passes the door of this building. What odds would you give that he would be exactly 67.7 inches tall? That is the average, you know.

Of course you would have to give pretty big odds. Obviously, the soldier could be anywhere between 59.9 and 75.5 inches in height. You would certainly try to collect if he varied from the average by even one thousandth of an inch!

Instead, suppose we bet that the next soldier would be between 65.1 and 70.3 inches tall. How would you figure the odds? We have already given you the answer. 68% of all the soldiers are between 65.1 and 70.3 inches tall. There are 68 chances in 100 that the next soldier

```
┌─────────────────────────────────┐
│         Men's Heights           │
│        ± I s  = 2.6"            │
│                                 │
│      67.7 - 2.6 = 65.1"         │
│      67.7 + 2.6 = 70.3"         │
│                                 │
│    ±2s  = 2.6" x 2 = 5.2"       │
│                                 │
│      67.7 - 5.2 = 62.5"         │
│      67.7 +5.2 = 72.9"          │
│                                 │
│    ±3s  = 2.6" x 3 = 7.8"       │
│                                 │
│      67.7 - 7.8 = 59.9"         │
│      67.7 + 7.8 = 75.5"         │
└─────────────────────────────────┘
```

would be within those limits. I would have to give you odds of 68 to 32, or approximately 2 to 1.

95% of all male soldiers are between 62.5 and 72.9 inches, so the odds are 95 to 5, or 19 to 1, that the next man will be neither shorter than 62.5 inches nor taller than 72.9 inches. There are only 2.5 chances in 100 that he will be taller than 72.9 inches and just 13.5 chances in 10,000, or 1 in 740, that he will be taller than 75.5 inches (Figure 3-64).

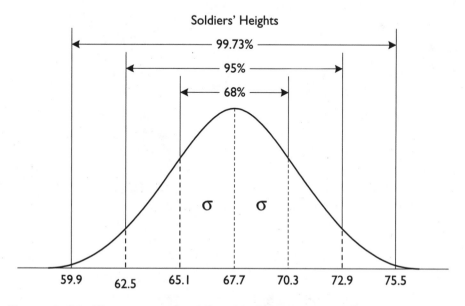

FIGURE 3-64. Histogram of soldiers' heights

Example 3

Let's go back to the world of business for another example. We want to cut a lot of widgets exactly 2 inches long using our special widget maker. (In case you do not know what a widget is, refer to Figure 3-65.) Yesterday we cut 500 widgets. We measured them all very carefully and made a histogram of what we found. As you see in Figure 3-65, the widget lengths vary in the bell-shaped pattern or normal curve. The mean is 2.00 inches, but individually the widgets vary from 1.91 inches to 2.09 inches. That is OK with our customers. Their specifications require an average of 2.00 inches with a tolerance of plus and minus 0.15 inches. That means they will accept anything between 1.85 inches and 2.15 inches.

Our problem is to keep the cutting machine at the center of 2 inches and not let the individual pieces vary much more than they did in yesterday's lot. Please note that the same logic applies to non-widget

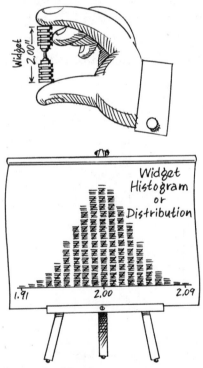

FIGURE 3-65. Histogram of widgets

numbers, such as the number of minutes required to process an invoice or the number of customers checked into a hotel during the day shift. We need to be accurate and precise to keep our customers happy.

All of our widgets were made at one time, on the same machines, by the same operator, and from the same lot of material, so we are quite sure that the pattern of their variation will almost exactly fit the normal curve. We also know that 99.7% of the widget variations will be within -3 and $+3$ standard deviations of the mean. That is a spread of 3 standard deviations $\pm 3\sigma$ or 6σ in total.

Additional Ammunition

Burr, Irving Wingate. *Statistical Quality Control Methods* (New York: Marcel Dekker, 1976)

Deming, W. Edwards. "Management of Statistical Techniques for Quality and Productivity." Management Seminar, 1981

Deming, W. Edwards. "On Some Statistical Aids Toward Economic Production," *Interfaces Magazine*, Vol. 5, No. 4, August 1975, p. 5

Deming, W. Edwards. *Out of the Crisis* (Cambridge, MA: MIT Center for Advanced Engineering Study, 1986)

Ernst & Young. *Advanced SPC* (San Jose, CA: Ernst & Young, 1989)

Ernst & Young. *Introduction to SPC* (San Jose, CA: Ernst & Young, 1989)

Ishikawa, Kaoru. *Guide to Quality Control*, 2nd edition (Tokyo: Asian Productivity Organization, 1982)

Leer, Robert E. "Statistical Methods Seminar." Rieker Management Systems, Los Gatos, CA, 1983

Montgomery, Douglas C. *Introduction to Statistical Quality Control* (New York: John Wiley & Sons, 1985)

Orr, Ellis R. *Process Quality Control: Trouble-Shooting and Interpretation of Data* (New York: McGraw-Hill, 1975)

Shewhart, Walter A. *Economic Control of Quality of Manufactured Product* (New York: D. Van Nostrand Company, 1931; reprint Milwaukee, WI: ASQC Quality Press, 1980)

Wadsworth, Harrison K., A. Blanton Godfrey, and Kenneth S. Stephens. *Modern Methods for Quality Control and Improvement* (New York: John Wiley & Sons, 1986)

Western Electric Company. *Statistical Quality Control Handbook*, 2nd edition (New York: Western Electric Company, 1958)

Not dealing with the waste monster is playing with dynamite

CHAPTER **4**

Basic Idea-Generation Weapons

You have good ideas. I have good ideas. Together we have great ideas.

Chapter Preview

You can improve your creativity by learning about and using tools that help you see and understand the world from new perspectives.

Everyone has good ideas. No one is void of ideas. Too often we are too busy to develop our own ideas, let alone generate new ones. As a result, we fall back on past experiences and the teaching of others to define our future activities. Of course, this leads to non-growth and no-improvement operations. Now, if we don't have the time to develop our own ideas, we certainly don't have the time to listen to other people's ideas and help them develop their good ones into great ones.

The margin between success and failure is very small today. You can go bankrupt implementing good ideas if your competition is implementing great ideas. To succeed in the 21st century, management needs to train people in how to be creative and how to generate new ideas, then provide them with an environment in which their ideas are nurtured and used effectively. Think of each idea as a $1000 bill dropped on your desk. Are you going to pick it up and put it in your wallet? Or are you going to let it fall off into the trash can? Although the value of ideas varies greatly, in an average service organization an individual idea is worth approximately $10,000 if it is implemented. This chapter is dedicated to weapons that help you and the organization's groups and teams create new ideas that will slay the monster called Waste.

The suggestion box is a vault full of money in the form of little slips of paper.

The idea-generation weapons presented in this chapter range all the way from the very simple to the very complex. The 12 WOW idea-generation weapons will be presented in the following order:

Chapter 4—Basic Idea-Generation Weapons

- ▶ 5W's and 2H's Approach
- ▶ Ask "Why" Five Times
- ▶ Brainstorming
- ▶ Cause-and-Effect Diagram (Fishbone Diagram)
- ▶ Force-Field Analysis
- ▶ Mind Map (Ideagram)

CD-ROM Section G—Specialized Idea-Generation Weapons

- ▶ Affinity Diagrams
- ▶ Negative Analysis
- ▶ Nominal Group Technique
- ▶ Other Points of View (OPV)
- ▶ Storyboarding

CD-ROM Section H—Mass-Destruction Idea-Generation Weapons
▶   Creative Thinking

Summary

An idea is a lot like a newborn baby. It is very fragile and needs a lot of care and feeding until it can stand on its own two legs. It is also a very personal thing. It is something its creator feels strongly about. You would never tell a mother, "What an ugly child you have." No, you'd be much more tactful and, even if the baby were not beautiful, you'd say something like "My, how healthy he looks!" or "Look at how active she is already!"

The same is true of ideas. Don't criticize bad ones; understand what the person who made the suggestion was trying to accomplish and try to help him or her develop the idea into a worthwhile concept or to the point that the person realizes there is a better approach. There are no bad ideas if the person is sincerely trying to help. There are only ideas that have not matured or not found their right application or for which the time is not right.

Sanyo's suggestion program generates 37.7 suggestions per qualified employee per year, of which 93% are implemented. That's better than three ideas per month per qualified employee. You should be implementing three times that quantity from your professionals and managers. We suggest that you keep a chart on your own ideas that are implemented. Use six per month as a minimum acceptable level and 18 per month as world-class (see Figure 4-1). For every idea you plot on your performance chart, record what the idea was and estimate the impact it had on the organization's performance. In a very short time you'll gain an excellent understanding of the worth of your ideas as well as your capabilities to create and contribute. Then set a challenge target to increase your monthly idea value by 100%. You can do that in three ways:

1. Increase the number of your implemented ideas.
2. Increase the value of your implemented ideas.

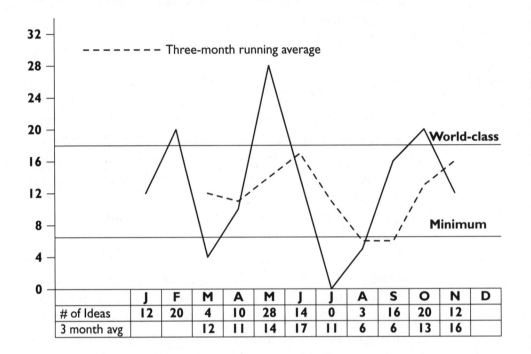

	J	F	M	A	M	J	J	A	S	O	N	D
# of Ideas	12	20	4	10	28	14	0	3	16	20	12	
3 month avg			12	11	14	17	11	6	6	13	16	

FIGURE **4-1. Idea implementation chart for Ken Lomax**

3. Increase both the number and value of your implemented ideas.

As an exempt employee, if the yearly value of your ideas does not exceed your annual compensation, both you and your employer should be concerned.

Introduction

Most people generate less than 1% of the ideas they are capable of generating.

This chapter presents weapons that are used to generate new, creative ideas to solve problems and take advantage of opportunities. These are weapons designed for use by all the organization's employees and should be part of every employee's basic training.

The WOW weapons that are included in this chapter are:

► **5W's and 2H's Approach**—A rigid, structured approach that probes into and defines a problem by asking a specific set of questions related to a previously defined opportunity or problem statement. The 5W's and 2H's stand for:
  - W1—What?
  - W2—Why?
  - W3—Where?
  - W4—Who?
  - W5—When?
  - How did it happen?
  - How much did it cost?

► **Ask "Why" Five Times**— A systematic technique used to search for and identify the root cause of a problem.

► **Brainstorming**—A technique used by a group to quickly generate large lists of ideas, problems, or issues. The emphasis is on quantity of ideas, not quality.

► **Cause-and-Effect Diagram**—A visual presentation of possible causes of a specific problem or condition. The effect is listed on the right-hand side and the causes take the shape of fish bones. This is the reason it is sometimes called a "fishbone diagram." It is also called an "Ishikawa diagram" after Kaoru Ishikawa, author of *Guide to Quality Control.*

▶ **Force-Field Analysis**—A visual aid for pinpointing and analyzing elements that resist change (restraining forces) or push for change (driving forces). This technique helps drive improvement by developing plans to overcome the restrainers and make maximum use of the driving forces.

▶ **Mind Map**—An unstructured cause-and-effect diagram. Also called mind-flow, Brain Web, or ideagram.

WOW WEAPON: THE 5W'S AND 2H'S APPROACH/ SITUATION DESCRIPTION TECHNIQUE

Definition: A rigid, structured approach that probes into and defines a problem by asking a specific set of questions related to a previously prepared opportunity or problem statement. The 5W's and 2H's stand for

▶ W1—What?
▶ W2—Why?
▶ W3—Where?
▶ W4—Who?
▶ W5—When?
▶ H1—How did it happen?
▶ H2—How much did it cost?

Classification: Basic Idea-Generation Weapon
Users: Teams, Groups, and Individuals

Just the Facts

The 5W's and 2H's approach (situation description technique) provides a very effective framework for systematically gathering information about a problem or a situation. The framework is to ask the 5W's and 2H's. The 5W's are Who, What, Where, When, and Why. The 2H's are How did it happen? and How much did it cost? A similar approach is used widely in journalism to ensure that all relevant information regarding a story is collected. It can be used similarly in industrial problem-solving applications. We like to add a third H, How do you correct it? (5W's and 3H's). This addition changes the weapon from a problem-definition weapon into a problem-solution weapon.

The following are typical questions that are asked related to the 5W's and 3H's:

- ▶ W1—Who: Who was affected?
- ▶ W2—What: What happened?
- ▶ W3—When: When did it happen?
- ▶ W4—Where: Where did it happen?
- ▶ W5—Why: Why did it happen?
- ▶ H1—How: How did it happen?
- ▶ H2—How much: How much impact did it have (cost, productivity, schedule slippages, etc.)?
- ▶ H3—How: How can the situation be corrected and prevented from recurring?

This approach is somewhat more time consuming to use than the Five Whys technique covered next in this section of the book, but it will develop different perspectives on a situation. It will also be more likely to uncover sub-problems that might be addressed separately (a form of stratification of the problem).

It is important to note that the order in which the five W's are applied is not critical in the 5W's and 2H's technique. We like to adjust them to the specific item being evaluated. Some people like to start by asking, "Who was affected?" Others prefer not to ask the "Who?" question until later in the process.

Using the 5W's and 2H's

Step 1. Write down an initial problem statement.
Step 2. Develop a set of questions. Ask Who, What, Where, When, Why, How, and How Much for any relevant part of the initial problem statement.
Step 3. Answer the questions developed in Step 2.

Step 4. Using the answers from Step 3, either alone or in combination, prepare a comprehensive problem statement that contains the information required to have a good understanding of the situation. This often leads to more than one problem statement, since many problems occur as a result of a number of interacting conditions.

Guidelines and Tips

When generating potential problem statements, do not include quantitative goals. This will narrow the perspectives that the approach can provide and reduce the number of alternative solutions. Use a problem statement that will open up a wide variety of alternative solutions, then select from those using another method, based on quantitative criteria.

As in brainstorming and other idea-generation techniques, defer judgment on the questions, responses, and alternatives. Only when a complete list of alternative problem statements is completed should you evaluate it to make a final selection.

Examples

The following is an example of how the 5W's and 2H's are applied to a problem.

Problem Statement

Our employees are not motivated to work harder.

What is motivation?

That which stimulates action and drives people to achieve a goal.

What does "work harder" mean?

Accomplishing more with limited resources, being more efficient while maintaining quality.

What motivates most employees?

Feelings of achievement, responsibility, recognition, money, food, security, confidence that they know how to do their jobs.

Where are employees motivated to work hard?

In their bosses' offices, in their work areas, at award ceremonies.

Where is employee motivation not a problem?

Where basic personal and work needs are taken care of, where employees do a task from beginning to end, at organizations X, Y, and Z.

Who are the employees?

Blue-collar and white-collar workers, workers who are perceived as not working as hard as they should be.

Who doesn't work hard?

Some employees with little direct supervision, employees who believe they are underpaid, employees who are physically sick on the job.

When are employees not motivated to work hard?

When they feel their contributions are not recognized and appreciated, when they don't have adequate resources to do their jobs, when their bosses are overbearing and exert too much direction and control, when their co-workers are uncooperative.

When do bosses try to motivate employees?

During scheduled performance evaluations, when employees make a mistake, when employees do something well, when they are under pressure to increase productivity.

Why motivate employees to work harder?

To increase productivity, to increase personal income through employee participation in profit sharing, to become more competitive with other organizations, to provide better customer service.

How can employees be motivated?

With rewards, with punishment, by being told why they should work harder, by being asked what they want and need to do their jobs better.

How much is it costing because employees are not highly motivated?

It is estimated that value added per employee per hour would increase by $8.50.

Alternative Problem Statements

▶ Our employees have poor perceptions about hard work.
▶ Certain employees need more supervision.
▶ Our hard-working employees don't receive enough compensation.
▶ Our employees' basic needs are not met well enough.
▶ Our employees are not involved in determining how to do their jobs.
▶ Our customer service is poor.

Many other alternative problem statements are possible.

Situation/Problem:	
Impact on the Process:	
Description	
What	**Why**
Who	**How**
When	**How Much**
Where	**How to Correct**

FIGURE 4-2. A typical 5W's and 3H's data form

Additional Ammunition

The Mescon Group, Inc. *Techniques for Problem Solving: Participant's Guide* (San Francisco: Pfeiffer and Company, 1996)

Scholtes, Peter R. *The Team Handbook* (Madison, WI: Joiner Associates, 1991)

Smith, Gerald F. *Quality Problem Solving* (New York: McGraw-Hill, 1998)

WOW WEAPON: ASK "WHY" FIVE TIMES

Definition: A systematic technique used to search for and identify the root cause of a problem.
Classification: Basic Idea-Generation Weapon
Users: Groups, Teams, and Individuals

Just the Facts

This technique asks the team members to ask "Why?" at least five times. When the team is no longer able to answer the "Why?" the possible root cause has been identified.

Steps:
Step 1. Start with a completed problem statement. The problem statement should be as specific as possible.
Incorrect: "The janitors are not emptying the trash in some rooms each night."
Correct: "The janitors are not emptying the trash in the main conference room each night."

Step 2. Ask, "Why does this problem/situation exist?"

Step 3. Continue to ask "Why?" until the root cause has been identified. In some cases it may not take five tries and in some cases it will take more. When the team can no longer answer the question "Why?" it will be time to consider if the root cause has been identified.

Step 4. Once the root cause has been identified, move to the next step in the problem-solving process.

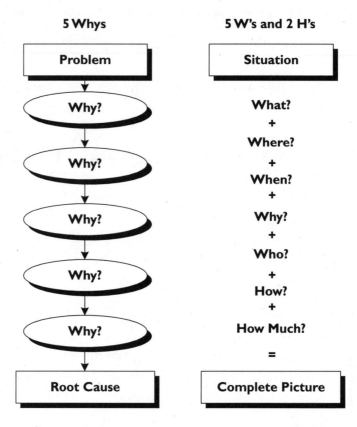

FIGURE 4-3. Comparing the 5 Whys and the 5 W's and 2 H's

Example

QC Team: Day Shift Production   **Date** 07/30/99

Problem Statement:

The janitors are not emptying the trash in the main conference room each night.

Why?   1. Why are the janitors not emptying the trash in the main
              conference room each night?

Response: The conference room has been locked after 5:00 P.M. for the
              last week.

Why?   2. Why is the conference room locked after 5:00 P.M.?

Response: Building maintenance was told to lock it at the end of the
              day shift.

Why?   3. Why was maintenance told to lock it?

Response: A special task team is working on a corporate issue and
              wants the door locked after they leave.

Why?   4. Why do they want the door locked?

Response: They are leaving planning charts on the wall and don't want
              them reviewed by the wrong parties or removed accidentally.

Why?   5. Why do they need to leave the charts on the wall?

Response: Since the charts are quite large, they don't want to have to
              take them down each night and put them up each morning.

Has the root cause of the problem been identified?   X   yes____   no

If "no," continue asking "Why?"

State the root cause: The janitors cannot empty the trash because they

                      temporarily don't have access to the room.

FIGURE 4-4. Example of an "Ask Why 5 Times" form

Additional Ammunition

Brassard, Michael. *The Memory Jogger Plus* (Milwaukee, WI: ASQC Quality Press, 1989)

Ernst & Young LLP. *Tools and Techniques Resource Guide* (Cleveland, OH: The Quality and Productivity Group, 1992)

Harrington, H. James. *The Improvement Process: How America's Leading Companies Improve Quality* (New York, NY: McGraw-Hill, 1987)

Ishikawa, Kaoru. *Guide to Quality Control* (Milwaukee, WI: ASQC Quality Press, 1986)

Smith, Gerald F. *Quality Problem Solving* (New York: McGraw-Hill, 1998)

WOW Weapon: Brainstorming

Definition: A technique used by a group to quickly generate large lists of ideas, problems, or issues. The emphasis is on quantity of ideas, not quality.
Classification: Basic Idea-Generation Weapon
Users: Groups and Teams

Just the Facts

Brainstorming is perhaps the most widely recognized technique used to encourage creative thinking. It is also one of the most important tools any individual can have in his or her improvement arsenal. Problem-solving groups can take advantage of brainstorming techniques during several phases of their operation.

Brainstorming is an intentionally uninhibited technique for generating the greatest possible number of ideas. Group members suggest as many ideas as they can about a given subject. The quantity of ideas is more important than their quality; each idea will be evaluated later.

Groups can use this idea-generating technique to identify work-related problems, their causes, and possible solutions.

A brainstorming group:

- ► Has 4 to 12 members
- ► Determines the problem to be addressed
- ► Understands the problem
- ► Records all suggestions
- ► Gives each member the same opportunity to express opinions
- ► Encourages all ideas without criticism
- ► Has a leader who conducts the meeting, keeping the group focused on the selected problem

Brainstorming uses the thinking resources of the entire problem-solving group. The ideas generated by a group are likely to be much more numerous and creative than those of any individual. The group generates a large number of ideas, accepts all of them, and writes them all down without discussion or judgment. At the end of the session, or later on in the problem-solving process, the group screens the ideas for the good ones.

Brainstorming is used to generate a large number of new and creative ideas. How can brainstorming help to determine the best solutions for important problems? Start with the assumption that people are conscientious, are aware of problems affecting the quality of their work, and have thought about solutions. There are many good solutions incubating in their minds. Brainstorming is an opportunity to bring these ideas out for consideration. This process helps to meet the unending challenge of finding the right solutions to real problems. It recognizes that—if certain conditions exist—people can participate in a creative process that is self-fulfilling, improves the quality of their work, and makes use of the organization's most valuable asset, the people in it.

Using Brainstorming

Groups use brainstorming when identifying and analyzing a problem and when looking for solutions. Constant attention must be given to the essentials of brainstorming:

- ▶ "Is everyone thinking about the same problem?"
- ▶ "Are all ideas encouraged and accepted without criticism?"
- ▶ "Are all ideas recorded?"
- ▶ "Do all of the group members have an equal chance to participate?"

If all of these conditions are not satisfied, it is not a brainstorming session. Brainstorming is not a meeting in which everyone is talking at the same time, nor is it an unorganized "bull session."

There are times when the group is faced with an unusual or difficult situation—one that cannot be solved through experience, formulas, or some other method. In these cases, a stronger technique is needed. Brainstorming facilitates diversity in thinking and the production of many ideas. It is not used to produce a single line of thought, nor is it the answer to a problem that has only one solution. Brainstorming is used when creative solutions are required. It is a cooperative, creative technique to be used when individual efforts do not yield satisfactory results.

Preparing for a Brainstorming Session

Brainstorming is worthwhile only after the subject to be brainstormed has been well defined. All the members of the group should be aware of what the problem is and they need to see all of the data relating to the present situation.

Select a suitable meeting place for the occasion. The room needs to be just large enough to accommodate the group comfortably. Too much room often leads to a loss of unity and makes it harder for the participants to coalesce into a group, a phenomenon critical to forming a collective intellect of diversified individuals to operate as a single entity.

A relaxed atmosphere, which can readily accommodate laughter, is best for a productive and creative session. It allows the participants to verbalize their "offbeat" ideas by presenting them tongue-in-cheek. Experience has proved that often in the resulting laughter a voice rises up: "You know, that's not such a crazy idea." Thus the unusual thought often leads to a viable avenue or idea.

Brainstorming Techniques

There are several techniques that can be used to guide and expand brainstorming.

1. **Idea-Spurring.** The leader can ask questions like "Can we make these smaller?" "What can we add?" or "What can we combine or package with this idea?" The questions are designed to break down any mental barriers the group may have, to open up thinking and encourage participation.

2. **Participation in Sequence.** It is a good idea to ask for ideas to be contributed in turn, beginning with one person and going all the way around the group. This technique can be used at the beginning of a session to ensure that everyone participates, even shy members. If a person can't think of anything to contribute, the appropriate response is "Pass." A good idea may occur before the next round.

3. **Incubation.** This is a process that may go on between brainstorming sessions. The initial brainstorming session gives the subconscious mind suggestions. The subconscious works on these suggestions slowly and sometimes generates very creative ideas. In the incubation process, the members of the group just let their minds work on the issue between sessions.

Guidelines for Brainstorming

Select an appropriate meeting place.

A place that is comfortable, casual, and the right size will greatly enhance a brainstorm session.

Determine if training is needed.

The team should have a very good understanding of the brainstorming process. If this is not the case, provide the required training.

Define and document the subject/problem to be brainstormed.

The team should clearly define the subject/problem that will be the focus of the brainstorming activity. It has often been said, "A problem well defined is a problem half solved."

Record all ideas.

Appoint a recorder to note everything suggested. The ideas should not be edited; rather, they should be jotted down just as they are mentioned. Keep a permanent record that can be read at future meetings. You may want to read through the list and take "inventory" a few times; this process sometimes stimulates more ideas.

Generate a large number of ideas.

Don't inhibit yourself or others; just let the ideas out. Say whatever comes into your mind and encourage others to do the same. The important thing is quantity.

Encourage freewheeling.

Even though one of your ideas may seem half-baked or silly to you, it has value for the group. It may provoke thoughts from other members. Sometimes making a "silly" suggestion can spur another idea you didn't know you had.

Encourage everyone to participate.

Everyone thinks and has ideas, so allow everyone to speak up. Speaking in turn helps: solicit ideas clockwise around the group. Encourage everyone to share his or her ideas.

Don't criticize.

This is the most important guideline. There will be ample time later to sift through the ideas for the good ones. During the session, you should not criticize ideas because you may inhibit other members. When you criticize, you reduce the potential for brainstorming to generate great ideas.

Let ideas percolate.

Once you've started brainstorming, ideas will come more easily. You are freeing your subconscious mind to be creative. Let it do its work by giving it time. Don't discontinue your brainstorming sessions too soon; let some time go by to allow those ideas to develop. Take a few minutes of quiet to be sure all the ideas have been voiced before moving on to the next phase of the brainstorming process.

What Inhibits Good Brainstorming?

Inasmuch as brainstorming is the most widely used idea-generation tool, it is also the most misused. If the rules for brainstorming are not conscientiously followed, the quality of the session will suffer. A frequent mistake made by a session leader is to allow discussion or criticism of suggestions during brainstorming. This turns off other members of the group and keeps the group synergy from building. Brainstorming is not effective unless all members of the group participate. The leader should be especially careful to see that everyone is given the opportunity to contribute to the brainstorm list. It is the responsibility of the leader of the brainstorming group to encourage the members to comply with the rules for brainstorming.

Brainstorming helps us release many subconscious creative ideas. Any problem-solving group may use brainstorming to identify problems in its work area. Brainstorming is an effective technique for directing the efforts and attention of a group in a systematic problem-solving process.

Examples

Problem Statement: What problems are we having related to shipping products?

- ▶ Dock is overcrowded
- ▶ Long lag time in getting orders changed
- ▶ Some products are hard to package and ship
- ▶ Many data entry errors

- Parts sent to the wrong shipper
- Bar code labels are damaged
- Many errors in the incoming shipping paperwork
- Damaged shipping boxes
- Wrong quantity shipped
- Paperwork not sent to shipping on time
- Errors in phone messages
- No labels on boxes
- Know defective parts shipped
- Can't read the handwriting
- Parts sent to customer

Problem Statement: What is causing the problems in shipping products?

- Hire freight carrier based on lowest rate
- Shipping does not know when they create an error
- When big customers push we switch labels
- No shipping procedures for some products
- Data entry is too complex
- High turnover among shippers
- High turnover in shipping
- Dock used to store material for return to suppliers
- Shipping sometimes takes instructions from sales representatives for rush orders
- The old shipping boxes are easily damaged
- Production department puts wrong count on box
- Shipping takes changes over the phone that do not get into the data base
- Handwritten changes are made because the computer is too slow
- No place to segregate customer returns
- Poor glue on the bar code labels
- Data entry people are poorly trained
- Shipping is a low-pay job
- Bonus is based on quantity shipped
- Bad environment on the back dock—cold in the winter and hot in the summer

Additional Ammunition

Ernst & Young Quality Improvement Consulting Group. *Systematic Participative Management: Team Member Manual* (San Jose, CA: Ernst & Young LLP, 1991)

Ernst & Young LLP. *Tools and Techniques Resource Guide* (Cleveland, OH: The Quality and Productivity Group, 1992)

WOW WEAPON: CAUSE-AND-EFFECT DIAGRAM

Definition: A visual of possible causes of a specific problem or condition. The effect is listed on the right-hand side and the causes take the shape of fish bones. This is the reason it is sometimes called a "fishbone diagram." It is also called an "Ishikawa diagram."
Classification: Basic Idea-Generation Weapon
Users: Groups, Teams, and Individuals

Just the Facts

You can improve your creativity by learning about and using tools that help you see and understand the world from new perspectives.

Cause-and-effect analysis is a structured analysis used to separate and define causes. The effects are the symptoms, which let us know that we have a problem.

The cause-and-effect diagram is very applicable to repetitive processes. For this reason, most of the craft operations can use cause-and-effect analysis. Processes under the control of one group or organization and where responsibilities are clearly defined are also good candidates for cause-and-effect analysis.

Not only are there several types of cause-and-effect diagram, but there are also two methods used to develop them. The random method is so called because members of the problem-solving group may suggest causes that apply to any of the major subdivisions of the diagram. Typically, just as in brainstorming, each session has a leader and a scribe is appointed to record the contributions of the members of the group. With the systematic method of developing a cause-and-effect diagram, the leader chooses one of the major subdivisions on which to focus the group's attention. The brainstorming process addresses the subdivision indicated by the leader. When that particular subdivision has been completed, the leader indicates the next one, and so on, until the cause-and-effect diagram has been systematically completed. The completed diagrams, whether generated by the random method or the systematic method, look alike.

Cause-and-effect diagrams have been variously called fishbone diagrams (as suggested by the shape of the completed diagram), Ishikawa diagrams (named after Professor Kaoru Ishikawa), and cause diagrams.

The process-analysis diagram is another type of cause-and-effect diagram. It looks much like a flow chart.

The solution-analysis diagram, in some ways, is much like the cause-and-effect diagram, except that it can be considered a backward fishbone.

Constructing a Cause-and-Effect Diagram

Constructing a cause-and-effect diagram (Figure 4-5) is a three-step process:

Step 1. Name the problem or "effect." Place this effect in a box on the right and draw a long process arrow pointing to the box.

Step 2. Decide on the major categories or subdivisions of causes. Place these major categories parallel to and some distance from the main process arrow. Then connect the boxes with arrows slanting toward the main arrow.

Step 3. Brainstorm for causes. Write these causes on the chart, clustered around the major category or subdivision that they influence. Connect them with arrows pointing to the main process arrow. Divide and subdivide the causes to show, as accurately as possible, how they interact. To have a little fun, use the format in Figure 4-6 to perform the analysis.

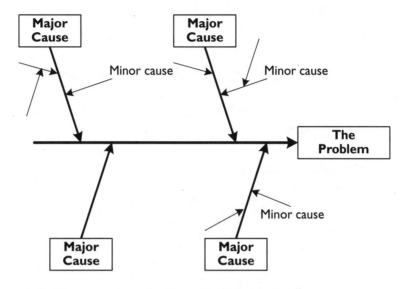

FIGURE 4-5. The cause-and-effect (fishbone) diagram

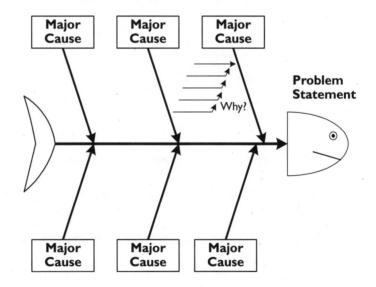

FIGURE 4-6. Fishbone diagram

Remember that either the random method or systematic method may be used to generate the fishbone diagram.

Constructing a Process-Analysis Diagram

There are three steps in constructing the process-analysis diagram (see Figure 4-7):

Step 1. List the series of tasks you wish to analyze, in the order in which they are done.

Step 2. Place each of these in a box, in the proper order. Connect the boxes with arrows to indicate the progress of the process.

Step 3. Brainstorm, using either the random or the systematic method, all of the causes that contribute to each step. List these causes on the chart and connect them with arrows to the box(es) containing the step to which they refer.

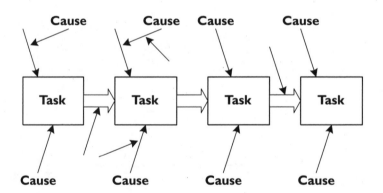

FIGURE 4-7. The process-analysis diagram

Constructing a Solution-Analysis Diagram

With the cause-and-effect diagram and process-analysis diagram, we start with the effect (problem) and analyze for causes. In the solution-analysis diagram (Figure 4-8), we do the reverse. Start with a single cause (a proposed solution) and analyze for all of the possible effects. If you have several possible solutions, you may wish to analyze them

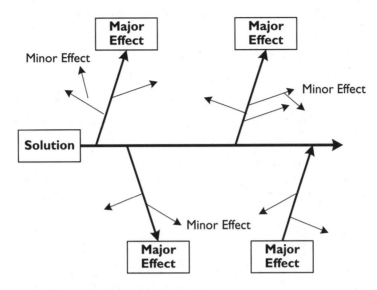

Figure **4-8. The solution-analysis diagram**

all. To best determine all the effects of a possible solution, use a solution-analysis type of cause-and-effect diagram. It will help to make better solution choices and to answer questions about your activities.

Step 1. Name the proposed solution and enclose it in a box. Place the box on the left side with a process arrow leading away from it. This arrow shows the direction of influence.

Step 2. Decide on the major categories or subdivisions of "effects." These are the areas the proposed solution is likely to influence.

Step 3. Brainstorm, using either the systematic or the random method, the likely effects (good and bad) of the proposed solution. Cluster these effects around the major categories, with smaller arrows leading away from the arrows indicating major categories.

Step 4. List the positive outcomes in one column and the negative in another.

Step 5. Compare the positive and negative results of the proposed solution. Use this information in deciding which solution to employ.

Use of Cause-and-Effect Diagrams

There are several uses for cause-and-effect diagrams. They can be used to:

1. Help both individuals and groups organize their ideas
2. Serve as a recording device for ideas generated
3. Reveal undetected relationships
4. Investigate the origin of a problem
5. Investigate the expected results of a course of action
6. Call attention to important relationships

Another aspect of diagramming causes and their effects is that one can tell at a glance whether the problem has been thoroughly investigated. A cause-and-effect diagram that contains much detail indicates how deeply a group has gone into the process of investigation, if that detail is legitimate. On the other hand, a bare cause-and-effect diagram might indicate that the problem was not significant or that the problem solvers were not exhaustive in their search. Likewise, if the solution-analysis diagram is complete, it will show the group's concern for the impact of a proposed solution.

Guidelines for Constructing Cause-and-Effect Diagrams

When constructing cause-and-effect diagrams, attention to a few essentials will provide a more accurate and usable result.

1. *Encourage everyone concerned to participate.* Full participation is necessary to ensure that all causes are considered. All members must feel free to express their ideas. The more ideas mentioned, the more accurate the diagram will be. One person's idea may trigger ideas from others.
2. *Do not criticize any ideas.* To encourage a free exchange, write down all ideas just as they are mentioned, in the appropriate place on the diagram.
3. *Make the diagrams visible.* Visibility is a major factor of participation. Everyone in the group must be able to see the diagrams.

Use large charts, print in large letters, and conduct diagram sessions in a well-lighted area.

4. *Connect related causes* as they are mentioned, so the relationships can be seen as the diagram develops.

5. *Understand where each cause is to be placed* on the diagram.

6. *Do not overload any one diagram.* As a group of causes begins to dominate the diagram, that group should be isolated and a separate diagram made for those causes.

7. *Construct a separate diagram* for each separate problem. If your problem is not specific enough, some major categories of the diagram will become overloaded. This indicates the need for additional diagrams.

8. *Circle the most likely causes.* This is usually done after all possible ideas have been posted on the cause-and-effect diagram. Only then is each idea critically evaluated. The most likely ones should be circled for special attention.

9. *Create a solution-oriented atmosphere* in each session. Focus on solving problems rather than on how problems started. The past cannot be changed—only the future can be affected by eliminating causes of undesired effects.

BOMB OUT THE CAUSE OF WASTE

Examples

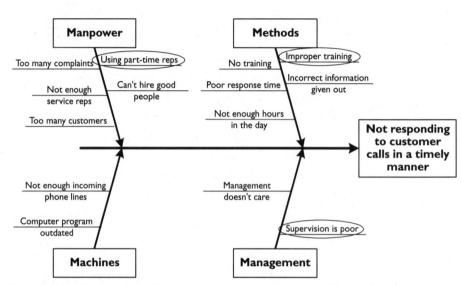

FIGURE 4-9. Example of a completed cause-and-effect diagram analysis

Additional Ammunition

Brassard, Michael. *The Memory Jogger Plus* (Milwaukee, WI: ASQ Quality Press, 1989)

Ernst & Young Quality Improvement Consulting Group. *Systematic Participative Management: Team Member Manual* (San Jose, CA: Ernst & Young LLP, 1991)

Fukuda, Ryuji. *CEDAC: A Tool for Continuous Systematic Improvement* (Portland, OR: Productivity Press, 1997).

Harrington, H. James. *The Improvement Process: How America's Leading Companies Improve Quality* (New York: McGraw-Hill, 1987)

Lynch, Robert F., and Thomas J. Werner. *Continuous Improvement Team and Tools: A Guide for Action* (Milwaukee, WI: ASQ Quality Press, 1991)

WOW WEAPON: FORCE-FIELD ANALYSIS

Definition: A visual aid for pinpointing and analyzing elements that resist change (restraining forces) or push for change (driving forces). This technique helps drive improvement by developing plans to overcome the restrainers and make maximum use of the driving forces.
Classification: Basic Idea-Generation Weapon
Users: Groups, Teams, and Individuals

Just the Facts

The force-field analysis technique has been used in a number of settings to:

1. Analyze a problem situation into its basic components
2. Identify those key elements of the problem situation about which something can realistically be done
3. Develop a systematic and insightful strategy for problem solving that minimizes "boomerang" effects and irrelevant efforts
4. Create a guiding set of criteria for the evaluation of action steps

The technique is an effective device for achieving each of these purposes when it is employed seriously.

Kurt Lewin, who developed force-field analysis, has proposed that any problem situation—be it the behavior of an individual or group, the current state or condition of an organization, a particular set of attitudes, or a frame of mind—may be thought of as constituting a level of activity that is somehow different from that desired. For example, smoking, as an activity, may become the basis for a problem when it occurs with greater intensity or at a higher level than one desires. Quality, as another example of an activity level, may become a problem when it is at a lower-than-desirable level. Depression or authoritarianism, as examples of attitudinal activity levels, become problems when they are too intense or at higher-than-desirable levels.

The level of the activity, to put it differently, is the starting point in the problem identification and analysis. In order to constitute a problem, the current level typically departs from some implicit norm or goal.

A particular activity level may be thought of as resulting from a number of pressures and influences acting upon the individual, group, or organization in question. These numerous influences Lewin calls "forces" and they may be either external to or internal to the person or situation in question.

Lewin identifies two kinds of forces:

1. Driving or facilitating forces, which promote the occurrence of the particular activity of concern, and
2. Restraining or inhibiting forces, which inhibit or oppose the occurrence of the same activity.

An activity level is the result of the simultaneous operation of both driving (facilitating) and restraining (inhibiting) forces. The two force fields push in opposite directions. Although the stronger of the two will tend to characterize the problem situation, a point of balance is usually achieved that gives the appearance of habitual behavior or a steady-state condition. Changes in the strength of either of the fields, however, can cause a change in the activity level of concern. Thus, apparently habitual ways of behaving, or frozen attitudes, can be changed (and related problems solved) by bringing about changes in the relative strengths of driving (facilitating) and restraining (inhibiting) force fields.

In order to appreciate just what kinds of forces are operating in a given situation and which ones are susceptible to influence, a force-field analysis must be made. As a first step to a fuller understanding of the problem, the forces—both facilitating and inhibiting—should be identified as fully as possible. Identified forces should be listed and, as much as possible, their relative contributions or strengths should be noted.

Basic Steps in Force-Field Analysis

Once the problem has been recognized, and commitment is made by the appropriate stakeholders to change the problem situation, there are four basic steps in force-field analysis:

Step 1. Define the problem and propose an ideal solution.
Step 2. Identify and evaluate the forces acting on the problem situation.
Step 3. Develop and implement a strategy for changing these forces.
Step 4. Re-examine the situation to determine the effectiveness of the change and make further adjustments if necessary.

Let's examine these steps.

Step 1: Define the Problem and Propose an Ideal Situation

The first step is to define the problem and propose the ideal situation.

1. Define the problem, stating exactly what it is. Be as specific as possible.
2. Propose an ideal situation in a "goal statement." It can be prepared by answering the question: "What will the situation be like when the problem is solved?" The answer must be tested to determine if it really gets to the heart of the problem. Another possible question is "What would the situation be like if everything were operating ideally?" (See Figure 4-10.)

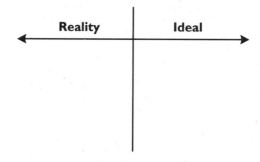

FIGURE 4-10. Reality versus the Ideal

Determining the precise goal statement is important because it guides the rest of the problem-solving steps.

Step 2. Identify and Evaluate the Forces

The second step is to identify and evaluate the forces that act on the problem situation. Forces that promote the goal are driving or facilitating forces: they tend to move the problem situation from reality toward the ideal. Forces that push away from the goal are restraining or inhibiting forces: they resist the movement toward the ideal state and, in a state of equilibrium, counterbalance the facilitating forces (Figure 4-11).

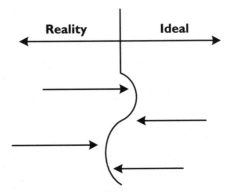

FIGURE **4-11. The as-is state in equilibrium**

Visualize a problem situation by drawing a line down a sheet of paper and listing the facilitating forces on one side and restraining forces on the other side. Each of these forces has its own weight and taken together they keep the field in balance (Figure 4-12).

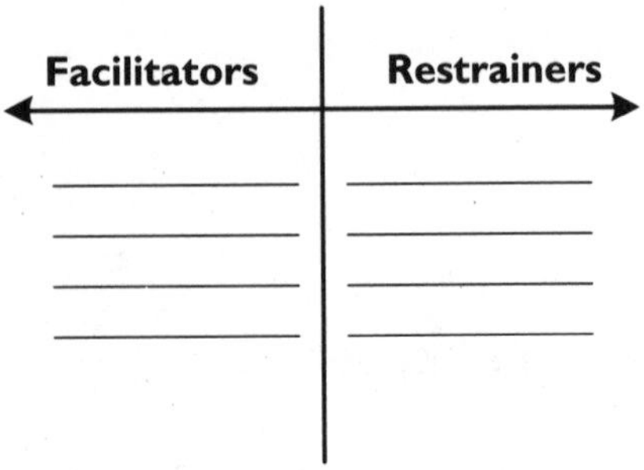

FIGURE **4-12. Force field in balance**

In addition to helping make the problem situation visual, force-field analysis provides a method for developing a solution. The most effective solution will involve reducing the restraining forces operating on the problem (Figure 4-13).

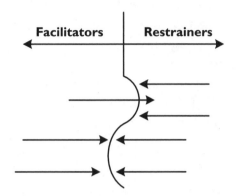

FIGURE 4-13. Reducing the restraining forces

There are two reasons for reducing the restraining forces:

▶ To move the problem toward solution.
▶ To avoid the effect of having too many facilitating forces.

Because the forces on each side of the situation are in balance, removing or reducing the restraining forces will cause movement of the problem toward solution. On the other hand, adding facilitating forces without reducing restraining forces will likely lead to the appearance of new restrainers. Remember, although you may change the situation by changing a force, you may not be improving the situation.

An effective strategy cannot be planned without evaluating the restraining forces for two factors: first, whether and to what degree a restrainer is changeable, and second, to what degree will changing a restrainer affect the problem. It is ineffective and a waste of energy to try to change an unchangeable force.

One way to begin planning a strategy is to evaluate each force to see how changeable it is. A simple three-point rating scale is sufficient:

1. A fixed, unchanging force
   Example: a contractual item, a law, a fixed budget.
2. A force changeable with moderate to extensive effort
   Example: an item that involves the efforts and cooperation of many departments.
3. A change that can be rather readily performed, perhaps by just revising a procedure, and is probably within the control of the group

The change or removal of some restrainers may have little or no impact. You must consider the effect that changing the force will have. It is good, then, to also rate the restrainers for their effect on solving the problem. A three-point rating scale can be used to rate the effect a change will have on the problem:

1. No significant improvement will occur with the change.
2. Some minor improvement will occur with the change—perhaps up to 20% of the improvement needed to solve the problem.
3. A major improvement results from changing this force, from 25% to 100% of the needed improvement.

After you have rated all of the forces operating on the problem situation, you can determine a priority for dealing with each force by adding together the ratings for each of the forces. The highest priority will be the restraining force that will have the most effect and that is most changeable. After this will come those forces that you judge to have a large effect but are less changeable, and so on.

Step 3: Develop and Implement a Strategy

At this point in the force-field analysis, you are ready to begin developing and implementing a strategy for changing the forces affecting a situation.

1. Prioritize the actions to be taken. In deciding the priority, strive for a balance between ease of change and the impact of the proposed change. Often the actions in dealing with any situation will require creative thinking. The ease of changing the facilita-

tors and the restrainers is a clue for deciding which forces to change.

2. Remove one or more of the restraining forces to allow the point of equilibrium to shift. If the new point is not satisfactory, examine the driving forces and determine which ones you can successfully change.

Step 4: Re-examine the Situation and Adjust as Necessary

The fourth step is to examine the situation once again. If you are still not satisfied with the new situation, determine which facilitating forces can be added. Each time a change is planned, take the time to estimate and determine whether the change will be worth it. Ask these questions:

1. Will it produce the desired results?
2. Which facilitating and restraining factors will be affected and how much?
3. How will the equilibrium point be affected?
4. Is there a better way of getting the same results?
5. Does the change have a negative impact on any other parts of the process?
6. What will be the return on the investment?

Force field analysis is a straightforward approach. Using it with diligence and an ongoing evaluation of solutions will ensure that it can work toward the achievement of your desired goal. Force-field analysis is valuable because it goes beyond brainstorming by helping to develop plans and set priorities.

Example

Consider a "real" example of "starting a TQM effort," shown in Figure 4-14.

In this example the organization would have to consider if the restraining forces might be too great to overcome. If the organization decides to continue with starting TQM, a great deal of effort must be expended to overcome the restraining forces.

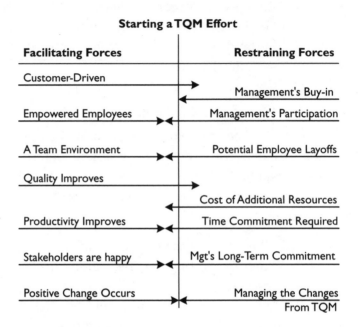

FIGURE **4-14. Example of a completed force-field analysis diagram**

Additional Ammunition

Brassard, Michael. *The Memory Jogger Plus* (Milwaukee, WI: ASQ Quality Press, 1989)

Harrington, H. James. *The Improvement Process: How America's Leading Companies Improve Quality* (New York: McGraw-Hill, 1987)

Lynch, Robert F., and Thomas J. Werner. *Continuous Improvement Teams and Tools: A Guide for Action* (Milwaukee, WI: ASQ Quality Press, 1991)

Tague, Nancy R. *The Quality Toolbox* (Milwaukee, WI: ASQ Quality Press, 1995)

WOW Weapons: Mind Maps/Ideagrams

Definition: An unstructured cause-and-effect diagram. It is also called mind-flows or Brain Webs.
Classification: Basic Idea-Generation Weapon
Users: Groups, Teams, and Individuals

Just the Facts

Mind Mapping™ was introduced in 1974 by Tony Buran. He recommended using it for creative writing, taking notes, and problem solving. The problem statement is written in the center of chart paper. Members of the group offer their opinions about possible causes, using brainstorming. These are drawn on the chart paper as "spinoffs" from the problem statement (see Figure 4-15).

After identifying all the causes, the group selects the most significant cause. A new mind map is created, with this cause now becoming the problem statement. This process is continued until it defines the root cause of the problem (see Figure 4-16).

When the root cause is defined, the mind map is then used to define potential solutions (see Figure 4-17). Sometimes the mind map is drawn with the problem statement in the circle and the "spinoff" lines are straight lines rather than curved lines.

These nine steps will help guide a team in constructing a mind map.

Step 1. Select an experienced mind-mapping facilitator.

Step 2. Select a meeting area that has a whiteboard. Flip charts will work, but a whiteboard works better.

Step 3. Determine if the team needs to be trained in the mind-mapping approach. Training should be provided if necessary.

Step 4. Select a scribe.

Step 5. The group selects a problem or opportunity to mind map.

Step 6. The scribe draws a circle in the center of the whiteboard and records the problem in the circle.

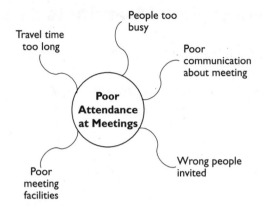

FIGURE 4-15. Mind map—level 1

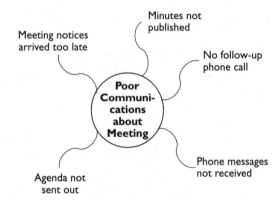

FIGURE 4-16. Mind map—level 2

FIGURE 4-17. Mind map—level 2

Step 7. The team brainstorms to define major causes (branches) and they are connected to the center.

Step 8. Each branch can become the center circle of a new mind map (see Figures 4-16 and 4-17) and the process is repeated. Another approach draws sub-branches ("twigs") that are connected to the major branches (see Figure 4-18). The team continues to add information with twigs until all the information is recorded.

Step 9. When no new ideas are being submitted, the facilitator conducts a final check of the team and concludes the exercise.

Sometimes branches that come out of the circle break out into twigs that define causes related to the branch. In the more complex mind maps, the twigs will even have sub-twigs that define causes related to the twigs. These are called "connected mind maps." Often symbols or icons are used to highlight general classifications of twigs (see Figure 4-17). For example

 = quality cause

 = cost cause

 = cycle time cause

GETTING TO THE HEART OF WASTE

Example

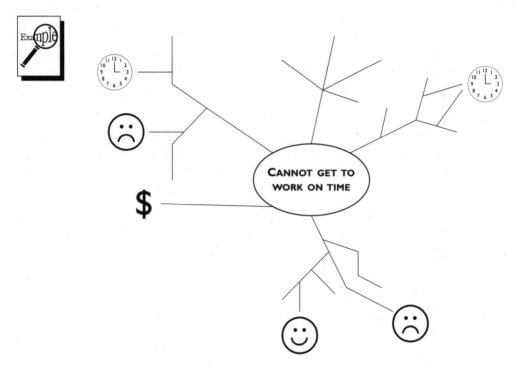

FIGURE 4-18. Connected mind map using symbols to denote causes

Additional Ammunition

Harrington, H. James. *The Improvement Process: How America's Leading Companies Improve Quality* (New York: McGraw-Hill, 1987)

King, Bob. *The Seven Management Tools* (Methuen, MA: Goal/QPC, 1989)

CHAPTER

5

Basic Decision-Making Weapons

A decision put off until tomorrow is a day wasted.

Chapter Preview

One of the biggest dollar-value waste drivers in industry today is lack of decision making at the proper time. It costs organizations within the United States billions of dollars every year. Few people realize the negative impact that putting off decisions has upon the organization. Not only does it stop progress, but it keeps us from doing other things more productive with our time because we clutter our minds with things that should have already been disposed of. Too many of us live in the mode, "Why do anything today if it can be put off until tomorrow?"

Is that you? Stop and make a list of things that you did in the last 24 hours that could have been done earlier. We hope that your list was a lot shorter than the one we made the first time we tried it. Think about the last ten times you sent something by express mail. How many of those items would you have sent out earlier if you didn't have express mail available to you? If your answer is more than two, then you are a procrastinator and need help making decisions.

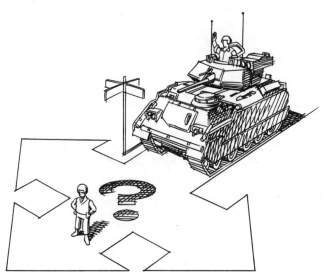

FIGURE 5-1. Making sound decisions: another weapon to reduce waste

Today's trend leads us to involve many people, teams, and groups in the decisions that relate to them. We want to get a consensus opinion, not a vote. As a result, we tend to blame others because decisions are not made rapidly. Many people argue that it takes time to get everyone involved and to reach consensus. We agree with this concern, but we cannot allow involvement to bring the decision-making process to a stop. Today there are many effective weapons that will help you quickly unite ideas and define a course of action. The team decision-making process is well-defined and should be understood by every individual who is a member of a team or a group. This part of the book will give you techniques to help your teams make decisions more efficiently.

The decision-making weapons presented in this chapter range from the very simple to the very complex. The decision-making weapons will be presented in the following order:

Chapter 5—Basic Decision-Making Weapons

▶ Consensus
▶ Delphi Narrowing Technique
▶ Management Presentations
▶ Matrix Diagrams/Decision Matrices
▶ Plus-Minus-Interesting

CD-ROM-Section I—Specialized Decision-Making Weapons

▶ Assumption Evaluation
▶ Solution-Analysis Diagram

CD-ROM-Section J—Mass-Destruction Decision-Making Weapons

▶ Best Value Future State Solution

Summary

Decisions, decisions, decisions. We're constantly faced with many decisions all the time as we go through life. We go to Baskin-Robbins and we have 31 flavors to select from, yet we can't find plain vanilla and chocolate. We turn on my television and the cable presents me with 98 channels. By the time we understand what's on at 8:00 p.m., it's 8:32 p.m. and we need to start all over again.

In today's fast-moving business environment, if you put off making a decision about a business opportunity today, your competition will make it and you'll lose the opportunity. Minimize risks. Make decisions based upon fact. Certainly, that is the theme today. If you don't have all of the facts, it may be best to take the risk and make the decision rather than sit around doing nothing. The tools are there to help you make decisions fast and effectively. Don't be afraid to make decisions, but understand the risk associated with each decision and stay close to the activities that have high risk associated with them. This will allow you to take quick corrective action if decisions result in problems.

A wise man once said, "Do something, even if it's wrong. It's better than doing nothing."

Introduction

Decisions are a lot like money. The more good ones you make, the richer you are.

This chapter presents weapons that are used to help employees and management make better decisions and to get improved buy-in from the people affected by the decision. These are relatively simple, straightforward weapons that everyone in the organization should be able to use effectively. These are weapons that should be part of the basic training for every employee.

The weapons that are included in this chapter are:

Consensus—An interactive process, involving all group members, where ideas are openly exchanged and discussed until all group members accept and support a decision, even though some of the group members may not completely agree with it. Reaching a consensus is often time-consuming and often involves individual compromising.

Delphi Narrowing Technique—A technique where team members' priorities are used to reduce a list of alternatives to a few of the most important alternatives.

Management Presentations—A special type of formal meeting of work groups and their managers.

Matrix Diagrams/Decision Matrices—A way to display data to make it easy to visualize and compare.

Plus-Minus-Interesting—An idea-evaluation weapon that analyzes the idea or concept by making a list of positive (+) and negative (-) things related to the idea or concept. It also uses a third column, called "interesting," where random thoughts about the item being evaluated are recorded, a technique often used to evaluate a solution that may initially seem like a bad idea.

WOW WEAPON: CONSENSUS

Definition: An interactive process, involving all group members, where ideas are openly exchanged and discussed until all group members accept and support a decision, even though some of the group members may not completely agree with it. To reach a consensus often is time-consuming and often involves individual compromising.

Classification: Basic Decision-Making Weapon

Users: Groups, Teams, and Management

Just the Facts

Consensus is a commitment by all team members to move forward in a particular direction. It is the alternative to voting to reach a group commitment.

Consensus does not mean that all members of the group agree with a decision. It does mean that all members of the group agree to act together with regard to a decision.

There is no formal procedure for reaching consensus. However, the following principles should guide whatever procedure is used:

Consensus is:	**Consensus is not:**
When team members	*When team members*
• Freely offer their knowledge and opinions	• Hold back their ideas for fear of ridicule
• Express and explore their disagreements	• Let their arrogance or dogmatism cause others to reject their ideas
• Question all underlying assumptions	• Misinform the group on a critical point
• Clarify all misunderstandings	• Mislead others by pretending to understand what is not clear to them

(Continued on the next page)

Consensus is not:
When team members

- Make unfounded assumptions
- Force a decision before all available information has been considered
- Let their emotions dominate their thinking
- Fail to pose all the questions they have

Consensus: When all members of the team participate in arriving at a common decision and can accept ownership as if it were their own idea. There are basically two types of consensus: *Hard Consensus*—When all members of the team absolutely agree with the outcome or solution. *Soft Consensus*—When some members would prefer a different solution but are willing to support the decision of the team.

Managing Meetings with Consensus—Guidelines and Tips

▶ Avoid arguing for your own priorities. Present your position as lucidly and logically as possible, but listen to other members' reactions and consider them carefully before you press your point.

▶ Do not assume that someone must win and someone must lose when discussion reaches a stalemate. Instead, look for the alternative next most acceptable to all parties.

▶ Do not change your mind simply to avoid conflict and reach agreement. When agreement seems to come too quickly and easily, be suspicious. Explore the reasons and be sure everyone accepts the solution for basically similar or complementary reasons. Yield only to positions that have objective and logically sound foundations.

▶ Avoid certain conflict-reducing techniques, such as majority vote, averages, coin flips, and bargaining. When dissenting members finally agree, do not feel that they must be rewarded by having their own way on some later point.

► Differences of opinion are natural and expected. Seek them out and try to involve everyone in the decision process. Disagreements can help the group's decision because a wide range of information and opinion increases the chance that the group will find adequate solutions.

Making Decisions by Consensus

Consensus will happen:

► When all team members participate in arriving at a common decision and support it as if it were their own idea.

Consensus is best when:

► Team and leader have skills of listening and negotiation.
► The team is not under pressure of time to make a decision.

Consensus can be dangerous because:

► It takes more time than other methods.
► It may result in compromise instead of agreement.

Example

Let's pretend we work in an office whose employees typically go out to lunch together. In the past, one of them has made a suggestion and the others have gone along with it, whether they wanted to or not. Today let's try to reach consensus.

Mary: Well, guys, where are we going to eat today?

Bob: I know this swell new Mexican restaurant over on the south side of town. I think we ought to go there.

Tom: I'm OK with that—let's go!

Mary: Wait a minute, you guys. What about the rest of you? Betty, what do you think about going for Mexican food?

Betty: Well, I don't mind Mexican food, but it will take us 10 minutes just to get there and since it's a new restaurant it will be packed. We probably won't get seated for 10 minutes. Add 10 minutes to get a server, then 20 minutes to get our food. That leaves us 10 minutes to eat and get back to work. I think we should consider other alternatives.

Bob: Gee, I never thought about how much time it would take. If everyone is OK with Mexican food, how about Joe's Taco Town?

Mary: That's OK with me. What about you, Betty?

Betty: I can go along with that. I'm just having a salad, but I can get that anywhere. What about you, Tom? Is that OK?

Tom: Yes, anywhere is OK! I'm hungry—let's go eat!

You might call this a soft consensus, because Betty still doesn't sound too sure about Mexican food. She has, however, agreed that she is OK with the solution and can support it. Tom will probably go along with anything. He is the type of member who can cause a team to take an unwanted trip. (Remember the Abilene Paradox? It's the story of a group of people who ended up driving miles to eat in a restaurant where none of them really wanted to go, simply because everyone wanted to get along with the others.) Always challenge the decision that is reached quickly and without much research or discussion.

This team has gone from a suggestion that was almost implemented (because one team member was in a hurry) to a much better solution that everyone could buy into.

Additional Ammunition

Bucholz, Steve. *Creating the High-Performance Team* (New York: John Wiley & Sons, 1989)

Ernst & Young LLP. *Tools and Techniques Resource Guide* (Cleveland, OH: The Quality and Productivity Group, Ernst & Young, 1992)

Ernst & Young Quality Improvement Consulting Group. *Systematic Participative Management: Team Member Manual* (San Jose, CA: Ernst & Young LLP, 1991)

Harrington, H. James. *The Improvement Process: How America's Leading Companies Improve Quality* (New York: McGraw-Hill, 1987)

Ishikawa, Kaoru. *Guide to Quality Control* (Milwaukee, WI: ASQ Quality Press, 1986)

Lynch, Robert F., and Thomas J. Werner. *Continuous Improvement Teams and Tools: A Guide for Action* (Milwaukee, WI: ASQ Quality Press, 1991)

PQ Systems, Inc. *Total Quality Tools* (Milwaukee, WI: ASQ Quality Press, 1996)

WOW WEAPON: DELPHI NARROWING TECHNIQUE

Definition: A technique where team members' priorities are used to reduce a list of alternatives to a few of the most important alternatives.

Classification: Basic Decision-Making Weapon

Users: Groups and Teams

Just the Facts

The Delphi narrowing technique is a method for selecting from a list of alternative problems, causes, or solutions. It is primarily a subjective method, used to reach consensus on a problem.

For our example, let's pretend our team has brainstormed a list of 38 items pertaining to an issue. The team has agreed to narrow the list down to a few significant issues using the Delphi narrowing technique. The following is a step-by-step approach to using the Delphi narrowing technique.

Step 1. *Agree on the criteria to be used as a basis for the narrowing.*
Possible Problem-Selection Criteria
a. Problem Type (extent of team control)
Type I: *Control*—Team has information, expertise, resources, and authority necessary to solve the problem.

Type II: *Influence*—Team does not have the full control necessary, but can influence the outcome, with assistance.

Type III: *Neither*—Team has neither control nor influence and should not take on this problem.

b. Frequency of Occurrence

The number of times the condition, event, or problem occurs. Consider what, where, when, or under what circumstances it occurs.

c. Cost of Poor Quality

Consider the costs to the organization: to prevent the problem from occurring, to inspect the problem when it occurs, to fix the problem if detected in process prior to shipment, to fix the problem if detected by the end user, and warranty and field repair costs. Consider also the loss of potential sales.

d. Number of Customers (Internal and/or External) Affected

How widespread is the impact of the problem?

e. Cost to Customer

Consider cost impact on the customer (internal or external) or end user when defect occurs during use.

f. Time Lost or Wasted

Consider schedule delays, waiting time, rework, duplicated effort, etc. resulting from the problem.

g. Measurability

Can the current state and future state be measured or quantified objectively? Will we have clear evidence of outcomes?

h. Complexity/Difficulty

Are the problem and its causes easy to understand? Or are there a large number of unknowns and variables? How much expertise will be required? Does the problem appear solvable?

i. Time to Solution
An estimate of both the labor hours required and the total elapsed time to implement the solution.

j. Durability of Solution
Once fixed, is the problem likely to stay fixed?

k. Applicability or Transferability
Is a solution to this problem likely to solve other problems as well? Be transferable to similar problems? Be usable by other units in the organization?

l. Management Priority
What importance does management assign to solving this problem? How relevant is the problem to attaining the organizational mission and goals?

Let's say we picked Number of Customers Affected, Cost to Customer, Frequency of Occurrence, and Time to Solution as our selection criteria. The team leader then would make sure that each team member clearly understands the criteria and how to apply it to the given problem and brainstormed items on our list.

Step 2. *Each team member individually ranks his or her top choices from our brainstormed list.*
Based on the number of brainstormed items, agree on the number of choices that each person gets to select, using the table below.

Number of Brainstormed Alternatives	Number of Choices
40-60	6
25-40	5
15-25	4
10-15	3
5-10	2

Since there are 38 items on our brainstormed list, each team member will be allowed to select five selections from the list.

Each person independently applies the criteria to the alternatives and records privately the ranking of the items he or she has selected, in priority order.

Step 3. *Each individual should rank-order his or her choices.* This means the top choice (or the one he or she feels is most important) would be ranked as a 5. The second choice would be a 4, and so on.

Step 4. *The individual rankings are recorded on the master list.*

Recording the choices is easy. Start with each team member's top choice. On the whiteboard, next to the brainstormed item that was selected as a top choice, place a 5. Go through each member's list until all rankings have been recorded.

Step 5. *Tally the number of responses given for each item and the total value given for each item chosen.*

For instance, if one of our brainstormed items were "Cost prohibitive to our customers" and seven team members ranked it as one of their five choices, the tally might look like this:

"Cost prohibitive to our customers" 5, 4, 5, 5, 3, 4, 5 = 7/31

The sequence of numbers records the seven rankings: four members ranked this item as most important, while two others ranked it second, and one member ranked it third. The total value of this item would be 31—the sum of the seven rankings.

Step 6. *Circle the choices that receive:*
- ▶ The highest total value
- ▶ The highest number of mentions
- ▶ A top priority ranking by any participant

Step 7. *Subject the alternatives to further discussion, investigation, data collection, verification, etc.,* leading to a consensus decision based on facts.

Out of our list of 38 potential concerns, the team will probably have selected a third or fewer for further review.

The purpose of the Delphi narrowing technique is just what the name says—to narrow, not select the final concern. Only additional review and investigation will help in the final selection.

Additional Guidelines and Tips

If the team is brainstorming possible causes to a problem, use the following possible cause-selection criteria:

1. *Extent of the Cause-Effect Relationship Correlation*
   Consider which of the possible causes are most highly correlated to the effect being analyzed. (Scatter diagrams may prove to be helpful.)

2. *Deviation from Standards or Specifications*
   Pay particular attention to the possible causes linked to current practices that do not comply with approved procedures or to goods that do not meet specifications. (Histograms may prove to be helpful.)

3. *Cause Type*
   Similar to *problem type*. Identify the possible causes over which you have the most control or influence, then focus attention on those.

4. *All Other Problem-Selection Criteria*
   Consider some of the same criteria identified earlier as potentially useful in selecting the problem, and collect data as needed. Those criteria were:

   ► Frequency of occurrence
   ► Quality cost
   ► Number of customers (internal/external) affected
   ► Customer cost
   ► Time lost or wasted
   ► Measurability
   ► Complexity/difficulty
   ► Time to solution

▶ Durability of solution
▶ Applicability or transferability
▶ Management priority

5. *For Solutions—Extent of the Solution-Cause Relationship Correlation*
Consider which proposed solutions are most likely to eliminate the cause.

6. *For Solutions—Requirements and Targets Relationship*
Consider which proposed solutions are most likely to meet the conditions set forth under the requirements and targets set by the team and/or management. Which will most likely achieve what we've set out to accomplish?

7. *For Solutions—Future State Relationship*
Consider which proposed solutions are most likely to result in the conditions set forth in our "Picture of the Future State."

8. *Solution Type*
Similar to *problem type* and *cause type*. Consider the proposed solutions over which you have the most control or influence.

9. *Cost-Benefit Analysis*
Evaluate potential costs and benefits of proposed solutions. For which solution is the ratio most favorable?

10. *Resources Needed*
Consider the extent of labor, material, information, and capital resources that may be required. What is the extent of the proposed change? The more energy required to produce it, the greater the potential for resistance to it.

11. *Time to Implement*
Consider the total elapsed time necessary to implement alternative solutions.

12. *Durability*

Which solutions are likely to have the most lasting performance effects?

13. *Applicability or Transferability*

Which solutions are likely to have the broadest applications? Which might solve other problems as well? Which might be usable by other departments?

Example

The problem statement is:

> *"The Administrative Department is not*
> *getting its work out in a timely manner."*

The following is a list of brainstormed potential solutions:

- ► Hire more people
- ► Distribute the work more evenly
- ► Take on fewer new tasks
- ► Change from word processors to computers
- ► Hire part-time workers
- ► Use management to fill in
- ► Take fewer breaks
- ► Take more breaks
- ► Buy new word processors
- ► Provide better training
- ► Provide any training
- ► Provide comfortable chairs
- ► Designate work-flow supervisors
- ► Use first-in, first-out system
- ► Outsource some of the work

There are five members of the team. Since there are 15 potential solutions proposed, each team member would get three selections.

Let's say each team member has made his or her selections and ranked them, giving a 3 to the top choice and a 1 to the bottom choice.

The following is the resulting prioritized brainstorm list, showing the rankings and totals. The fraction at the end of the line shows the number of team members selecting that item and the sum of the votes.

- Hire more people   1,3,2 = 3/6
- Distribute the work more evenly
- Take in fewer new tasks
- Change from word processors to computers   2,3,3,3,3 = 5/14
- Hire part-time workers
- Use management to fill in
- Take fewer breaks
- Take more breaks
- Buy new word processors   1 = 1/1
- Provide better training   1,1,2,2 = 4/6
- Provide any training
- Provide comfortable chairs
- Designate work-flow supervisors
- Use first-in, first-out system
- Outsource some of the work   1,2 = 2/3

In this example, the team would select the following items for further review:

- Change from word processors to computers (note: this item got the most votes and the largest sum of ranking points)
- Hire more people (note: this was one team member's top selection)

Remember: the purpose of the Delphi narrowing technique is not to determine the correct solution or cause, but to narrow a list of many possibles to a few probables.

Additional Ammunition

Bucholz, Steve. *Creating the High-Performance Team* (New York: John Wiley & Sons, 1989)

Ernst & Young LLP. *Tools and Techniques Resource Guide* (Cleveland, OH: The Quality and Productivity Group, 1992)

Harrington, H. James. *The Improvement Process: How America's Leading Companies Improve Quality* (New York: McGraw-Hill, 1987)

WOW WEAPON: MANAGEMENT PRESENTATIONS

Definition: A special type of formal meeting where the work groups present their activities to their managers.
Classification: Basic Decision-Making Weapon
Users: Groups, Individuals, and Teams

Just the Facts

You can improve your creativity by learning about and using tools that help you see and understand the world from new perspectives.

Management presentations are held to show a group's achievements or to present proposals to managers for approval.

Benefits of Management Presentations

The management presentation is a mechanism from which both group members and management receive benefits. The members benefit through the personal development and experience they receive in preparing for and giving the presentation. They also benefit through management's recognition of their accomplishments. Management benefits by becoming personally acquainted with the valuable improvements being made by the group and by witnessing the quality-consciousness and dedication of their employees. They also can hear accounts from the group as to the beneficial experiences from working together to systematically solve problems.

Purposes

There are several purposes that can be served by a management presentation. Fundamentally, the presentation is a demonstration of effective participation; it is itself an exercise in participative management.

Ultimately, the purpose of the presentation is communication. The structure of your presentation can help serve this purpose, by making certain that the environment is conducive, that you are well prepared, and that there is an opportunity for a two-way conversation.

Areas Needing Special Attention

Some people by virtue of experience and/or position are accomplished public speakers. They know how to present their ideas clearly and persuasively; they know how to use visual aids effectively. Others need to work at acquiring or improving these competencies. The more accomplished can aid those who must work harder to make an effective presentation. They can listen to rehearsals and offer constructive criticism, assist in the preparation of visuals, and help in the proper use of audio-visual equipment. Such assistance is a continuation of the cooperative activities that precede any formal presentation.

What follows are a few ideas to serve as a reminder or a guide to an effective presentation.

Oral Presentation

Regardless of experience, it is always wise to rehearse an oral presentation. Benefit can come from speaking out loud in front of a mirror, as you can both see and hear yourself. When possible, practicing before another person can also provide constructive feedback. You want to be particularly aware of clarity and speed of delivery.

There are those who perform best speaking from notes; others prefer a written script. Use the method with which you are most comfortable. It is normally better to avoid reading a script to your audience. Should this be necessary, practice can lead to a delivery that minimizes the stiffness often associated with reading a presentation. The same can be said for those who choose to memorize their presentations.

Eye contact with the audience is very important. You want to be able to "read" their responses as you proceed. You will be able to tell if the listeners are understanding you, if they are with you, and if questions or objections are forming. Their faces will give you immediate and ongoing feedback. Make sure that they are following and understanding you.

Visual Aids

The following are some guidelines that will help with using visual aids:

▶ Whatever diagrams, lists, graphs, or slides you present should be accurate, neat, and uncluttered. Each should tell the story you want it to tell.

▶ Overhead transparencies (foils) are a particularly effective visual aid, leading to participation, interaction, and efficiency in your meetings. Here are some proven uses of these visual tools:

• Announce topics and elicit feedback
• Balance discussions by showing the issues
• Avoid digressions by re-displaying the issues or purposes of the meeting
• Regain control by focusing attention on projected information
• Stimulate attention with bold print and use of color
• Refer to agenda to ensure that all items are covered
• Project conclusions and action plans

▶ Use the overhead projector with the room lights on for better group attention and participation.

▶ Face your audience. This enables you to remain in control and pick up any group reactions quickly.

▶ Make certain the projector shows what you are saying, when you say it.

▶ The on-off technique directs attention to information on the screen or to you. In other words, turn off the projector when you want attention focused on you and not on the screen.

▶ Reveal material point by point so you can control the pace and flow of your presentation.

▶ Become familiar with how the projector operates. Make sure it is easy to use, quiet, not distracting.

AV Equipment

The overhead projector is not the only piece of AV equipment you may want to use. Today we have many computer presentation aids that make the presentation look more professional. Whatever types of equipment you use, make sure that you or an assistant know how to operate them and that each is working properly. Nothing can destroy an otherwise well-prepared presentation as completely as malfunctioning equipment or ineptness in using the equipment. This is particularly true when making a computer presentation for the first time. Although time-consuming, we recommend having a set of overhead transparencies as a backup.

Summary

As a communication device, the management presentation provides opportunities for everyone in attendance. Those who prepare and give the presentation benefit in both personal development and experience. They also benefit from everyone's recognition of their accomplishments. Those hearing the presentation benefit by becoming personally acquainted with the valuable improvement and accomplishments being made by those making the presentation and by witnessing the quality-consciousness and dedication of their employees.

There are several things to be achieved in a management presentation. Any of the following results might be expected:

- ▶ It displays the group's problem-solving skills.
- ▶ It shows the accomplishments of the team.
- ▶ It demonstrates the personal accomplishments and leadership skills of the presenters.
- ▶ It provides an opportunity to request necessary approval to implement the solution to a problem.
- ▶ It allows for communication of decisions.
- ▶ It opens lines of communication between employees and management.

A management presentation is an occasion that can be both beneficial and enjoyable for all the participants. When well prepared and well delivered, it will be well received.

Examples

Figure 5-2 shows a typical team invitation to management to attend the presentation. The figures following track the presentation, based on the agenda.

Invitation to Attend a Management Presentation on:

Proposed Solution for Eliminating Improper Price Quotes on the ABC Product

Team: The ABC Product Team
Time: Friday, April 17, 1998 10:00 AM - 11:00 AM
Place: West Wing-Executive Conference Room
Attendees: ABC Product Manager, VP Production, VP Sales and Marketing, Director of Sales and Marketing, ABC Product Engineering Supervisor, ABC Product Team Members

Proposed Agenda

10:00-10:05 Present Team Members to Management Staff
10:05-10:30 Present Problem Statement and Problem-Solving Process
10:30-10:45 Present Proposed Solution and Cost-Saving Analysis
10:45-11:00 Questions and Answers
11:00   Adjourn

Please contact the team leader (Ms. Ida Knowles) if you are unable to attend this very important meeting.

FIGURE 5-2. Example of an invitation to attend a management presentation

Figure 5-3 is an example of an overhead introducing the team to the management staff. Never assume that management is aware of who the team members are—or even that a team exists!

Figure 5-4 shows a typical overhead that states the problem assigned to the team and its revision of that problem statement after analysis.

Figure 5-5 shows the proposed solution and cost-savings analysis overhead. Note that it does not go into great detail. A handout should be available to show any detailed analysis (see Figure 5-6, page 235). Keep the overhead simple.

Introducing the ABC Product Team

Member's Name	Work Location
Bobbie Lyn Baker	Customer Service
Ms. Ida Knowles	ABC Product Line (Team Leader)
Sally Scales	Customer Service
John Smith	Sales
Dorothy Yamamoto	Marketing
Dan Dinkles	Improvement Management (Facilitator)

FIGURE 5-3. Example of overhead showing team members

The ABC Product Team Presentation

1. Original task given to the team was to review customer complaints about the ABC Product and recommend a solution.

2. Original Problem Statement:

   "The ABC Product is generating numerous customer complaints."

3. Analysis:

   The customers don't have a problem with the ABC Product. They do, however, have a problem with the original price quotes provided by Sales and Marketing. 97% of the customer complaints pertained to discrepancies between the original price quotes and the final price on the billing invoice.

4. New Problem Statement:

   "Improper price quotes are generating numerous complaints and returns on the ABC Product."

FIGURE 5-4. Example of a team's revised problem statement

The team could also add a "Recommendations" overhead as well as others showing one- to three-year projections. The level of detail is dependent upon the issue and the audience.

In any case, the team should require an answer from its management on the proposed solution. Meeting wrap-up questions could include:

- ▶ Is the proposed solution acceptable as presented?
- ▶ Will the present team be empowered to implement its recommendations?
- ▶ When should the solution be implemented?
- ▶ What measures will be used to track its progress?
- ▶ What is the next step?

The ABC Product Team Presentation

Proposed Solution and Cost-Savings Analysis

Proposed Solution: Redefine costs for the ABC Product to include all typical add-ons. Sales and Marketing will inform customers that the basic price of this product includes the basic add-ons.

Cost-Savings Analysis:

• Profit due to return rate reduction	= $282,658
• Added profit on previously returned units	= $42,908
• Total profit per month	= $325,566

(Note: The organization also makes an additional profit of $68 on every unit sold and not returned.)

FIGURE 5-5. Proposed solution and cost-savings analysis overhead

If you follow this simple process, your management presentation will be a productive and rewarding event for you and your audience.

Additional Ammunition

Brassard, Michael. *The Memory Jogger Plus* (Milwaukee, WI: ASQ Quality Press, 1989)

Bucholz, Steve. *Creating the High-Performance Team* (New York: John Wiley & Sons, 1989)

Ernst & Young Quality Improvement Consulting Group. *Systematic Participative Management: Team Member Manual* (San Jose, CA: Ernst & Young LLP, 1991)

Harrington, H. James. *Business Process Improvement: How America's Leading Companies Improve Quality* (New York: McGraw-Hill, 1991)

The ABC Product Team Presentation

Proposed Solution and Cost-Savings Analysis Report

Proposed Solution: Redefine costs for the ABC Product to include all typical add-ons. Sales and Marketing will inform customers that the basic price of this product includes the basic add-ons.

Rationale: While the initial cost of the product will increase from $1,500 to $1,725, we feel the customer will more readily accept the cost increase since including the add-ons later would typically increase the cost to $1,850.

Cost Savings: Our company is currently losing long-term clients due to this pricing issue. The cost to implement this solution is less than $20,000. This includes changing the price in the new edition of the company catalog, providing distributors with new price labels, and training the telemarketers in how to present the new price to customers.

We are currently processing 650 returns monthly pertaining to this specific problem. Our analysis shows that approximately 97% (631) of current returns will be eliminated. We do predict a loss of 3% due to the newly increased price.

- Profit due to return rate reduction = S

- Previous loss due to returns = PO

- PO = 650 (no. of returns) × $450 (old profit) = $292,500

- New loss due to returns = PN

- PN = 19 (no. of returns) × $518 (new profit) = $9,842

- S = PO - PN = $292,500 - $9,842 = $282,658

- Added profit on previously returned units = PA

- Difference between old and new return rates = R

- R = 650 (old return rate) - 19 (new return rate)   = 631

- Difference between old and new profits = D

- D = $518 (new profit) - $450 (old profit) = $68

- PA = R × D = 631 × $68 = $42,908

- Total profit = profit on returns + added profit = $282,658 + $42,908 = $325,566

(Note: The organization also makes an additional profit on every unit that is sold and is not returned of $68.)

FIGURE 5-6. Cost savings analysis report, used as a handout

Ishikawa, Kaoru. *Guide to Quality Control* (Milwaukee, WI: ASQ Quality Press, 1986)

Lynch, Robert F., and Thomas J. Werner. *Continuous Improvement Teams and Tools: A Guide for Action* (Milwaukee, WI: ASQ Quality Press, 1991)

WOW Weapon: Matrix Diagrams/Decision Matrices

Definition: A systematic way of selecting from larger lists of alternatives. They can be used to select a problem from a list of potential problems, select primary root causes from a larger list, or select a solution from a list of alternatives.
Classification: Basic Decision-Making Weapon
Users: Teams and Individuals

Just The Facts

The matrix diagram is a weapon that assists in the investigation of relationships. While there are many variations of matrix diagrams, the most commonly used is the decision or prioritization matrix. This comes in two basic formats, L-shape and T-shape.

L-Shaped Decision Matrix

We will start by showing a relatively simple L-shaped decision matrix that compares two sets of information (Figure 5-7).

As you can see from the example, we are comparing several automobile dealers (our choices) with a predetermined set of decision criteria. Now all that remains is to determine which type of ranking method we will use. There are four basic types of ranking methods:

1. **Forced Choice.** Each alternative is ranked in relation to the others. The alternative best meeting the criteria gets a score

Criterion / Choice	Recommended by Friends	Good Selection of Cars	Good Service Department	Free Loaner Cars	Free Drop-off and Pick-up
Dealer 1					
Dealer 2					
Dealer 3					
Dealer 4					
Dealer 5					

FIGURE 5-7. Example of an L-shaped decision matrix

equal to the number of alternatives. Since we have five dealers in our example, the worst would get a 1 and the best a 5.

2. **Rating Scale.** Each alternative is rated independently against an objective standard. For example, a 1–10 scale would have 1 = very low (does not meet the standard at all) and 10 = perfect (absolutely meets the standard).

3. **Objective Data.** Here we enter actual data, rather than the opinions of the individual(s) doing the ranking.

4. **Yes/No.** If the criteria are expressed in absolute terms, so an alternative either meets each criterion or not, a "Y" for yes or an "N" for no may be entered to indicate conformance or non-conformance.

Figure 5-8 shows our automobile dealership example using the simple Yes/No ranking method.

As you can see, while it is the easiest ranking method, the Yes/No approach often leaves the user with little information on which to make a decision.

Let's try ranking our choices, using the Forced Choice method (Figure 5-9). Remember: this method ranks each alternative in relation to the others. In this case the dealer meeting our criteria the best will get a 5, since we have five choices, and the worst will get a 1.

Criterion / Choice	Recommended by Friends	Good Selection of Cars	Good Service Department	Free Loaner Cars	Free Drop-off and Pick-up
Dealer 1	(Y)	(Y)	N	N	(Y)
Dealer 2	(Y)	N	(Y)	(Y)	N
Dealer 3	N	(Y)	(Y)	N	(Y)
Dealer 4	(Y)	(Y)	(Y)	N	N
Dealer 5	(Y)	N	(Y)	(Y)	N

FIGURE 5-8. Example of an L-shaped decision matrix using the "yes/no" ranking method

Criterion / Choice	Recommended by Friends	Good Selection of Cars	Good Service Department	Free Loaner Cars	Free Drop-off and Pick-up	Totals
Dealer 1	5	4	1	2	5	17
Dealer 2	3	1	2	5	3	14
Dealer 3	1	3	3	1	4	12
Dealer 4	4	5	5	3	1	(18)
Dealer 5	2	2	4	4	2	14

FIGURE 5-9. Example of an L-shaped decision matrix using the "Forced Choice" ranking method

Now we have information that might allow us to make a decision. As you can see, Dealer 4 scored the highest, with 18. Does this mean you should automatically buy your car from him? Not necessarily. Although Dealer 4 scored the highest overall, he scored the lowest on "Free Drop-off and Pick-up." If this were a critical element to the potential buyer, he or she might want to consider the second choice, Dealer 1.

This is where using the Objective Data method might be of assistance. The person or group doing the ranking might even consider using a combination of ranking methods. This is certainly an option, but it makes the final selection a bit more complex.

T-Shaped Decision Matrix

The second format we mentioned was the T-shaped decision matrix. While the L-shaped matrix compares two sets of information, the T-shaped matrix compares two sets of information with a third.

An example of this could be a corporation's training program. We could compare the type of training available with departments that need the training and training providers. Figure 5-10 shows an example of this matrix format.

There are many approaches to designing and developing a matrix diagram. Listed below are five steps you may find useful in developing a matrix diagram that's just right for your purpose.

Step 1. Determine the task. Are you looking at two elements or three? What should the desired outcome look like? Is the matrix to be used

Training Providers		TQM Tools	Computer Skills	Specific Job Skills	Team Building	Effective Meetings	Leadership Skills
	OD Dept			✓			✓
	Quality Group	✓			✓	✓	
	Direct Supervisor						
	Outside Resource	✓	✓	✓			
Training Available		TQM Tools	Computer Skills	Specific Job Skills	Team Building	Effective Meetings	Leadership Skills
Departments Requiring Specialty Training	Engineering	✓			✓		
	Manufacturing	✓			✓		✓
	Finance	✓	✓	✓			
	Sales	✓			✓	✓	
	Marketing	✓			✓		

FIGURE 5-10. Example of a T-shaped decision matrix

as a problem-solving tool or a planning graph? Is it a stand-alone tool that leads us to action? Or will we use it in conjunction with other tools, such as a tree diagram or relation diagram?

Step 2. Select the matrix format. If you are reviewing the relationships between two elements, you may want to use the L-shaped matrix. If you add a third element, you will want to use the T–shaped matrix.

Step 3: Determine the criteria for evaluating alternatives. A typical list of criteria is presented below:

- ► Customer Impact
- ► Number of Customers Affected
- ► Within Control of the Team
- ► Within Influence of the Team
- ► Cost of Quality
- ► Rework
- ► Frequency of Occurrence
- ► Cycle-Time Impact
- ► Revenue Impact
- ► Return on Investment
- ► Complexity of Analysis
- ► Time to Develop a Solution
- ► Durability of Solution
- ► Cost to Implement Solution
- ► Availability of Measurements

The criteria should be worded in terms of the ideal result, not worded neutrally. For example, a criterion could be "Easy to implement," but not "Ease of implementation."

Step 4: Determine the weights for the individual criterion or use equal weighting.

Step 5: Determine how the individual alternatives will be ranked.

- ► *Forced Choice:* Each alternative is ranked in relation to the others. The alternative best meeting a criterion would get a score equal to the number of alternatives and the worst alternative would get a 1.

- ▶ *Rating Scale:* Each alternative is rated independently against an objective standard. For example; a 1 – 10 scale would have 1 = very low (does not meet the standard at all) and 10 = perfect (absolutely meets the standard).
- ▶ *Objective Data:* Enter actual data, rather than the opinions of the individual(s) doing the ranking.
- ▶ *Yes/No:* If the criteria are expressed in absolute terms, so an alternative either meets each criterion or not, simply enter Y or N to indicate conformance or non-conformance.

Step 6: Review the results and take action as required.

Guidelines and Tips

Whenever comparing alternatives (Forced Choice or Rating Scale), the group must agree on the relative importance of the alternatives and criteria for scoring purposes. Relative importance can be established either through consensus discussion or through voting techniques. You will usually want to reach agreement rather quickly on this. The amount of time you spend should be based on the importance of the problem/solution and on the number of alternatives and criteria. If there are a large number of alternatives and/or criteria, you can reach agreement more quickly if you keep in mind that the impact of each individual item on the list is smaller.

Depending on the nature and impact of the problem, this process can be simplified for quicker and easier use. For example, the process can be simplified by assuming that the criteria are of equal importance and therefore the ranking of alternatives can be skipped. You can look for other simplifying assumptions. Just be aware of their impact on results.

There is no one best way to weight criteria or alternatives. In the Forced Choice method, you rate each element against the other, based on the number of choices. This is a time-consuming method, though.

The Rating Scale method is quick, but has the drawback that people tend to rank every criterion as very important or high on the scale of 1 through 10.

Again, there is no one best method. Use the method that provides the most information. Before using any of the alternative approaches described here, however, think about the implications of the various schemes.

If you plan to use prioritization matrices repeatedly, you might set up a simple spreadsheet to assist you with some of the calculations.

Example

The examples are included in the text.

Additional Ammunition

Asaka, Tetsuichi, and Kazuo Ozeki, eds. *Handbook of Quality Tools: The Japanese Approach* (Portland, OR: Productivity Press, 1998)

Eiga, T., R. Futami, H. Miyawama, and Y. Nayatani. *The Seven New QC Tools: Practical Applications for Managers* (New York: Quality Resources, 1994)

King, Bob. *The Seven Management Tools* (Methuen, MA: Goal/QPC, 1989)

Mizuno, Shigeru, ed. *Management for Quality Improvement: The 7 New QC Tools* (Portland, OR: Productivity Press, 1988)

GET RID OF THE WASTE MONSTER

WOW WEAPON: PLUS-MINUS-INTERESTING (PMI)

Definition: An idea-evaluation weapon that analyzes the idea or concept by making a list of positive (+) and negative (-) things related to the idea or concept. It also uses a third column, called "interesting," where random thoughts about the item being evaluated are recorded. A technique often used to evaluate a solution that may initially seem like a bad idea.
Classification: Basic Decision-Making Weapon
Users: Groups and Teams

Just the Facts

Plus-minus-interesting (PMI) is an idea-evaluation and selection technique. It is used to objectively evaluate proposed solutions to problems and to mitigate the effects of initial emotional reactions to ideas and premature judgments. A side benefit of using the technique may be generation of new ideas.

Here are the basic advantages of PMI:

▶ PMI helps you avoid rejecting a valuable idea that seems bad at first sight.

▶ PMI is likely to reveal the disadvantage of an idea you like very much.

▶ PMI shows that ideas are not just good or bad, but can also be interesting if they lead to other ideas.

▶ PMI helps base judgments on the value of the idea, not on your emotions at the time.

▶ With PMI, you decide whether you like the idea *after* you have explored it instead of *before*.

PMI uses a structured brainstorming approach and is best used in group processes, although individuals may also find the framework useful. Figure 5-11 presents the worksheet for using this technique.

Problem Statement: _____	
Alternative Solution: _____	

Plus	**Minus**

Interesting

FIGURE 5-11. A worksheet for using the PMI decision-making technique

Steps to Prepare a PMI

Step 1. Write down the problem statement.

Step 2. Write down a solution idea. Alternative solutions should have been generated previously.

Step 3. Conduct a brainstorming session on the pluses of the idea. Write down the positive aspects of the proposed solution (why you like it).

Step 4. Conduct a brainstorming session on the minuses of the idea, analogous to the pluses session in Step 3.

Note: If at any time in using this technique, a thought occurs that is not clearly a plus or a minus for the idea, record it in the "interesting" category.

Step 5. Do a gross appraisal of the idea at this time. Is it still worth pursuing? If not, evaluate the next idea. If so, go on to Step 6.

Step 6. Evaluate the pluses. Do they include the outcomes that you want from the solution? Does it appear that it will achieve the targeted improvement? Do the pluses include any meaningful unforeseen benefits?

Step 7. Evaluate the minuses. Are any both unavoidable and of sufficient magnitude to warrant eliminating the idea from the list of alternatives? Can modifying the idea mitigate some of the minuses? Identify the minuses that will need specific attention in the implementation, should the idea be pursued.

Step 8. Repeat Steps 2 through 7 for a new solution idea.

Step 9. Compare the analyses for all of the alternatives evaluated.

Step 10. Select an alternative to implement.

Guidelines and Tips

To the extent possible, quantify the benefits of the pluses and the impact of the minuses in your evaluation. However, remember that creative problem-solving techniques are often used because it is not possible or practical to obtain complete information. If some elements of the pluses and minuses are quantified and others are not, be sure not to discount the importance of the factors not quantified. They may be just as significant in determining the best solution.

Summary

- ▶ P = Plus: the good points of an idea—why you like it
- ▶ M = Minus: the bad points of an idea—why you don't like it

▶ I = Interesting points that are important to consider, but neither obviously good nor obviously bad

Example

You and a co-worker are assigned to work on a marketing study. She prefers to work by herself; you want to pool resources and cooperate in order to get quicker results and greater productivity. She is adamant about working alone. You would like her to be a bit more flexible. So you suggest that you both do a PMI on the idea of cooperating on the project. The resulting PMI is shown in Figure 5-12 on the next page.

Additional Ammunition

Ernst & Young LLP. *Tools and Techniques Resource Guide* (Cleveland, OH: The Quality and Productivity Group, 1992)

Ernst & Young Quality Improvement Consulting Group. *Systematic Participative Management: Team Member Manual* (San Jose, CA: Ernst & Young LLP, 1991)

I'VE GOT IT IN MY SIGHTS

Problem Statement: Would it be more effective to work together on this marketing study?

Plus

- Better, more effective results.

- Better results could lead to benefits for both.

- Less lonely than working alone.

- It might be fun.

- You might discover a whole new opportunity.

- Cooperation on projects might become the new trend in the company, which could benefit everyone.

Minus

- Credit for work done well has to be shared with someone else who might not have contributed much.

- One might have to wait for the other person's thinking before going ahead.

- You might not always agree and then there would be conflict.

- Personality differences might interfere with the work.

- One might stifle or otherwise inhibit the other's creativity.

- Overconfidence by the team might lead to stubbornly pursuing the wrong course.

Interesting

- Perhaps work separately most of the time, then get together at certain times and make a fresh decision each time whether to pool results.

- Work separately throughout the project; get together at the very end and decide how to confine the results.

- We may discover that we make an excellent team and decide we both should quit the company and go into business for ourselves.

- The project should be defined to give credit to the person who does the work.

- Which approach will minimize the cycle time?

- Which approach will require fewer resources?

- If the job does not get done on schedule, we both will fail.

FIGURE 5-12. PMI on the idea of cooperating on the project

6

Basic Action/Execution Weapons

Just do it!

—NIKE SLOGAN

Chapter Preview

We have talked a lot about planning, data analysis, idea generation, and decision making. This is all a waste of effort and time if the output from these activities is not implemented. By now, you should have a long list of things that should be done. Let's get with it.

The weapons that are presented in this chapter are all weapons that do not fit into the planning, data-analysis, idea-generation, or decision-making categories. These are weapons like bureaucracy elimination, project management, and error proofing. As you can see, they are all action items designed to transform the organization. We suggest that you look at these weapons carefully, as they are very effective at cutting right to the heart of waste. The action/execution weapons presented in this chapter range from the very simple to the very complex. The 12 action/execution weapons will be presented in the following order.

Chapter 6—Basic Action/Execution Weapons

- ▶ Cycle-Time Analysis and Reduction
- ▶ Executive Error-Rate Reduction
- ▶ Five S's
- ▶ Problem-Tracking Log
- ▶ Process Simplification

CD-ROM-Section K—Specialized Action/Execution Weapons

- ▶ Arrow Diagrams/Activity Network Diagrams
- ▶ Bureaucracy-Elimination Methods
- ▶ Error Proofing
- ▶ Project Management

CD-ROM Section L—Mass-Destruction Action/Execution Weapons

- ▶ Quality Function Deployment

CD-ROM Section M—Strategic Action/Execution Weapons

- ▶ Process Qualification
- ▶ Reverse Engineering

Summary

We have presented fewer than 10% of the weapons that make up the performance improvement arsenal. The ones presented are the ones that we find are the most effective and commonly used. This is just the tip of the iceberg. In order to customize your performance improvement process, maximize the organization's competitive position, and optimize the return on investment from your performance improvement activities, you will have to gain an understanding of some of the other 1001 performance improvement weapons.

Remember that, unlike the stories about Aladdin's *1001 Arabian Nights*, these cannot be considered passing fantasies that bring you joy for one night or even for one month. These are weapons that, once selected, should become part of the way the organization is managed and have a very significant impact upon the organization's culture. As the knight who guarded the Holy Grail in the movie *Indiana Jones and the Last Crusade* said to Harrison Ford as he tried to select the cup that Jesus drank from at the Last Supper, "You must choose, but choose wisely, for just as the true Grail will bring you life, the false Grail will take it from you."

This book does have something in common with Aladdin's *1001 Arabian Nights*. It's a lot like the magic lamp. Rub it to bring out the genie—but be careful what you wish for. Your organization will have to live with it.

Introduction

The benefits occur only when you convert plans into action.

This chapter presents weapons that are used to implement performance improvement activities. These are weapons that should be widely used and understood throughout the organization. Weapons 1, 3, and 4 should be part of everyone's basic training. Weapon 2 should be part of every manager's basic training.

The weapons that are included in this chapter are:

Dd

This is a sample of the text for the definition, or these are more synonyms and usages that are commonly found in the English language.

Cycle-Time Analysis and Reduction—An approach to reduce the time that it takes to move an item through a process.
Executive Error-Rate Reduction (E²R²)—A way to establish acceptable executive behavior standards and measure compliance with them.

Five S's—A systematic approach to bring organization to the workplace. A translation of the original Five S terms from Japanese to English went like this:

▶ Seiri-Organization
▶ Seiton-Orderliness
▶ Seiso-Cleanliness
▶ Seiketsu-Standardized Cleanup
▶ Shitsuke-Discipline

Problem-Tracking Log—A systematic way to categorize, monitor, and measure progress of the corrective action process. It is designed to ensure that the correct resources are applied to solving all important problems.

Process Simplification—A methodology that takes complex tasks, activities, and processes and bisects them to define less complex ways of achieving the defined results.

WOW WEAPON: CYCLE-TIME ANALYSIS AND REDUCTION

Definition: An approach to reduce the time that it takes to move an item through a process.
Classification: Basic Action/Execution Weapon
Users: Groups, Teams, and Individuals

Just the Facts

Based upon the International Quality Study conducted by Ernst & Young LLP and the American Quality Foundation, there are only six world-wide best practices.

▶ Top management involvement
▶ Strategic planning
▶ Supplier certification

- ▶ Process simplification
- ▶ Process value analysis
- ▶ Cycle-time analysis

Time is money. Every time anything is not moving forward, it costs you money. To date, most of our focus has been on reducing processing time because we see it as added labor cost. But cycle time is also very important. Reducing time to market, time to respond to a customer request, and time to collect an outstanding bill can mean the difference between success and failure.

Critical business processes should follow the rule of thumb that time is money. Undoubtedly, process time uses valuable resources. Long cycle times delay product delivery to our customers and increase storage costs. A big advantage Japanese auto companies have over American companies is their ability to bring a new design to the market in half the time and cost. Every product has a market window. Missing the early part of the product window has a major impact on the business. Not only does the company lose a lot of sales opportunities, but it then faces an uphill battle against an already established competitor. With the importance of meeting product windows, you would think that development schedules would always be met. Actually, few development projects adhere to their original schedule.

Applications of Cycle-Time Analysis and Reduction

The object of this activity is to reduce cycle time. This is accomplished by focusing the process improvement team's attention on activities with long time cycles and activities that slow down the process. The time-line flowchart provides valuable assistance in identifying the problem activities. The team should look at the present process to determine why schedules and commitments are missed, then reestablish priorities to eliminate these slippages, and then look for ways to reduce the total cycle time. Typical ways to reduce cycle time are:

▶ *Do activities in parallel rather than serially*. Often, activities that were done serially can be done in parallel, reducing the cycle time by as much as 80%. Engineering change review is a good example. In the old process, the change folder went to manufacturing engineering, then to manufacturing, then to field services, then to purchasing, and finally to quality assurance for review and sign-off. It took an average of two days to do the review in each area and one additional day to transport the document to the next reviewer. The engineering change cycle took 15 working days, or three weeks, to complete. If any of the reviewers had a question that resulted in a change to the document, the process was repeated.

By using computer-aided design, all parties can review the document simultaneously and eliminate the transportation time. This parallel review reduces the cycle time to two days. A less equipment-intensive approach would be to hold weekly change meetings. This would reduce the average time cycle to 3.5 days and eliminate most of the recycling, because the questions would be resolved during the meeting.

▶ *Change activity sequence*. The geographic flowchart is a big help to this activity. Often, output moves to another building and then returns to the original building. Documents move back and forth among departments within the same building. In cycle-time analysis, the sequence of activities is examined to determine whether a change would reduce cycle time. Is it possible to get all the signatures from the same building before the document is moved to another location? When a document is put on hold waiting for additional data, is there anyone else who could be using the document now, saving cycle time later on?

▶ *Reduce interruptions*. The critical business process activities should get priority. Often less important interruptions delay them. People working on critical business processes should not be located in high-traffic areas, such as near the coffee machine. Someone else should answer their phones. The office layout should allow them to leave their work out during breaks, over lunch, or at day's end. The employee and the manager should agree on a time when the employee will work uninterrupted, and the manager should help keep these hours sacred.

▶ *Improve timing.* Analyze how the output is used to see how cycle time can be reduced. If the mail pickup is at 10:00 a.m., all outgoing mail should be processed before 9:45 a.m. If the computer processes a weekly report at 10:00 p.m. on Thursday, be sure that all Thursday first-shift data are input by 8:00 p.m. If you miss the report analysis window, you may have to wait 7 more days before you receive an accurate report. If a manager reads mail after work, be sure that all of that day's mail is in his or her incoming box by 4:30 p.m. It will save 24 hours in the total cycle time. Proper timing can save many days in total cycle time.

▶ *Reduce output movement.* Are the files close to the accountants? Does the secretary have to get up to put a letter in the mailbox? Are employees who work together located together? For example, are the quality, development, and manufacturing engineers located side by side when they are working on the same project? Or are they located close to other people in the same discipline?

▶ *Analyze locations.* Is the process being performed in the right building, city, state, or even the right country? Where an activity is performed physically can have a major impact on many factors. Among them are:
  • Cycle time
  • Labor cost
  • Customer relations
  • Government controls and regulations
  • Transportation cost
  • Employee skill levels
  Performing an activity in less than the optimum location can cause problems, from a minor inconvenience all the way to losing customers and valuable employees. The approach and con-

sideration for selecting the optimum location vary greatly from process to process.

As a general rule, the closer the process is located to the customer, the better. The restraints to having the process close to the customer are economy of scale, stocking costs, equipment costs, and inventory considerations. With today's advances in communication and computer systems, the trend is to go to many smaller locations located either close to the supplier or close to the customers. Even the large manufacturing specialty departments (machine shop, welding department, tool room, etc.) are being separated into small work cells that are organized to fit a process in which a lot size of one is the production plan. Often, the advantages of quick response to customer requests, increased turns per year, and decreased inventories far offset the decreased utilization costs.

Questions like "Should we have a centralized service department or many remote ones?" require very careful analysis. A graphic flowchart helps make these decisions, but the final decision must be based on a detailed understanding of customer expectations, customer impact, and cost comparisons between the options.

▶ *Set priorities.* Management must set proper priorities, communicate them to employees, and then follow up to ensure that these priorities hold. It is often a big temptation to first complete the simple little jobs—the ones that a friend wants worked on, the ones someone called about—and let the important ones slip. It's the old "squeaky wheel" principle. As a result, projects are lost, and other activities delayed. Set priorities and live by them.

Cycle-Time Analysis and Reduction Process

The cycle-time analysis and reduction process consists of 16 activities:

1. Flowchart the process that is being studied.
2. Conduct a process walk-through to understand the process and to verify the flowchart.

3. Collect cycle-time data related to each activity and task. It is often advisable to collect minimum and maximum cycle times in addition to average. This is necessary because, typically, an organization loses customers not over averages but over worst-case conditions.
4. Collect data that define the quantity flow through each leg of the flow diagram.
5. Construct a simulation model that includes all of the data that have been collected.
6. Perform a replication analysis, using the simulation model to define the cycle-time frequency distribution.
7. Classify each activity or task as *real-value added, business-value added*, or *no-value added*. Eliminate as many of the *business-value-added* and *no-value-added* activities as possible. (To understand how to eliminate business-value-added and no-value-added activities, see the section of this book related to process redesign.)
8. Define the average cycle time's critical path through the process, using the simulation model.
9. Using the cycle-time reduction principles, eliminate the critical path.
10. Repeat activities 8 and 9 until the minimum cycle time is obtained.
11. Define worst-case critical path through the process using the simulation model.
12. Using the cycle-time reduction principles, eliminate the critical path.
13. Repeat steps 11 and 12 until the minimum worst-case cycle time is obtained.
14. Develop a plan to change the process to be in line with the modified simulation model.
15. Pilot the modifications as appropriate.
16. Implement the new process.

Replication Analysis: A statistically significant number of cycles through a simulation mode using random values for the specified variables.

Example

IBM's RPQ or special bid process provides modifications to computers so that they can meet an individual customer's unique needs. Typically, the cycle time to take a customer's special requirement and design and price out the modification was taking an average of 90 days. The business was very profitable as 20% of the bids were closed. IBM decided that 90 days was too long and a team was put together to reduce the cycle time. As a result, 24 months later, any place in the world, it took an average of 15 days to complete a special bid process. In addition, the cost related to preparing the bid was decreased by 30%. But that was not the big payoff. Along with the quick response to customer requests, the bid closure rate jumped from 20% to 65%—a 325% improvement. Customers love companies that respond quickly to their special requests.

Additional Ammunition

Harrington, H. James, and James S. Harrington. *Total Improvement Management: The Next Generation in Performance Improvement* (New York: McGraw-Hill, 1995)

Harrington, H. James, Glen D. Hoffherr, and Robert P. Reid. *Area Activity Analysis: Aligning Work Activities and Measurements to Enhance Business Performance* (New York: McGraw-Hill, 1998)

Harrington, H. James. *Business Process Improvement: The Breakthrough Strategy for Total Quality, Productivity, and Competitiveness* (New York: McGraw-Hill, 1991)

Northey, Patrick, and Nigel Southway. *Cycle Time Management* (Portland, OR: Productivity Press, 1993)

WOW WEAPON: EXECUTIVE ERROR-RATE REDUCTION (E²R²)

Definition: A way to establish acceptable executive behavior standards and measure compliance to them.
Classification: Basic Action/Execution Weapon
Users: Groups, Teams, and Individuals

Just the Facts

You can improve your creativity by learning about and using tools that help you see and understand the world from new perspectives.

If we had only $10,000 to invest in improving the total organization's performance, we would invest it in establishing an executive behavior error-rate measurement system. We would make this our first priority because the behavior of the total organization changes as the executives' behavior changes.

Top management are all for change, as long as it is someone else who changes. But the No. 1 improvement rule is: Top management must change first.

Why should top management change? Aren't the managers already successful? Look at all the money they are making. In truth, more than 99.99% of top managers have a lot of opportunity to improve. In fact, none of us are perfect and most of us have many opportunities to improve our own personal behavioral patterns.

To prepare their personal performance indicators, top managers need to define what they do. I don't mean things like "motivate employees" or "manage R&D." These are their assignments. Examples of what managers do are:

Example

▶ Attend meetings
▶ Read and answer mail
▶ Answer telephone calls
▶ Make decisions
▶ Delegate work
▶ Chair meetings

Once top managers have completed a personal list of what they do, they need to define behavioral patterns related to these activities that could be improved. For example:

- ► Start meetings on time.
- ► Do not attend meetings that can be delegated to employees.
- ► Return all telephone calls within eight hours.
- ► Don't set items aside that can be done quickly.
- ► Always show up on time for meetings.
- ► Read all new mail each day.
- ► Don't use overnight mail if the project can be finished earlier and sent by regular mail.
- ► Talk with three customers each day.
- ► Make a minimum of three one-hour tours of employee work areas each week.
- ► Read five technical articles each week.
- ► Have the office organized so well that there is no need to search for lost or misfiled items.
- ► Have a clean desk at the end of the day.
- ► Stop doing things that can be delegated.
- ► Stop using bad language in the workplace.
- ► Arrive at work on time.
- ► Have an agenda in each attendee's hands a minimum of eight hours before a meeting is held.

We recommend that the executive team meet to select a group of about eight activities that it wants to focus on improving and set performance standards for each of these activities. For example, most executives select as one of the eight improvement activities "improving the way meetings are conducted." In this case, they should ask themselves such questions as:

1. How late is it acceptable to start a meeting?

- ► 2 hours?   Answer: no
- ► 1 hour?   Answer: no
- ► 30 minutes?   Answer: no
- ► 5 minutes?   Typical answer: at the most.

The executive team then agrees that the preferred start time is on schedule but never more than 5 minutes after the scheduled start time. As a result, if the person who called the meeting starts 5 minutes late, he or she has caused an error. Anyone who arrives at a meeting more than 5 minutes late has also caused an error.

2. Should there be meeting agendas and when should they be sent out?
3. Should commitments made at meetings be kept?
4. Should people who attend meetings be prepared to discuss the items on the agenda?
5. Should the meeting end on schedule?

As a result of asking questions like these, all the executives develop and agree to a complete list of behavioral performance standards. We like to have the executives report their personal error rates once a month at the executive meeting.

Each selected behavioral pattern should be recorded on a card similar in size to an airplane ticket, which can be carried easily in a purse or a coat pocket. Each time the executive does not behave as defined, he or she has made an error and should place a check mark behind the appropriate behavioral pattern. Once a week the total number of check marks should be counted and plotted on a run chart.

We recommend that each executive set an improvement target of 10% of the first month's average error rate. When all the executives reach this target, it is time to add eight more behavioral patterns to the list and start over again. In organizations where top managers have a high degree of confidence and credibility, they are each encouraged to post their personal performance run chart in their offices, demonstrating to their fellow workers that the top managers accept the fact that they personally need to change and improve. Eventually all managers and employees will use this same approach to measure their personal improvement.

The executives are each also encouraged to define their personal set of values that govern their behavior at work and in their personal lives. These values are seldom mirror images of the organization's values or principles because they reflect the total person. We encourage every top manager to post these value statements in a very visible place in their offices and/or conference room. Sharing these personal values with their fellow managers and employees and posting them where they can influence each executive's behavior has a major positive influence on the individual and the organization. Don't be afraid to let your employees know you are human. Of course, any time that an executive does not live up to a personal value, it is also an error and should be recorded on his or her error record.

Figure 6-3 is a creed written by an unknown author that H. James Harrington has adopted as his personal set of values. We hope it will start you thinking about your values.

Examples

Behavioral Category	Number of Errors	Total
End meeting on schedule	⫽⫽⫽ ⫽⫽	7
Start meeting on time	⫽⫽⫽	5
Read 5 technical articles each week	/	1
Read all new mail each day	⫽⫽⫽ ///	8
Talk to customers each day	⫽⫽⫽ ⫽⫽⫽	10
Work out 3 times each week	//	2
Delegate work	///	3
Minimize use of overnight mail	////	4
Total		40

Figure 6-1. Bob Maas, CFO, personal error log

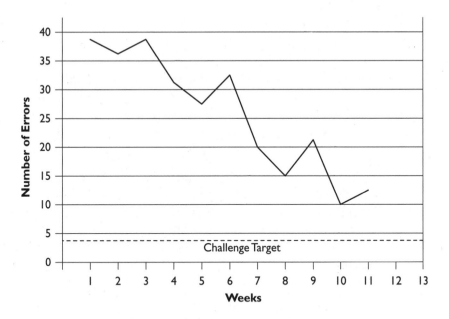

FIGURE 6-2. Bob Maas's personal performance chart

The Person I Want to Be!

A person who would be concerned with how he could help me instead of himself/herself, who would give me loyalty instead of demanding of me, who would think of himself/herself as my assistant, instead of my boss, who would think it was his/her job to help me do my job better.

A person whose pride was peculiar because his/her pride was in the team. A person who would walk around saying, "Yes, it was well done but not by me. I just happen to be lucky enough to have the best bunch of people in the whole organization." That is where his/her pride lies. Anything worthwhile that comes out of the organization, the team did. If something goes wrong, this person feels that maybe he/she was not on the ball. Maybe he/she had not directed or taught or led the people properly. This person will take the blame for anything that goes wrong.

A person who never made a promise he/she didn't intend to keep, merely to slough me off. I would pick a person who might say, "Gee,

I'm so busy, Jim, I just don't know if I'll ever get done. But let's not wait until tomorrow when it is more convenient for me. Let's sit down right now and go at it. Now is the time."

A person who knew that I was not a genius. If I come to him/her with an idea, I don't want him/her to give me that objective stuff. I don't want to hear "You have a suggestion. Here is the form. Stick it here. Stick it in the box and three months later if it is any good we will give you an award for it."

This person gets excited about my brainchild and treats my brainchild very carefully, because it is the most wonderful idea in the world at the moment. I gave birth to this child of mine. I want this person to treat it tenderly. Especially tenderly if it is a feeble-minded brainchild. The person who is going to get an award, doesn't have to worry. It is I. If I don't get one, I will feel low. I want my boss to pick me up and encourage me.

A person who would handle every grievance right now, not like the person who has a 40-room mansion, but no garbage pails, and who says, "We just kick it around until it gets lost."

A person who in many ways reminded me of my father whom I loved dearly, but who had the knack if I stepped out of line, of lowering the boom so fast I wouldn't know what struck me until too late. But who if he thought I had been pushed around, would fight for me every step of the way up the line even to the president of the company and the chairman of the board if necessary to see that I got a fair shake and a square break.   —*Author Unknown*

FIGURE 6-3. H. James Harrington's personal set of values

Additional Ammunition

Forsha, Harry I. *The Pursuit of Quality Through Personal Change* (Milwaukee, WI: ASQ Quality Press, 1992)

Harrington, H. James, and James S. Harrington. *Total Improvement Management: The new Generation in Performance Improvement* (New York: McGraw-Hill, 1995)

Nadler, David A., and Janet L. Spencer. *Executive Teams* (Milwaukee, WI: ASQ Quality Press, 1991)

WOW WEAPON: FIVE S'S

Definition: The Five S's or Five Pillars is a systematic approach to bring organization to the workplace.
Classification: Basic Action/Execution Weapon
Users: Can be used by Teams but most often by Individuals

Just the Facts

The concept of the Five S's originated in Japan by Hiroyuki Hirano. A translation of the original Five S terms from Japanese to English went like this:

- ► Seiri—Organization
- ► Seiton—Orderliness
- ► Seiso—Cleanliness
- ► Seiketsu—Standardized Cleanup
- ► Shitsuke—Discipline

In order to help users of this tool remember the elements, the original terminology has been retranslated to the following Five S's.

- ► Sort
- ► Set in Order
- ► Shine
- ► Standardize
- ► Sustain

Since several books have been written on this tool, it should be noted that the terms Five Pillars and the Five S's can be used interchangeably. Figure 6-4 is a way to visualize the the Five Pillars and the Five S's.

In the original book, *Five Pillars of the Visual Workplace,* the word "pillar" is used as a metaphor to mean "one of a group of structural elements that together support a structural system." In this case, the five

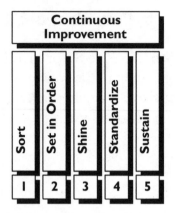

FIGURE 6-4. The Five Pillars and Five S's

pillars are essential in supporting a continuous improvement process within the organization.

The five pillars are identified as Sort, Set in Order, Shine, Standardize, and Sustain. The most important elements of the five are Sort and Set in Order. The success of all improvement activities depends upon them. The figure below gives a good overview of this very beneficial tool.

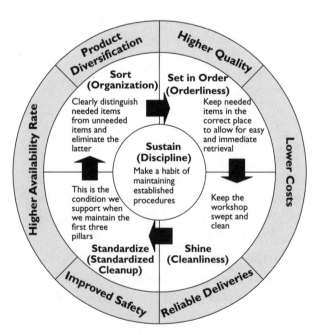

FIGURE 6-5. Overview of the five pillars (This figure modiifed from a similar figure in the book *Five Pillars of the Visual Workplace* by Hiroyuki Hirano, Productivity Press, 1995.

An Overview of the Five Pillars

Have you visited a manufacturing plant that seemed cluttered and unorganized? These organizations value the employee who can find items that are missing. These missing items could be tools, parts, equipment, and even documentation. The employees look at the "search for resources" as a part of their daily task. Now add the additional unsavory element of a plant that is dirty with spilled oils and other trash.

This represents a factory that has neglected to implement the first two pillars or S's, Sort and Set in Order. Very likely this factory will produce a high level of defective products. It may miss delivery deadlines, resulting in loss of business and a decline in employee morale.

Why the Five Pillars Are the Foundation of Five S Improvement Activities

As stated earlier, the five pillars are essential in the support of continuous improvement activities. However, people may still have a hard time fully understanding the need for the Five Pillars.

Each of us practices the Five Pillars in our personal lives without really noticing it. We practice Sort and Set in Order when we keep things like wastebaskets, towels, and tissues in places that are convenient and comfortable to us. When our home becomes crowded and disorganized, our efficiency and effectiveness deteriorate.

Few manufacturing plants are as organized with the Five-Pillar (Five S) process as is the home life of a well-organized person. This is unfortunate since, in the daily work of a factory, just as in the daily life of a person, routines that maintain organization and orderliness are essential to a smooth and efficient flow of activities. The Sort and Set in Order elements are the foundation for achieving zero defects, cost reductions, safety improvements, and zero accidents. The Five S system sounds so simple and normal that we often dismiss its importance. However, the fact remains that:

- ▸ A neat and clean factory has higher productivity.
- ▸ A neat and clean factory produces fewer defects.
- ▸ A neat and clean factory meets deadlines better.
- ▸ A neat and clean factory is a much safer place to work.

Description of the Five Pillars

Now let's look at each of the Five Pillars, one at a time.

The First Pillar: Sort

Sort: Removal of all items from the workplace that are not needed for the current operation.

As easy as this seems, it is often difficult to identify what is *needed* versus what is *wanted*.

Getting rid of items in the workplace can be stressful. People tend to hang onto parts, equipment, and/or tools, thinking that they may be needed for the next order or operation. This causes inventory and equipment to accumulate and get in the way of everyday production activities. If everyone does this, it can lead to a massive buildup of waste organization-wide.

The following types of waste lead to errors, defects, and an unmanageable work space.

- ▸ Unneeded inventory creates extra costs, such as storage space and management.
- ▸ Unneeded transportation of parts requires extra pallets and carts.
- ▸ The larger the amount, the harder it is to sort out needed inventory from unneeded inventory.
- ▸ Large quantities of stocked items become obsolete due to engineering changes, limited shelf life, etc.
- ▸ Quality-related defects result from unneeded in-process inventory and machine breakdowns.

► Unneeded equipment poses a daily obstacle to production activities.

The presence of unneeded items makes designing equipment layout more difficult.

The Second Pillar: Set in Order

Set in Order: Arranging needed items so that they are easy to use and labeling them so that they are easy to find and put away.

This activity should always be implemented with Sort. Once everything is sorted through, only what is necessary to the task remains. Next it should be made clear where these things belong, so that anyone can immediately understand where to find them, as well as where to return them. For example, the outline of every tool can be painted on the surface where it should be stored.

The Third Pillar: Shine

Shine: Keeping the workspace clean.

The third pillar includes sweeping floors, emptying trash, wiping down machinery after use, cleaning up spills, etc. In a manufacturing organization, this activity is closely related to the ability to produce quality products. Shine also includes saving labor by finding ways to prevent dirt, dust, and debris from piling up in the manufacturing areas.

Shine should be designed into the preventive maintenance process to combine cleaning checkpoints with maintenance checkpoints.

The Fourth Pillar: Standardize

Standardize: Do it the same way each time.

The Standardize activity differs from Sort, Set in Order, and Shine in that the first three pillars can be thought of as activities, as something we do. However, Standardize is the activity you use to maintain these first three pillars.

This activity is related to each of the first three pillars, but it relates most strongly to Shine. It results when we keep machines and their surroundings free of debris, oil, and dirt. It is the condition that exists after we have practiced Shine for some time.

The Fifth Pillar: Sustain

Sustain: Making a habit of properly maintaining correct policies and procedures.

The first four pillars can be implemented without difficulty if the workplace is one where the employees commit to sustaining Five S conditions. Such a workplace is likely to have high productivity as well as high quality.

In many organizations much time and effort are spent in vain sorting and cleaning because the company lacks the discipline to maintain and continue Five S implementation on a daily basis. As with all continuous improvement tools, if the process does not have the Sustain pillar the other pillars will not last long.

Benefits of Five S Implementation for You and Your Organization

Five S implementation should have many benefits for you.

- ► It can give you an opportunity to provide input regarding how your workplace should be organized and laid out and how your work should be done.
- ► It can make the workplace more pleasant to work in.
- ► It can make the job more satisfying.
- ► It can remove some of the obstacles and frustrations related to the work.
- ► It can make it easier to communicate with everyone in the workplace.

Your organization can also experience many benefits from implementing the five pillars. It can:

► increase product diversity
► raise quality
► lower costs
► encourage reliable deliveries
► promote safety
► build customer confidence
► promote organizational growth

Example

Equipment Cleanliness Checklist	Yes	No	Comments
Are the gauges working and readable with no cracks in the glass?			
Are V-belts broken or loose?			
Is oil leaking from the equipment?			
Is there oil on the floor?			
Is the oil in the oil tanks murky?			
Are there oil or air leaks from hydraulic and pneumatic devices?			
Are there any nuts or bolts loose or missing?			
Are there chips on the floor?			
Is there abnormal vibration or noise?			
Are the motors abnormally hot?			
Has the total machine been cleaned in the last 24 hours?			
Are the tools hanging in their indicated location?			
Are the parts to be processed and the already processed parts in a location where dirt or oil cannot drop or be blown on them?			
Is the paperwork in oil-proof folders?			

Comments:

Checked by _____   Date ___ / ___ / ___   Time_____

FIGURE 6-6. A Five S checklist

Additional Ammunition

Greif, Michel. *The Visual Factory: Building Participation Through Shared Information* (Portland, OR: Productivity Press, 1991).

Hirano, Hiroyuki. *Five Pillars of the Visual Workplace* (Portland, OR: Productivity Press, 1995)

Nikkan Kogyo Shimbun, Ltd. *Visual Control Systems* (Portland, OR: Productivity Press, 1998)

Productivity Press Development Team. *5S for Operators* (Portland, OR: Productivity Press, 1995)

Productivity Press Development Team. *The Visual Factory* (Portland, OR: Productivity Press, 1993)

WOW Weapon: Problem-Tracking Log

Definition: A systematic way to categorize, monitor and measure progress of the corrective action process. It is designed to ensure that the correct resources are applied to solving all important problems.
Classification: Basic Action/Execution Weapon
Users: Organizations, Groups, Teams, and Individuals

Just the Facts

The problem-tracking log, while simple in concept, is one of the most important weapons in our "War on Waste" arsenal. Too many problems or important issues get lost on somebody's desk and forgotten until—you probably have guessed where we're going with this—the boss wants to know the status of the issues.

There are five key elements to a problem-tracking log. Let's look at them in order.

▶ What (Description of the problem)

▶ Where (Department or process that owns the issue or problem)

▶ Who (Responsibility for overseeing or correcting)

▶ Why (Level of seriousness of the issue or problem)

▶ When (Due date of final corrective action)

Pretty simple, right? If so, why don't we use this important action/execution WOW weapon more often? We think the answer is that people really intend to complete in a timely manner the tasks given to them or for which they have volunteered. The priorities of their normal day-to-day activities, however, get in the way and the "problem" gets pushed to the side.

At an IBM site in California, problem response time was cut by 75% just by installing a problem-tracking process. This is best accomplished through the organization's computer network, but can be just as effective in a small organization to generate a problem log that is reviewed by management once a week.

Our example (Figures 6-7 and 6-8) shows a problem-tracking log (also called a "corrective action log") that lists all the problems or issues being tracked. Figure 6-8 shows how a detail log tracks an individual problem. You will note that the problem has not been solved in the 50 days it was assigned to J. Smith; it has now been reassigned to Bob Reid.

One of the key pieces of information on the log is the "Problem Slip-to Date" or, as some computer programs have it, an "Action Aging Report." This information lets the reviewer know when the original corrective action was supposed to be complete and the actual date of compliance.

Another type of report that can be very helpful in problem tracking is the exception report. We like to send out the following reports:

▶ A list of problems that are due next week to the person responsible

▶ A list of problems that are overdue by three weeks or more to the second-level manager

- A list of all overdue problems to the person responsible and his or her manager
- A list of problems that have missed the target date more than three times to the second-level manager. The second-level manager is made responsible for defining why his or her management process is not working effectively and what action he or she will take to correct it.

There are many more value-added reports that can be generated by a good problem-tracking computer program, such as:

- action detail reports
- problem Pareto reports
- action Pareto reports
- problem summary reports
- problem trend reports
- action trend reports
- problem aging reports
- action aging reports

You want to remember—the desire is to drain the swamp, not count alligators. If the reports don't add value to your situation, don't use them. If a problem is tracked, it tends to be corrected. If not, it tends to be neglected.

Example

Figure 6-7 shows a page from a problem-tracking log for an employee in the customer service department, showing all the problems or issues assigned to this individual. You will note that the overdue items are highlighted and that 50% of the items are behind the original target date. This reflects the realities of life. We used to track action items based upon target dates. When a target was missed, the person responsible set a new target that was tracked. As a result, it took months to correct a problem that could have been solved in days.

You will also see that the problems listed in Figure 6-7 are symptoms, not root causes. Often these types of problems are answered like this:

▶ Operator is notified
▶ Order is found
▶ Parts are cleaned
▶ Supplier is notified
▶ Sent out replacement parts

These are reaction responses, not corrective action, let alone preventive action. By reviewing the problems during the last one to three months, the major problems can be defined and addressed. We recommend that the same problem not be answered the same way more than once. If the action that was taken didn't correct the problem the first time, it will not correct it the second time.

Problem - Tracking Log(List all problems assigned to John Smith)							**Date of Log:** 8/12/98
Tracking Number	**Problem Description**	**Dept #**	**Problem Date**	**Person Resp.**	**Due Date**	**Slip-to Date**	**Status**
P-0001	Customer complaints not handled in a timely manner	31	4/1	John Smith	7/14/98	10/19/98	In process
P-0002	Customer No. Q23670 order never arrived at destination	31	7/1	John Smith	7/16/98	N/A	Order misrouted, delivered 7/12
P-0003	Product B5439 shipping containers arriving damaged	31	7/1	John Smith	7/18/98	8/21/98	Vendor working on Correct-Act.
P-0004	Customer complaints not handled from 12 - 1:30 P.M.	31	7/30	John Smith	8/5/98	N/A	New CS rep covers lunch hour
P-0005	Product B5439 returns are not processed in a timely manner	31	7/30	John Smith	8/7/98	8/13/98	Eng. design team looking into
P-0006	Customer No. H53985 order return not received for shipping	31	8/6	John Smith	8/7/98	N/A	Found— shipped same day

FIGURE 6-7. Example of a problem-tracking log (highlighted item covered in more detail in Figure 6-9)

Figure 6-8 shows an example of how additional information about a specific problem, identified on the Problem-Tracking Log, is stored. This report is often called the "Problem-Tracking Detail Log" and is available on most of the more detailed PTL computer programs (see Additional Ammunition). The purpose of this report is to provide the reviewer with a deeper level of detail about what took place or is taking place to close out the item. Note that a change to the original corrective action (C/A) date requires an explanation. Any time the original C/A date changes, or "slips," an explanation should be provided. This does two things: it gives the reviewer the reason for the missed target and it cuts down on dates that are missed for frivolous reasons. If the person responsible for the problem has to provide reasons for missing a target date, he or she is more likely to try and make it.

Problem-Tracking Detail Log		Date of Log: 8/12/98

Problem Owner Identified by: Andrew Jones   **Date of Original Notification:** 7/1/98
Problem Owner: Customer Service Department
Problem Tracking Number: P-0003   **Assigned to:** John Smith   **C/A Due Date:** 7/18/98
Part Code: 175   Problem Code: 062___   **Cause Code:**___

Slip-to Date (Explanation required): 8/21/98

Date	Person	Comments
7/1	A. Jones	Product B5439 shipping containers arrived damaged at the back dock. John Smith will look into the problem and report status on 7/4.
7/6	J. Smith	Containers were inspected. It looks like a forklift backed into them. We need to understand if our forklifts did it or if it is a supplier problem. Target date for corrective action is 7/18.
7/30	J. Smith	Our forklifts are too high to have caused the problem. I will discuss the problem with the supplier. New target date for corrective action is 8/21.
8/5	J. Smith	Picture sent to the supplier and containers are being returned. They should get to the supplier by 8/10.
8/15	J. Smith	Receiving notified me that the lot delivered on 8/10 had the same problem.
8/20	J. Smith	Supplier notified me their forklift couldn't be causing the problem. Bob Reid from Purchasing will visit the supplier to inspect the way they are handling the containers. Trip planned for 9/15. This problem is being reassigned to Bob Reid. He will provide a new corrective action target date.

FIGURE 6-8. Example of a problem-tracking log

You will note that the form in Figure 6-9 contains a part code, a problem code, and a cause code. These are used with group problems and corrective actions to detect trends. They can be either word codes or number codes. With computers, word codes work well. In order to ensure the correct grouping, a list of problem words and cause words is generated and used by everyone. You will note that the part and problem codes are filled in. This is usually done by the person who detects the problem. The cause code cannot be filled in until the root cause of the problem is known.

Additional Ammunition

Corrective Action 5 (C/A 5 Problem Tracking System), software, Richard Harrington (Orlando, FL: The Harrington Group, 1998)

Ernst & Young Quality Improvement Consulting Group. *Systematic Participative Management: Team Member Manual* (San Jose: CA: Ernst & Young LLP, 1991)

Ernst & Young Quality Improvement Consulting Group. *Total Quality: An Executive's Guide for the 1990s* (Homewood, IL: Business One Irwin, 1990)

Harrington, H. James, and James S. Harrington. *Total Improvement Management: The Next Generation in Performance Improvement* (New York: McGraw-Hill, 1995)

Harrington, H. James. *Excellence—The IBM Way* (Milwaukee, WI: ASQC Quality Press, 1988)

WOW Weapon: Process Simplification

Definition: A methodology that takes complex tasks, activities, and processes and bisects them to define less complex ways of accomplishing the defined results.
Classification: Basic Action/Execution Weapon
Users: Groups, Teams, and Individuals

Just the Facts

Based upon the International Quality Study conducted by Ernst & Young LLP and the American Quality Foundation, there are only four world-wide best practices:

- ▶ Top management involvement
- ▶ Supplier certification
- ▶ Cycle-time reduction
- ▶ Simplification

It's obvious that simplification is an extremely important weapon. Let's begin by trying to understand the term. We live in a world of ever-present and increasing complexity and rapid change. Complexity means that life has more of everything: more parts, more systems, more relationships, more dependencies, more problems, and more imperatives. This applies in particular to our business processes. Business processes are typically designed to support goals, requirements, and current volume. Their design is usually limited by the degree of technology that is available.

However, goals, requirements, volume, and technologies are changing rapidly, so the processes must adapt accordingly. More steps, more tasks, more people, and more interdependencies are added. When new tasks are added, support tasks usually follow (for example, preparation, filing, or putting away work), making the process more complex.

The increase in complexity results in increasing difficulties every-where, as activities, decisions, relationships, and essential information become more difficult to understand and more difficult to manage. In an era of rapidly increasing complexity, it is essential to be engaged actively and continuously in simplification as a counterforce to evolving complexity.

So what does simplification mean? It means to reduce complexity wherever feasible. It leads to fewer stages, fewer tasks, fewer interdependencies, etc. It means making everything easier: easier to learn, easier to do, easier to understand.

When you apply simplification to business processes, you evaluate every element in an effort to make it less complex, easier, and less demanding of other elements. When an organization fails to make continuous simplification efforts a major part of the managing process, it invites difficulty and poor performance. The natural evolution of complexity will eventually stifle the ability to manage the system and the processes effectively.

Applications of Simplification

The following list illustrates the application of the concept in relative-ly simple but time-consuming everyday activities:

- ▶ *Reduce duplication and/or fragmentation of tasks.* Identify duplication and fragmentation anywhere in the process, then combine related tasks and eliminate redundancies. Most organizations are shocked at the savings possible in this area.
- ▶ *Streamline complex flows and bottlenecks.* Change the order of tasks, combine or separate tasks, and even balance the work loads of different individuals.
- ▶ *Reduce memos and other correspondence.* Simplify by making these documents shorter, more direct, better formatted, more readable. Thousands of employee hours are saved by decreasing time writing, reading, and interpreting words. Less rework is required because of better understanding.

▶ *Minimize meetings.* An agenda (sent well in advance) is a basic simplification device. Presentation materials should be simple and easily understood. Meeting protocol should be established; meeting participants should be trained in protocol and follow it. It's best to have fewer meetings and spend less time in each meeting. Don't schedule meetings in whole increments (1 or 2 hours). In a one-hour meeting, 80% of the work gets done in the last 15 minutes. Look at the meeting agenda schedule to determine the amount of time required. Some meetings should be 25 minutes, others 80 minutes. Too many meetings are scheduled by the hour (8:00 a.m. to 9:00 a.m.). Try to schedule your meetings by the minute (8:18 a.m. to 8:52 a.m.). Then always start them on schedule. It will make a big difference in the way the team reacts to your meetings.

▶ *Combine similar activities.* Can similar or consecutive activities be combined to make one job more rewarding to the person performing the assignment and reduce cost, errors, and cycle time?

▶ *Reduce the amount of handling.* Can you reduce handling by combining responsibilities? Can the person doing the activity evaluate the output to ensure that it is correct? Can a phone call eliminate the need to mail a document to another building? Can a list of documents processed replace copies of the documents that are mailed?

▶ *Eliminate unused data.* Do you use all the data that are recorded? If not, why record them? Each piece should be challenged.

▶ *Eliminate copies.* Are all the copies of letters and computer reports used? In most cases, they are not. Every six months, you should question the usefulness of all regularly scheduled reports. Send out a letter notifying the recipients that they will be eliminated from the mailing list unless they request otherwise in writing. Tell them that the cost of generating the report will be shared equally among the people who receive copies. You will be surprised how many reports are not needed.

▶ *Refine standard reports.* Meet frequently with the people who receive standard reports to find out what parts of the report they use and how they use them. Put all the standard reports in a similar formats. This reduces the time to read the reports and reduces errors in the interpretation of the reports. When graphs are used, draw an arrow indicating which direction is good. (For example, if a graph shows defects per million, the trend line is good when it goes down, but if it shows profits per unit sold, good is up.) Remove unused parts of the reports.

Method

Start the simplification process by flowcharting the process and then thoroughly understanding what the process's customers need and expect related to the output. Then apply simplification principles to the process.

In trying to find ways to apply the principles of simplification, we suggest you ask questions such as:

▶ Is the process effectively systematized? Or is it performed haphazardly?

▶ Would a different process be more effective, more efficient?

▶ Would a different layout make work smoother and easier, with less handling and less wasted motion?

▶ Can the forms be filled out without adding another document?

▶ Do people make errors in filling out the forms?

▶ Can this activity or stage of the process be eliminated?

▶ Can this activity or stage be combined with another?

▶ Could a single activity produce a combined output?

▶ Are instructions immediately available, easy to understand, self-explanatory?

▶ Would a backup process eliminate rework or wait time?

▶ Does this activity require someone to stand by idly while the task is being done?

▶ Would simpler language speed up reading, improve understanding?

- ► Does the way it is done create more unnecessary work downstream?
- ► Is time lost looking for information or documents?
- ► Is the computer system really needed?
- ► Do interruptions of the work flow add to complexity?
- ► Could a template be used to simplify performing the activity?
- ► Does the work flow smoothly around the area?
- ► Can a computer system make it easier?

And the list goes on and on ....

Sometimes it is helpful to start your simplification analysis for an activity by asking the question, What is your output? Then design a process for the simplest way of generating that output and compare this new process design with the original process. After making the comparison, combine the two processes, taking the best of each.

One of the mistakes North American organizations have made since World War II is that they have looked to technology as their first line of defense to handle the increased complexity in the business world. On the other hand, Japan Incorporated has been looking for the simplest ways to handle these increased demands. Simple solutions to complex problems have some very distinct advantages over information technology solutions. Typically:

- ► They cost less.
- ► They are implemented faster.
- ► They require less skill to operate.
- ► They are more user-friendly.
- ► They break down less often.

Japan Inc.'s first approach to improving a process is to evaluate what can be done to make it:

- ► Less complex
- ► Less demanding
- ► Fewer pages
- ► Fewer steps
- ► Fewer tasks

- Fewer interruptions
- Easier to learn
- Easier to do
- Easier to understand

Of course, you should always ask the basic question—Does it need to be done at all?

The simple way is usually the best way. Try to combine similar activities. Try to reduce the amount of handling. Is the office laid out in the best possible way? Should job assignments be changed? Do you need more detail? Can you get away with less documentation?

Examples

Let's look at an example of the simplification concept: writing checks, recording the transactions in a journal, and tracking the receipts. With the traditional, old-fashioned manual method, these are three separate activities, tedious and time-consuming. Simplification combines them into one activity. The method is called the *one-write* system of check writing. Simultaneously, you can write a check, make a duplicate, and record the transaction in a journal. This system achieves the same objective with less effort, in less time, and with less chance for error. Also, keeping track of receipts is easier because they are attached to a duplicate check that can be filed numerically. Coupling this to a computer database makes the whole process even more effective. This method has proved to be an important part of the process, yet it is so basic.

The Toyota just-in-time approach is an excellent example of simplification. While the U.S. Big Three were installing very complex inventory management computer programs and the associated data-collection and data-analysis systems, Toyota chose to simplify its inventory process. Instead of spending millions of dollars on computer programs and systems, the company decided to rely on sending back empty containers to the area that produced the item as soon as the parts were used. When an empty container arrived in a sub-assembly area, new parts were manufactured and the full container was returned to final assembly. Toyota's just-in-time system was simple, dependable, and very effective, while minimizing inventory and eliminating the expensive computer systems.

Another auto industry example is the way suppliers were paid. The conventional method is a complicated information technology system that collected data related to the number of good parts received from each supplier and then compared this number with the invoice submitted from the supplier to determine how much the supplier would be paid each month. Toyota decided to drop the system entirely. Suppliers were told not to send invoices. The auto manufacturer just counted the number of cars shipped each month. Using information about the quantity of each part number that was used in the cars, the auto manufacturer paid the supplier based upon the number of parts in the cars that were shipped during the month. This resulted in paying the supplier much faster and reduced the cost for the auto manufacturer and the supplier—a real win-win situation for everybody.

Some examples of paperwork simplification are:

- ▶ Boeing cut six manuals down to one that was smaller than any of the original six.
- ▶ IBM-Brazil eliminated 50 procedures, 450 forms, and 2.5 million documents per year.
- ▶ McDonnell-Douglas F-4 airplane specification was documented on two sheets of paper in 1955. Just 25 years later, the C-12 proposal consisted of 92 books made up of 13,560 pages and more than 30,000 pieces of artwork. This is an excellent example of what happens when organizations allow complexity to creep into their processes.

Additional Ammunition

Harrington, H. James. *Business Process Improvement: The Break-through Strategy for Total Quality* (New York: McGraw-Hill, 1991)

Harrington, H. James, and James S. Harrington. *Total Improvement Management: The Next Generation in Performance Improvement* (New York: McGraw-Hill, 1995)

Ernst & Young LLP. *The International Quality Study-Best Practices Report* (New York: American Quality Foundation and Cleveland, OH: Ernst & Young LLP, 1992)

Ishikawa, Kaoru. *Guide to Quality Control* (Milwaukee, WI: ASQ Quality Press, 1986)

CHAPTER

7

Performance Improvement Teams

Teams build teamwork. Teamwork builds successful organizations.

Introduction

Since the topic of *teams* will be covered in the book *Making Teams Hum* that is part of this series, we will not duplicate that work. However, since the subject covered by this book is *improvement weapons* and since it is primarily teams that use these weapons, it makes sense to understand about the different types of teams.

The concept of teams has been around for a long time but really came to light in the '70s and '80s. Although not the panacea executives had hoped for, quality control circles, developed by Kaoru Ishikawa of Japan, set the stage for a quantum leap forward in overall organizational improvement. From this start we have gone from small groups of departmental employees solving their own issues and problems to self-managed work teams that do their own hiring and are responsible as a profit center.

Yes, teams have come a long way, but we're not through with them yet. The idea of a participatively managed, empowered group of individuals helping management in decision making is alive and well, and we hope it will be around for a long time to come.

Types Of Teams

We have identified what we believe are the six types of teams most often used in organizations today:

- ▶ quality circles (QC)
- ▶ task forces (TF)
- ▶ task teams (TT)
- ▶ department improvement teams (DIT)
- ▶ process improvement teams (PIT)
- ▶ self-managed work teams (SMWT)

Quality Circles

The *quality circle* is the team concept that allowed Japan to excel in the 1970s and 1980s. Ishikawa started the quality control movement in Japan to train foremen and workers to use the quality tools. This concept also started the participative management movement in North America, as we know it today. Unfortunately, quality circles (QC)—sometimes called quality control circles, QCC—got a bad reputation in the late '70s and early '80s because most North American organizations used the concept incorrectly. Management did not provide the required skill training, direction, and support for successful implementation. In addition, management expected the quality circle teams to solve problems that management had been unable to solve for years. As a result, management became discouraged with circles because they did not rack up big dollar savings. Dr. Yoshio Kondo, one of Japan's leading quality professors and consultants, stated, "Quality Control Circles are to motivate employees, not to reduce cost."

Japan has been very effective in using quality control circles to train employees to solve problems. In North America, the quality control circle movement failed not because of the employees, but because of management's lack of understanding of the process; as a result, it was misused. As North American management matures, managers will understand why these types of teams are so important to their overall improvement success. The self-managed team concept is based upon the quality circles concept.

This type of team is mostly made up of volunteers who hold short meetings over a definite period of time and work on either departmental or organizational issues. Management direction tends to be low for this type of team. This is probably what got the QCC teams into trouble in the first place. We have found that the more interest management shows in the process, the more likely the team is to succeed. Most U.S. organizations have moved away from calling a team a "quality circle" and, even if they are the exact same thing, call them something else. If and when U.S. organizations start to empower their employees, these are the types of teams that will most often be used.

Task Forces

A *task force* is a team most often formed to work on a very important issue or problem. The members meet for long periods, sometimes as much as twelve hours a day, seven days a week, for a short duration (typically 30 days or less). This team is usually called on to solve "survival" issues or issues that must be corrected or resolved as soon as possible. Usually, this team's activity takes precedence over all other activities going on in the organization. Typically, task force-type teams are formed when a manufacturing process is closed down for what could be a long period of time due to problems or a customer safety issue.

Management usually forms the task force, with memberships being mandatory and the leader and members being selected based on experience in the issue at hand. Direction from management is as high as the urgency of resolving the issue.

The use of task forces indicates that management has major problems with the organization's processes. We know of organizations that use the decrease in the number of task forces to measure the improvement in their processes. Organizations that have good business processes should never need to use task forces to manage and correct the organization's problem, because problems will be eliminated or recognized before they become critical.

Task Teams

A *task team* is put together to resolve an issue, then disband. Management identifies the team members who are selected, based on experience with the issue.

The issue or problem is usually not urgent. The length of team assignment may be short meetings over long periods (e.g., one hour per week for 30 days or more) or, if the issue is of a more immediate nature, longer meetings over a short period.

Department Improvement Teams (DIT)

One of the most valuable teams in the entire process, the *department improvement team* is made up of the employees in a particular department reporting to the same manager. DITs are also called *natural work teams*.

This team tends to focus on Type I problems only. These are problems the team has knowledge about, has resources to use, and is empowered to solve with little or no outside approvals. The department manager or supervisor normally leads this team. In cases where the department has more than 10 employees, membership in the team that meets periodically may rotate every 90 to 180 days. This gives everyone a chance to participate.

The team normally meets for about one hour, once a week for an indefinite period. Departmental problems are identified and prioritized. Management has the final veto in case the team selects a problem that is outside its scope or does not meet the ROI requirements.

Since this team is looking at issues that affect its own efficiency and effectiveness, there are huge opportunities for saving organizational resources.

Process Improvement Teams (PIT)

Another very valuable team to any organization is the *process improvement team*. While other teams tend to have more of a task-oriented mission, the process improvement team is allowed to focus on a specific process. These teams are also called *cross-functional teams*.

Membership in this team is directed by management but usually consists of individuals intimately involved in the particular process. In some cases, short meetings are held over a long period of time (typically one to two hours per week for six months or more). These types of PITs very often will identify process issues that can be corrected through the use of a task team. While the process team remains together, the task team would meet only until the particular process issue is resolved.

Often organizations will prioritize their critical business process and assign PITs to redesign or reengineer one to three processes at a time. In these cases, the PIT members usually are assigned to the PIT for between 50% and 100% of their time for three to six months.

Like the department improvement team, the process improvement team has great opportunities to reduce internal costs by making the process more efficient, more effective, and more adaptable.

Self-Managed Work Teams

The *self-managed work team* seems to be the "brass ring" many organizations are grabbing for. We believe there is a big future for self-managed work teams in the U.S., but we don't believe it's here quite yet.

We have heard this type of team called everything from an *autonomous work team* to *self-directed work team*. In the truest sense, the self-managed work team is one that manages its own business without outside interference from upper management. The team is responsible for setting its own departmental budget, managing its own resources, and even hiring and firing its members.

Most organizations in the U.S. that use this type of team allow them to function with little direction from management—and they function very effectively in most cases.

A word of caution: although self-managed work teams can be a real moneymaker for certain organizations, they don't work for every organization. Before an organization implements this type of structure, it should be very far along with its quality improvement initiative. This type of organizational structure is not for neophytes.

We have included some information that may help you identify the team that is right for you and your situation (see Figure 7-1). This chart is designed to guide you in understanding basic team characteristics.

Characteristics	Task Force	Task Team	Process Improvement Team	Department Improvement Team	Quality Circle	Self-Managed Work Team
Membership	Membership based on experience	Membership based on experience	Members involved in the process	Department members	Department members	Department members
Participation	Mandatory	Mandatory	Mandatory	Mandatory	Voluntary	Mandatory
Management Direction	High	Moderate	Moderate	Moderate	Low	Low
Task Selection	By management	By management	By management	By team	By team	By team
Urgency	High	Moderate	Moderate	Moderate	Low	Moderate
Scope of Activity	Organization-wide	Organization-wide	Process-wide	Department-wide	Department-wide	Department-wide
Activity Time	Long meetings, short periods, no other assignments	Short meetings, long periods	Short meetings, intermediate periods	Short meetings, intermediate periods	Short meetings, ongoing	Short meetings, ongoing
Process Facilitator	Optional	Optional	Recommended	Recommended	Recommended	Optional
Team Leadership	Appointed	Appointed	Process owner or designate	Supervisor	Supervisor or designate	Shared or rotated
Implementation	By others	By team or others	By team or others	By team	By team	By team

FIGURE 7-1. Types of teams and their characteristics

Setting and/or Approving Team Structure

For organizations just starting their improvement efforts, we recommend that the executive improvement team (EIT) or other executive structure set up and/or approve each individual problem-solving team. Yes, this causes more work for an already overburdened executive team, but we believe in the long term it will pay off in huge dividends.

The executive team identifies and/or approves the issue the team is to focus on, picks a team leader (typically someone with knowledge of the issue), and, with the leader's assistance, identifies the team members.

This approach tends to conserve the organization's limited resources while allowing the overall team process to "settle down." After the organization has been involved in teams for six months to a year, the executive team can (and should) start empowering lower-level management to establish teams.

Establishing the Team Mission

The executive team should either pick or approve the task the team is to focus on. Once this is decided, the EIT should determine the mission of the team. The team mission should simply give the team a clear perspective of why the team exists.

One of the most frustrating experiences a team can have is to be assigned an unclear task or problem by the EIT. An example of this is forming a team to look at the "communication issue." This is referred to as a *divergent* problem, a problem that tends to grow in size and complexity as the team moves forward in its efforts to solve or control it. It's up to the EIT to ensure the team is working on problems that are *convergent*, problems that tend to become more clearly defined as the team moves toward solution and implementation.

In the case of "communication," a more convergent problem would be, "We have a problem communicating between management and the employees." The EIT would then give the team a mission that might say:

> *The mission of the Communication Task Team is to iden-*
> *tify ways to enhance communication and understanding*
> *between management and employees.*

The mission sets the stage for how you want the problem or issue to change. It should be very brief, no more than two or three sentences.

Once the mission is set, the team can establish its own team charter. The charter consists of three key elements:

- ▶ The Mission (Why the team exists)
- ▶ Team Goals (What the team hopes to accomplish)
- ▶ Team Guidelines (or Code of Conduct) (How the team will manage and measure itself)

As you can see, the clearer the team mission the easier it will be for the team to complete the task. Once the team charter is established, typically each team member and the team's EIT sponsor sign off on it. This sign-off shows "ownership" by both the team and its sponsor and helps the team identify team process issues that may inhibit its performance.

Another element that is not typically (but certainly could be) a part of the team charter is the project plan. This plan gives the team specific direction in the following areas:

- ▶ team meeting schedule
- ▶ resources required
- ▶ schedule of activities
- ▶ completion time frame
- ▶ measures of success

Both the finalized team charter and the draft team project plan should be reviewed and approved by the EIT. This review and approval authorizes the use of the organization's resources for a specific period of time to complete a specific task.

Providing Resources

Chances are, no matter what problem or issue the team is working on, the team will expend some resources. Not providing adequate resources to the team will send a very clear and negative message as to how much the EIT supports its efforts.

It is the EIT's responsibility to understand enough about the team's problem or issue to adequately budget the money, staff, time, etc. to complete the task. It is not a good idea to expect the team to accomplish corporate or organizational miracles on the members' own time.

If the EIT is concerned or unsure about the resources it will take to complete the task, the team should be asked to complete a cost analysis. This analysis should include, but not be limited to:

▶ Estimated time away from the job (for each team member)
▶ Estimated cost of outside analysis (if any)
▶ Estimated cost of team supplies
▶ Estimated cost of outside consulting (if required)
▶ Potential savings

The cost analysis should not include any implementation estimates at this time, since the team would not have progressed far enough in the problem-solving process to make any implementation estimates.

After the team has completed its task and is ready for implementation, it should conduct a new cost analysis and present it to the EIT. This analysis will help the EIT identify and plan for the resources needed to implement the solution.

Note: If the EIT has a limited budget for implementation, it is imperative to make that known to the team before the team identifies a solution. This will prevent hurt feelings later on, particularly if the EIT rejects a proposed solution due to a lack of resources.

Approving Team Projects

 After an organization's improvement efforts have been under way for a while, teams will be formed to solve organizational problems. Approval of these projects may take place at several levels. But first, let's look at the three basic types of problems:

- ▶ **Type I**—*Team controls*: The team has information and knowledge about the problem as well as expertise, resources, and authority to solve the problem. These types of problems are the ones on which teams should spend most of their time.
- ▶ **Type II**—*Team can influence*: The team does not have full control of the problem or issue, but can influence the outcome, with some outside assistance.
- ▶ **Type III**—*Team neither controls nor influences*: The team can do nothing about this problem or issue and should not take on a task of this type.

If the team and the project are at the department or work unit level, the manager or supervisor may be empowered to approve the task. This would be a Type I problem. If outside resources are required, the task would be a Type II problem and the project may need to be approved at the senior management level. The team should not undertake any Type III problem, since this problem type is outside its scope. The Type III problem should be turned over to management to form a new team to correct the problem if it is justifiable.

Any project requiring cross-functional team membership should be approved by the EIT. In cases where the organization is multi-divisional, any project requiring cross-divisional teams may have to be approved at the corporate level.

In Ernst & Young Technical Report #TR 93.021 HJH, *The Collapse of Prevailing Wisdom*, H. James Harrington provides us insight into the controls placed upon the formation of teams in different parts of the world. Figures 7-2a and 7-2b show some interesting results from his report:

Country	Past (-3 years)	Present	Future (+3 years)
Canada	34%	18%	10%
Germany	41%	31%	28%
Japan	68%	68%	64%
United States	45%	30%	21%

FIGURE 7-2A. Percentage of companies in the automotive industry in which it is "always or almost always" management that approves the formation of teams

Country	Past (-3 years)	Present	Future (+3 years)
Canada	38%	24%	11%
Germany	24%	24%	15%
Japan	68%	68%	72%
United States	24%	14%	5%

FIGURE 7-2B. Percentage of companies in the computer industry in which it is "always or almost always" management that approves the formation of teams

Using this data, it is easy to see that Japanese management maintains strict control over the formation of new teams and plans to continue the practice. In contrast, the other countries are reducing their controls. The tight controls Japan is applying are consistent with management's desire to reduce the percentage of people now involved in teams.

Japan started the quality circles movement to educate its employees on quality concepts. This trend could mean the process is complete. On the other hand, in Canada, Germany, and the United States, the education and training process is still under way. The other countries should assess the value-added content that their teams are providing to determine if the added controls over the formation of teams would improve their teams' performance.

Executive Support for Teams

The executive improvement team (EIT) should be willing to run interference for the team and guide it on policy issues and potential barriers.

On an ongoing basis, the EIT should meet with team leaders and facilitators to provide:

- ▶ Advice
- ▶ Encouragement
- ▶ Suggestions
- ▶ Progress reviews
- ▶ Assistance in overcoming potential barriers

As the team progresses, the EIT should hold periodic reviews on progress to eliminate any surprises during the solution and implementation stages. Team recommendations should be reviewed and approved by the EIT prior to implementation. This should not make the team feel less empowered. Remember: the EIT still has final responsibility for using the organization's resources wisely.

Last, but certainly not least, the EIT helps drive the implementation effort. This becomes much easier, even for a team totally empowered, when management has been a part of the process from start to finish.

How to Implement a Team Process

There are many ways to implement a team process within an organization. Some organizations train all their employees and send them on their way. Other organizations do it without training anyone. More organizations do it by selecting a few people who will be trained and assigned to teams. The combination of task teams, process improvement teams, department improvement teams, and executive improvement teams provide many other options.

There is no one right way to implement the team process. The team implementation plan is always unique to the personality of the organization. The single best practice that we want to impress on you is always to provide formal training before you assign anyone to a team.

The following is the approach that we recommend if it is applicable to the organization:

1. *Form an executive improvement team (EIT) and train the members in basic team, meeting, and problem-solving skills.*

2. *Have the EIT define some quick-win problems that will have significant impact on the organization.* The EIT should then assign task teams (TT) to solve these problems.
To get the TTs started:

   ▸ The team members should be provided with basic team, meeting, and problem-solving skills training.
   ▸ Task team leaders should also have team leadership skills training.
   ▸ Trained facilitators should be assigned to work with the task teams. (Before an individual is trained to be a facilitator, he or she should have experience using all of the team key tools. Because of this, it is often necessary to use facilitators from outside the organization.)

   As problems are solved, expand the task team concept to address other specific problems or issues that need to be studied or corrected in a short period of time.

3. *Train facilitators.* After the task team members have experience in using the team tools, interested people should be selected to be trained as facilitators to work with the department improvement teams, quality circles, and other task teams. As more and more people become experienced in the team methodologies through their activities with the various types of teams, additional facilitators will be trained. A facilitator can be assigned to more than one team. In addition, a monthly meeting will be held so facilitators can share implementation experiences and exchange ideas.

4. *Conduct management-level Area Activity Analysis (AAA)*. In this case, each manager who has managers reporting to him or her should prepare an AAA with those managers.

Take, for example, an organization with four levels of management:

Position	People in the Position	Average Span of Control	Number of Areas
President	1	10	1
Vice President	10	8	10
Project Managers	80	12	80
First-Level Managers	960	20	960
Employees	19,200	1	0
Total	20,251	-	1,051

In this example, a total of 91 areas that are made up of only managers and key staff people would do individual AAAs. To accomplish this, all managers and key staff would be trained in basic team leader skills, meeting skills, team leader skills, and AAA methodology. Assuming an average of five activities per area (department), a minimum of 455 effectiveness and 455 efficiency measurements and requirements will be developed.

5. *Develop management department improvement teams (DITs)*. Now that the deviations from requirements are defined, management DITs can be formed to work on these deviations. All managers now will receive problem solving training. A facilitator should be assigned to each DIT.

6. *Form process improvement teams (PITs)*. As a result of the measurements that were defined in Step 4 and the business needs, key processes should be selected by the executive improvement team and PITs assigned to streamline these processes. The PIT members will be trained on basic team, meeting, and problem-solving skills. In addition, the PITs will be trained to use the Business Process Improvement Ten Fun-

damental Tools and selected Advanced Tools. A facilitator should be assigned to each PIT.

7. *Train the trainers*. After the management team has experience with the team methodologies, interested managers and/or key staff should be selected to be trained as team methods instructors.

8. *Establish employee department improvement teams (DITs)/natural work teams*. When management has confidence in the team process and the ability of the groups to exist in the team environment, the process will be expanded to all first-level areas (departments). To start, each area will do an AAA. All employees will be trained in basic team skills and AAA methodology before the AAA activities are started. After the efficiency and effectiveness measurements and requirements have been established for each major activity, the employees on the DITs will be trained in problem-solving methodology and start the problem-solving phase of the team activities. A facilitator should be assigned to each DIT.

9. *Form quality circles (if applicable)*. As the team and problem-solving cycles become integrated throughout the organization, groups of employees will be encouraged to identify problems that they would like to work on that the DITs are not addressing. In these cases, the employees will be encouraged to submit a request to form a quality circle. These requests define the problem to be worked on, the members of the team, the leader, the cost of the problem, and the number of hours that the quality circle would like to be authorized to expend in developing a recommended solution. The quality circle leader will be trained in team leadership skills. A facilitator may be assigned to help the quality circles get key points in the process.

10. *Develop self-managed work teams*. With the proper management support, the employees who are members of the quality circles become more and more effective at correcting their own problems. As this occurs, they can take over more and

more of the manager's responsibilities. With proper financial and general operations training, the normal day-to-day activities for the work group can then be turned over to the employees, allowing them to evolve into self-managed work teams.

How to Measure Team Success

The measurement of team success depends largely on the strategic business objectives of the organization. What does the organization hope to accomplish through its team process? What are management's goals? Are the managers interested strictly in raising quality awareness? Or do they want teams that can assist in problem solving, such as reducing customer returns, reject rates, and defects? Or do they perhaps include eliminating communication barriers between employees and management? What about reducing employee absenteeism and raising productivity?

As you can see, there are as many ways to measure teams as there are teams. It is pointless to try to devise a single way to measure team success. Some teams, such as a reject rate reduction team, may be easily measured and have tangible results while others, like a management support improvement team, may not.

No matter the type of team or the problem or issue it is working on, measurement systems must be developed and applied during the start-up of the team. Some simple measurements may be applied to almost any team, regardless of type:

- ▶ Meeting team milestones
- ▶ Proper use of problem-solving tools
- ▶ Team member attendance
- ▶ Meetings start on time and end on time
- ▶ Effective use of time and other resources

Other, more complex measurements may be:

- ▶ Process cycle-time reduction
- ▶ Reject rate reduction

> ► Customer satisfaction increase
> ► Cost savings

In measuring a team, the important thing is to show that the team is adding value to the overall organizational improvement effort. The team should be able to prove that it plays an important role in improving the performance of the organization, its work environment, product and/or service quality, and—very important—the people.

There are many reasons for measuring teams. Looking at some of those reasons will provide a foundation for what and how to measure. First of all, measuring is the expected, management thing to do. After all, if you don't measure it, you can't manage it. Some other possible reasons to measure are to:

> ► Convince management to broaden the team process into other areas.
> ► Convince management to continue to support teams.
> ► Convince employees to continue to support teams.
> ► Assist in deciding whether to implement a given solution.
> ► Assess the need to modify a team or the team process to make it more efficient and effective.
> ► Determine the cost-effectiveness of a process.
> ► Justify the allocation of limited budget funds.
> ► Be able to identify "winning teams" to attend national or international conferences.
> ► Determine amount of monetary awards for teams having solutions implemented.

The common denominator in all these possible reasons has to be *dollars*. To be value-added to an organization, teams must show a positive return on investment (ROI). The difficult part is determining how much the team has affected the ROI. Teams do not exist in a vacuum. Ultimate team success will be directly attributable to the way the process is managed and supported.

Most organizations with an existing team process have already determined the cost-effectiveness of the effort. This cost-effectiveness is a key measurement of the overall team effort. The cost-effectiveness measured is the return on investment ratio of cost reduction and savings resulting from team suggestions compared with the cost of the process.

The ratios of cost savings and process costs for the *return* figures are established by the annual figure of dollar savings resulting from the implementation of a team solution to a problem or improvement suggestion. These include all savings related to labor costs, material and/or equipment costs, methods and process costs, etc.

The ratios for the *investment* figures are determined by the accumulated month-by-month accounts of actual expenditures for the wages paid to team members while in meetings and other organizational staff while supporting the team's efforts, for any outside consulting, for training (including materials), for team supplies, materials, etc. It also includes the cost of implementing the suggested changes.

Often the figures used for both categories have already been established (or projected) by the financial and accounting departments of the organization.

Organizations report a cost-effectiveness ranging from a low of 2-to-1 to a high of more than 10-to-1. The average seems to be around 6-to-1.

The following are items that can be measured for various types of teams. Remember: one of the keys to successful teams is being able to prove they provide value to the organization's improvement efforts.

Possible Measurements for Manufacturing/Shop Areas

- ► Cost savings per theme or problem
- ► Cost savings from producing the same or more in less time and/or with less material
- ► Reduced cycle time
- ► Meeting schedules more frequently
- ► More effective use of equipment or supplies
- ► Reducing customer complaints
- ► Reducing or eliminating omissions and oversights
- ► Reducing errors, scrap, waste, or rework
- ► Reducing equipment downtime

- ▶ More effective use of employees
- ▶ Reducing employee lost time
- ▶ Improving labor cost per unit
- ▶ Reduced poor-quality cost

Possible Measurements for Employee Relations Issues

- ▶ Reducing absenteeism, tardiness, turnover
- ▶ Regularity of attendance at team meetings
- ▶ Improved employee opinion indexes
- ▶ Number of grievances
- ▶ Number of transfer requests
- ▶ Participation in team meetings

Possible Measurements for Establishing Team Rewards

- ▶ Based on the ingenuity of the solution
- ▶ The use by the team of special assistance (consultants, specialists, and administrators)
- ▶ The professionalism of the team's presentation on the issue to management
- ▶ Overall return on investment
- ▶ Based on the difficulty of the problem
- ▶ The enthusiasm and full participation of the team
- ▶ Time from problem identification to solution

How to Deal with Problem Teams

Every organization that has ever had teams and every organization that will have teams will sooner or later face this question—"What do we do about our problem team?" Organizations that tell us they have "never had a problem team or a major problem with a team" are either not paying close enough attention to their teams, or they're not telling the truth! Anytime you involve individuals in a process, the potential for conflict exists.

Realizing there are many dynamics affecting group process, from individual personalities to basic communication failures, let's look at 13 of the most common problems with teams. We've listed the problems in what we feel is a "priority" order. A team may have any one of the problems listed below but some are the effect of other causes.

1. *The team doesn't have a good charter (mission, goals/objectives, and operating guidelines).*
   As we mentioned in the beginning of this section, a good team charter will not only help the team get started but also help the team focus on the task. It also helps the facilitator focus on the team. Most teams that fail or have serious problems within the first 30 to 60 days probably do not have a good team charter.

2. *The team or team members don't understand the mission.*
   If the team or management has not been diligent in establishing the team charter, very often the mission will be very vague. If management has established the team to look at a certain task, it is imperative that management give the team as clear a mission as possible. Once the mission has been set, the team leader should ensure not only that each team member understands the essence of the mission but also that any ambiguous words are clarified.

3. *The team hasn't learned or isn't using the tools and techniques.*
   One of the most important elements of a good team process is the up-front training of members in the use of the basic team tools and techniques. Teams must not only learn and use the basics but continuously study and learn new more advanced team tools.

4. *The team has failed to set goals and measure results.*
   While the debate rages over the propriety of measuring teams, experience has proven that unless teams set out to accomplish something worthwhile in a specific period of time and unless they have the ability to prove or confirm they have achieved

their goals, they are likely to stray from their task and slowly
but surely deteriorate.

5. *There are too many goals with unrealistic expectations.*
   Often a team's goals are too broad, general, or vague. Goals must
   be specific, concise, and measurable. Sometimes teams will
   attempt more than they can accomplish and expect success prematurely. When they don't achieve the goals or success doesn't
   come soon enough, these expectations cause frustration and
   lead to team members losing interest and/or dropping out.

6. *There is a lack of team leadership and accountability.*
   Management sometimes fails to understand that team activities continue during the period between meetings. Day-to-day
   work schedules can cause members and leaders to come to the
   team meetings unprepared. The team leader must communicate and follow up on action items and other team-related
   tasks. Team members should be held accountable for completing their assignments on time and to the best of their ability.

7. *The team runs out of new ideas or problems.*
   At some point, team progress will start to stop or slow down due
   to a lack of creative or innovative ideas. When teams first start
   up, members are interested, enthusiastic, and full of expectations. They have received their training and are applying it to
   their team task. Later, when there seems to be less and less to
   do, the team begins to become boring. At this time, new ideas,
   different approaches, and fresh viewpoints must be developed
   to revitalize the team. Additional training may be helpful. Bringing someone in from outside the team may provide different
   insights and restore enthusiasm.

8. *The team mission or task is causing difficulties.*
   Sometimes a team will be assigned or take on a task that just
   isn't right for it. Often the task is a divergent problem and
   keeps getting bigger as the team goes forward. It is very important that management guide the team in picking projects or
   problems involving work the team understands. The team
   should have experience, knowledge, and the expertise to work

on the problem. It should also work on only one problem at a time. The project or problem should be meaningful and important to the team members involved.

9. *The team isn't integrated with the organization's vision.*

Here we are most concerned with teams that do not function as an integral part of the organization-wide improvement effort or are not an integrated part of a work group's way of doing business. The team activity becomes effective and useful only when management establishes definite plans with respect to the organization's improvement effort and overall team process.

10. *The team is isolated from other employees.*

There is a tendency for team members to become isolated from their own management and the other employees in their department. This often leads to disastrous results, because there is a breakdown of communication among workers and suspicion and mistrust on the part of the manager. For teams to work properly, employees must be willing to step up and fill in for other employees away from the job on team assignments. Managers must be continuously convinced that what the team is doing is worthwhile and meaningful and fits in with not only the organization's vision, but also that of the individual work group.

11. *There is a lack of understanding or support from management.*

Teams are most effective when management shows an interest in their projects. Top management must not only understand the team process but also the issues the teams are working on. Providing the needed resources will motivate a team; not providing them will cause a team to rapidly lose interest in the project.

12. *There is a lack of team recognition and rewards.*

This is a big problem. As a team becomes more sophisticated in improving the organization and conserving its resources, team members expect and deserve proper recognition and, in many cases, rewards. If a team improves a process that saves the organization hundreds of thousands of dollars per year, you can be sure the team will not be happy with just a "pat on the back." There is a time for a pat on the back, but there is also a time for a pat on the wallet. Organizations should establish a rewards and recognition process that covers individuals as well as team activities.

13. *The team becomes inactive or dormant.*

   This problem is last because all of the preceding problems cause teams to become inactive or dormant. There are certainly other things that cause this, but we have mentioned the key issues. You will be able to quickly recognize this type of team behavior. The team will start to exist in name only. Few meetings will be held and even these meetings usually end up as social gatherings that have nothing to do with improvement. If this situation occurs when a team has been operating for a long time, the team needs some changes.

Problem teams must be dealt with swiftly and efficiently. The sooner you deal with the problems, the sooner the team can start earning its keep. Tackle the problems like any other organization issue. Identify the problem and the cause and then develop a recovery plan for the team.

Will Teams Have a Place in the Future?

The human mind, once stretched by a new idea, never regains its original dimensions.

—Oliver Wendell Holmes

Do teams have a place in the future of an organization's improvement efforts? The Ernst & Young *Best Practices Report* makes a point worth considering. It states that "building the human resource infrastructure is essential." According to the report, lower-performing organizations show less than 5% of the workforce participating on teams, while higher-performing organizations show over 25%.

The United States was introduced to participative management and the team concept almost three decades ago. It has changed the way we do business. Richard M. Davis, president of Martin Marietta's Manned Space Systems, has stated:

Ten years ago, when our employee involvement effort started, we had varying ideas about the program and expected results. Few of us envisioned the atmosphere and attitude of participative problem solving and cooperation that we have at Manned Space Systems today.

Ford Motor Company almost cut the Mustang automobile from its lineup. A team known as the "Gang of Eight" researched innovative ideas and changes, then presented the changes to top management. After very tough questioning from CEO Harold Poling, the eight got the go-ahead. The team promised a 37-month turnaround. This was several months quicker than any previous turnaround on new car design. Working together, the eight slashed bureaucracy and delivered the new Mustang in just 35 months. Will Boddie, Ford's Mustang boss, said, "We made decisions in minutes around the coffee pot that would normally take months."

Richard DeVogelaere and the folks at GM took a team approach to taking on water leaks in the Camaro and Firebird model automobiles. They called themselves the "F-car SWAT team." Not only did they fix the water leaks but also that "screee" noise made when a window glass rubs wrong against the rubber. They also took care of some shakes and squeaks in T-top models by using underbody braces. DeVogelaere commented:

You say to yourself, "If we'd done this five years ago, how many more could we have sold? How many more thousands of owners would be out there saying what a great, exciting car this is?" We thought we were meeting the customer's expectations, but we weren't really listening, I guess.

The stories go on and on. Every organization involved in teams can give you success stories like the ones above. Do they also have failures? Of course. To succeed you have to try, and to try is to sometimes fail. From our failures we learn to improve.

One thing all these examples have in common is they all show some type of problem-solving process that used a number of problem-solving tools. This is one of the reasons there are so many tools and techniques designed to assist us, both in our jobs and in day-to-day life.

In Summary: Do We Recommend the Use of Teams?

Of course we do! However, there are several questions to consider, such as the following:

- ▶ Does executive management sponsor the team?
- ▶ Does the team have a well thought-out charter?
- ▶ Is a measurement system in place to validate team progress?

We might also add—Is the team expected to succeed? In other words, is there a process in place within the organization that holds the team both responsible and accountable?

Having teams in your organization is a good way to facilitate the overall improvement effort. Teamwork is always a value-added activity. However, having teams just for the sake of having teams is a bad idea and can seriously harm the improvement effort.

Good luck with your organization's team-based improvement effort. Remember that the first step toward improvement is recognizing the need to improve. The next step is to do something about it.

I use not only the brain I have but all I can borrow.

—Woodrow Wilson

Additional Ammunition

Ernst & Young LLP. *Best Practices Report* (Cleveland, OH: Ernst & Young, 1992)

Harrington, H. James. *The Collapse of Prevailing Wisdom*, Ernst & Young Technical Report #TR 93.021 HJH (Cleveland, OH: Ernst & Young, 1993)

8

Measurement Systems

Only the poor performer doesn't want to be measured.

Introduction

Measurements are crucial to an organization's survival. We need to measure in order to know what's working in the organization and what needs to be fixed. Measuring is the only way that we can come to a conclusion about the performance of a person, a product, or a process. For example, an employee cannot be matched against his or her own fellow workers if we do not have some way of rating each and every individual. Even more basic, without measurements, an organization would have no way of knowing how well it is doing in the marketplace. If it were not for measurements, an organization would not even know how much money it is making.

We must be able to identify how we are performing before we can improve. To identify how the organization is performing, we need to be able to choose among a variety of alternatives. The only way to continued success in making right choices is to have a proper, repeatable system of measurements set up in the organization.

Measurements are important in every walk of life, from the weight of the vegetables you buy in a grocery store to the distance you have to commute to and from work every day. Our life is run by measurements, hence the phrase, "How do you measure up?" As important as measurements are to common, everyday events, they are even more important to the war on waste. In fact, the entire success of the war on waste effort is placed upon this building block. Without the right measurement system, the structure will fall.

Before you build a better mousetrap, it helps to know if there are any mice out there.

—Mortimer B. Zucherman

Figure 8-1 is a flow diagram for developing a measurement plan for a business process, product, equipment, or manufacturing process. In the following discussion, for the sake of simplicity, we will use the generic term *item*.

Item—Any process, system, product, or service.

The activity charted in the flow diagram consists of seven tasks:

1. Examine typical measurements.
2. Select categories of measurements.
3. Define business process measurements.
4. Define product measurements.
5. Define equipment measurements.
6. Define manufacturing (production) process measurements.
7. Develop a required measurements chart.

Task 1–Examine Typical Measurements

Don't measure too much or too little. Invest lots of careful, deliberate thought in establishing your measurement system. Hours should be spent mulling over the most crucial area(s) to be improved in order for

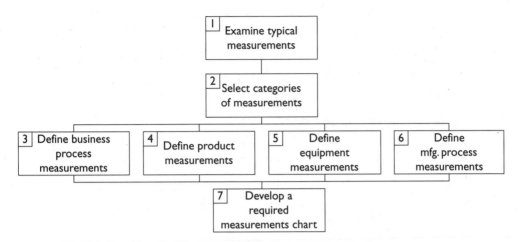

FIGURE 8-1. Flow diagram—develop the measurement plan

your organization to start down the path toward eliminating waste. Your organization may be poised to make a quantum improvement leap. However, what good are all of these improvement weapons without a proper set of measurements in place? None.

How could General Motors ever compare the Camaro with the Dodge Stealth or Pepsi compare its advertising effectiveness with Coca-Cola's if they did not have standardized measurement data? They could not. No organization would ever get a precise picture of its place in the market, compared with its competitors, if it were not for the use of measurement systems.

If we are going to improve performance, we first have to define what performance is and how we can measure it. Improvement occurs only when there is a change in the positive direction of a measurement. Too often, when we rely on gut feelings about improvement, we are led astray, thinking things are improving, only to find out later things are getting worse. Without measurements, we cannot effectively know if we are improving. In other words, without adequate measurements, performance improvement fails. Measurements are the military intelligence of our war on waste.

The measurement plan is prepared to characterize business performance as a total entity or in its individual parts. Typically when we think about measurements, we think about:

► **Quality**
  Product quality
  • Errors per item
  • Process first-time yield
  • Mean time between failures
  • Percent defective
  Service quality
  • Billing error rates
  • Customer satisfaction ratings
  • Percent of repeat service calls
  • Unplanned maintenance
  • Cycle time to react to a customer complaint
  • Percent of special requests honored

► **Productivity**
  • Output per employee
  • Value-added per employee
  • Customers served per hour
  • Patents issued per five-year period
  • Sales volume per salesperson
  • Lines of code per week
  • Orders processed per hour

► **Time**
  • Service response time
  • Cycle time
  • Percent of real-value-added time
  • Percent of items delivered on schedule
  • Required lead times
  • Set-up time

► **Resources**
  • Capacity utilization
  • Inventory turns
  • Theoretical capacity vs. actual equipment usage

- Percent of overtime
- Average inventory value
- Maximum production capacity

▶ **Costs**
- Poor-quality cost
- Warranty cost
- Value-added per item
- Profits
- Cost per unit
- Cost per service call
- Labor overhead rate
- Return on investment
- Labor cost as a percent of sales
- Material cost as a percent of sales

▶ **Management**
- Employee opinion survey ratings
- Percent of missed commitments
- Safety accidents per 10,000 hours
- Average equipment age
- Percent of total sales reinvested in research and development
- Span of control
- Number of unscheduled changes
- Budget cycle time
- Turnover rates
- Percent of new employees who leave within the first 12 months
- Quantity of "open doors" per month
- Profits over a five-year period as a percent of total sales
- Layers of management
- Average yearly training hours per employee
- Percent of employees' suggestions implemented
- Number of suggestions per employee

Once you have decided which item(s) will be measured, you need to crisply define how to measure the performance of the item(s). It is not enough to say that you are going to compare your order-fulfillment process with L.L. Bean's; you must clearly define the measurements needed in order to accomplish this task.

Types of Data

The performance improvement team (PIT) will spend much of its time and effort collecting data, analyzing data, and transforming it into usable information. There are two basic types of data information:

This is a sample of the text for the definition, or these are more synonyms and usages that are commonly found in the English language.

1. *Qualitative data*—Qualitative data define how the item operates, in terms of the selected factor(s), and are usually expressed in words or pictures. They are usually more difficult to interpret than quantitative data because they require much more judgment. This type of data is extremely important to the PIT, as it is a key input to the improvement process.
2. *Quantitative data*—Quantitative data define how the item performs, in terms of the selected factor(s), and are usually expressed in numbers.

Qualitative Data

Qualitative data are subjective. They are often used to reflect opinions or to define the way something is done. They are used to develop insight about the nature and content of things. They are usually expressed in words. Flowcharts or graphs are typical ways to express qualitative data. By selecting a larger population, individual qualitative data can be expressed in frequency distributions, percentages, or indices. This is often accomplished through the use of surveys or focus groups.

Some situations require information that cannot be considered quantitative in a classic sense. For example: The district manager of Gap clothing stores in San Francisco wants to measure how well the stores look, compared with those in Los Angeles. He or she might be looking at such things as how elaborate the displays are, how neat the racks are, or how well the employees are dressed—all important aspects of running a Gap store, but that cannot be measured on any standardized scale. One person might think that a store with a few displays looks elegant, while another person who likes flashier designs would think the same store looked rather bleak.

What's needed in this case, and in others like it, is the use of qualitative data. Qualitative data are most often used when trying to answer the question, "What do you think about something?" But they should be used only when quantitative measurements cannot be used, because qualitative information is not fact-based and is therefore open to debate. An individual answering a customer survey is recording qualitative data when you ask him or her to rate the organization's quality on a scale of 1 to 10. In most cases a qualitative measurement needs to be repeated many times, using different people, to obtain meaningful data. In some cases, an accepted expert can be used as the measurement standard, thereby reducing the sample size. Often, however, there is no accepted expert; you may have to survey a number of "experts." (For example, Roger Ebert and the late Gene Siskel, well-known film critics, both had highly regarded opinions on films, compared with those of the average moviegoer, but even these two experts often didn't agree.)

Often, qualitative data are needed to compare management approaches. Typically, qualitative data are used for comparing:

- Operating systems
- Cultures
- Environments
- Techniques
- Practices
- Structures
- Process flows

To help with the analysis of these management approaches, flowcharts, simulation models, and pictures are constructed and compared.

Quantitative Data

Quantitative data measurements can be expressed in quantities or amounts. Quantitative data define how the item is performing. Quantitative data are usually expressed in numbers and are the primary measurement process used in the war on waste.

There are two subcategories of quantitative data—*attributes* data and *variables* data. One of the first areas to address is whether the measurement system should stress variables data or attributes data.

Variables Data

This quantitative measurement focuses on actual measurements that are based on a standardized scale. Any individual measuring the same item should get the same results.

This measurement relates to an accepted standard, may be repeated at any time, and can be thought of as fact. This is the most desirable measurement because it is universally acceptable and transferable (centimeters can be converted into inches, kilograms into pounds, etc.).

It is preferable to have all measurements taken in variables terms. Variables measurements are normal when the PIT is recording weight, distance, time, speed, volume, depth, or anything else that can be measured on a standardized scale.

Attributes Data

Attributes data are often referred to as go/no-go data. They reflect the status of the item being measured, rather than the exact value. Attributes measurements ask: Is this good or bad? Does the item meet requirements or not? Do you like it or don't you like it? Attributes data are often expressed in terms like percent defective, errors per unit, and percentage of items correct. Attributes data are usually collected by counting the number of acceptable (or unacceptable) items and expressing them as a percentage of the total sample size. Attributes data can also be used to produce control charts.

You must decide early on whether measurements are going to be quantitative or qualitative, because that decision will definitely affect how much data you will need to collect. Do not make the mistake of thinking that these two types of measurements are mutually exclusive. You often will use both quantitative and qualitative measurements on the same item. For instance, the Gap district manager concerned about the appearance of his or her stores may want to add to his or her measurement list such quantitative figures as the dollar value of the stock on hand and the number of inventory turns per year.

Starting the Measurement Plan

To establish a measurement system, you need to first define what items will be measured.

In all organizations, there are many measurements that make up the organization's balanced scorecard. Typically, a measurement system starts with defining the objectives of the organization and then defines the measurements that will be used to determine if those objectives are being met—for example, return on investment, customer satisfaction level, market share, morale index, etc. Then you need to define the process that drives each of these key measurements and the measurement that defines the performance of each of those processes. Then define the subprocesses that feed the major processes and their relevant measurements. Repeat this cycle until your measurement system is completed and all of the important items have relevant measurements related to them (see Figure 8-2).

To start developing the item's measurements, define the item's primary customers and then find out what the customers' expectations are. Unfortunately, the customers' inputs are often not measurable. Typical customer expectations are:

- ▶ Tastes good
- ▶ User-friendly
- ▶ Looks nice

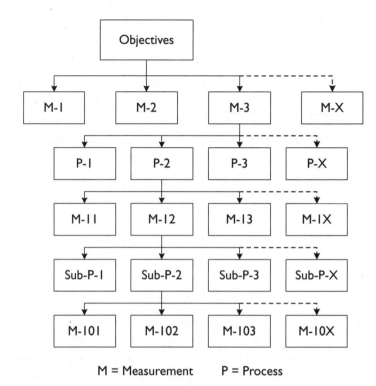

M = Measurement   P = Process

FIGURE **8-2. Flowchart of processes and measurements**

▶ Minimum wait time
▶ Low cost

Customers define their expectations as a combination of things that can be measured (minimum wait time or lowest cost) and things that are subjective expectations (tastes good, looks good, user-friendly). Subjective expectations are based upon opinions. What one person classifies as user-friendly may not be user-friendly from another person's standpoint.

Effectiveness—The extent to which the outputs of the item meet the needs and expectations of its customers. Effectiveness includes all the quality requirements and more. Effectiveness is having the right output at the right place, at the right time, at the right price. Effectiveness impacts the customer.

Typical effectiveness measurements evaluate the item's performance as it relates to the following:

- Appearance
- Timeliness
- Accuracy
- Performance
- Reliability
- Usability
- Serviceability
- Durability
- Costs
- Responsiveness
- Dependability

With subjective expectations, the organization needs to define how to measure performance according to subjective criteria. For example, survey customers to obtain their opinions on how user-friendly an item is or measure how long it takes a sample group of customers to learn the applications. These customer-related measurements are called *effectiveness measurements* because they measure how effectively the item is meeting the customer's expectations. Typical effectiveness measurements are:

- Product cost
- Mean time between failures
- Time waiting in line
- Number of times the telephone rings before it is answered
- Product return rates
- Repeat purchases

The other types of primary measurements are *efficiency measurements*. They evaluate how efficiently the item uses resources to produce the desired results. Efficiency measurements are of great concern to an organization because they make the difference between profit and loss—between staying in business and going out of business.

Efficiency—The extent to which resources are minimized and waste is eliminated in the pursuit of effectiveness. It is usually measured as the total amount of resources used to process one unit of output. Efficiency includes all the productivity measurements and more.

Typical efficiency measurements are:

- ▶ Cycle time
- ▶ Yields
- ▶ Processing time
- ▶ Processing cost per item
- ▶ Value-added cost per unit of output
- ▶ Scrap cost per item
- ▶ Value-added per unit of output
- ▶ Resources expended per unit of output
- ▶ Percentage of real-value-added time
- ▶ Items produced per employee
- ▶ Poor-quality cost
- ▶ Percent utilization
- ▶ Wait time per unit
- ▶ Value-added per employee
- ▶ In-process stock value

Once the organization has defined the item's primary measurements, it should define the secondary measurements that support or impact the primary measurements. We find that a fishbone diagram is an effective way to define secondary measurements. Secondary measurements are generally used to define what needs to be changed to improve the primary measurements' performance. By using the fishbone diagram, the PIT can systematically analyze what needs to be changed to improve overall performance.

Figure 8-3 is a fishbone diagram for a typical inventory management roadblock analysis. This diagram was prepared by management consultant Sy Zivan, a key individual in the development of Xerox's benchmarking process.

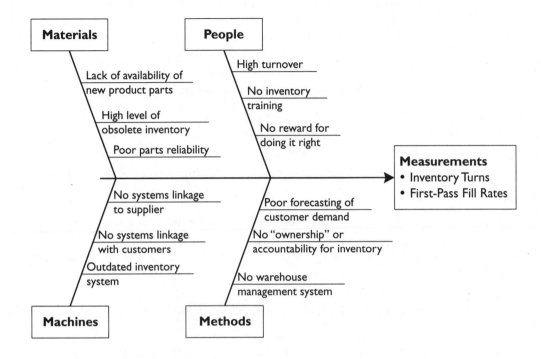

FIGURE 8-3. Inventory management roadblocks analysis

You will note in Figure 8-3 that Zivan defines two primary measurements that he wants to improve:

1. Inventory turns
2. First-pass fill rates

Four major branches define what can impact each of these two measurements:

1. Materials
2. People
3. Machines
4. Methods

Zivan then looks at each of the four branches and attaches related factors that could have a negative impact on inventory turns and/or first-pass fill rates. For example, the people branch has three related impact factors:

1. High turnover rates for people doing the work.
   Measurement: The area's turnover rate per year.
2. Assigning employees to the inventory process without adequate training.
   Measurement: Hours of training per new employee.
3. No reward system in place that reinforces desired behavior.
   Measurement: Percentage of employees who receive rewards per year.

You will note that all three measurements are quantitative. Admittedly, it takes a little time to develop fishbone diagrams for the primary measurements, but the efforts are well worthwhile for the following reasons:

▶ It helps the PIT identify when there is an improvement opportunity.
▶ It helps the PIT develop comparison measurement plans.
▶ It helps the PIT understand the interrelationships within the item.
▶ It helps the PIT in developing improvement plans.

Task 2–Select Categories of Measurements

When you begin to establish your own measurement system, it is important to have a point of reference and examples of typical measurements other than effectiveness and efficiency measurements that are made during an improvement process. Following are measurement categories that you might find useful.

Adaptability—The flexibility of the process to handle future, changing customer expectations and today's individual, special customer requests.

Adaptability is an area largely ignored, but it is critical for gaining a competitive edge in the marketplace. Customers always remember how you handled—or didn't handle—their special needs.

Typical adaptability measurements are:

▶ Percentage of special orders entered within 3 hours
▶ Percentage of special orders produced and delivered within 24 hours
▶ Percentage of special orders processed
▶ Percentage of special orders processed by the first person asked

Physical—Measurements that can be verified using equipment. They are often related to evaluating hardware to determine if it conforms to requirements.

Typical physical measurements are:

▶ The size of a hole
▶ The hardness of a steel plate
▶ The width of a room
▶ The number of ounces of water in a glass
▶ The number of volts in a battery

Operational—These are ways to understand how the item functions or is created. Typically, operational measurements take on the form of a flowchart that many of the other measurements are tied into.

Most of the items that are improved will be flowcharted as part of the measurement process.

Typical types of flowcharts that could be used are:

▶ Block diagrams
▶ American National Standards Institute (ANSI) standard flowcharts
▶ Functional flowcharts

- Data flowcharts
- Geographic flowcharts
- Word flowcharts

You should identify typical measurement categories that apply to the item, to provide valuable assistance in establishing measurements. For a more extensive list of typical measurements, see Dorsey J. (Jim) Talley's book *Total Quality Management.*

Following are some specific examples of measurements.

Cost

This category is an excellent beginning point for establishing measurements for your war on waste. Everyone understands the importance of saving money and being cost-competitive, and therefore can easily get behind efforts to measure the item's cost. This category deals with plain and simple dollars and cents, and is most often measured in the following ways:

- Cost per unit/order
- Cost per maintenance/service call
- Labor overhead rate (%)
- Return on assets
- Ratio of customer administration to revenue
- Ratio of service to revenue

Equipment/Vehicle Reliability

- Run time between repairs (up time)
- Capacity utilization
- Planned maintenance
- Unplanned maintenance
- Equipment age

Layout

- Travel distance between workstations
- Repeat visits to a process
- Material handling—cost, people
- Operation size

- Space for growth
- Percentage of floor space devoted to stock

Organizational Considerations

- Turnover rates
- Headcount by department as percentage of total
- Hourly employee/supervisor ratio
- Layers of management
- Average annual training time (hours per employee)
- Number of employees trained by topic, as percentage of total headcount
- Number of ideas recorded per employee per year
- Percentage of ideas implemented
- Number of autonomous work teams
- Average span of control

Processing Time

- Total lead time
- Backlog time
- Value-added vs. non-value-added activities
- Employee hours per unit
- Percent of overtime worked

Production Cost (Manufacturing)

- Labor cost as percentage of sales
- Material cost as percentage of sales
- Contractor costs as percentage of total cost

Production Procedures (Manufacturing)

- Maximum production capacity
- Frequency of physical inventory counts
- Number of schedule changes per month
- Compliance with daily scheduling
- Number of inventory turns annually
- Average inventory value
- Accuracy of inventory runs

Quality

- ▶ Process variability
- ▶ In-process errors
- ▶ Process yield
- ▶ Customer satisfaction index
- ▶ Warranty costs
- ▶ Service calls
- ▶ Customer complaints
- ▶ Inspection results
- ▶ Poor-quality cost
- ▶ Billing error rate
- ▶ Quality improvement effort ROI
- ▶ Elapsed time to solve a problem

Sales

- ▶ Sales growth last five years (dollar or volume)
- ▶ Advertising budget as percentage of sales
- ▶ Percentage of repeat sales
- ▶ Percentage of sales force time with customers
- ▶ Market share

Service

- ▶ Service response time
- ▶ Repeat service visits to correct the same problem
- ▶ Percentage of spare parts available when required

Supplier Management

- ▶ Number of suppliers
- ▶ Percentage of lots delivered within plus or minus 2 days of scheduled delivery date
- ▶ Delivery performance
- ▶ Cost performance
- ▶ Percentage of rejected lots at incoming inspection
- ▶ Percentage of suppliers with error-free performance for a minimum of 12 months

- ► Average cost to maintain a supplier
- ► Cost per procurement cycle

Unused Machining Capacity

- ► Scrap/rework lost time
- ► Theoretical capacity versus actual load
- ► Number of problem-free machines

Miscellaneous

- ► Profit for past five years in dollars, and as a percentage of sales
- ► Safety problems per million hours worked
- ► Number of open doors per year
- ► Number of grievances per year

There are four distinct and different types of items that can be improved:

1. Business Processes
2. Products
3. Equipment
4. Manufacturing Processes

Each of these four different types requires different types of measurement systems to define its performance. Because their measurement systems are so completely different, each of these types must be looked at separately. Based upon the type of item that the PIT will be improving, it will select Task 3, 4, 5, or 6.

Task 3—Define Business Process Measurements

The key to successfully improving business processes, whether you are redesigning, reengineering, benchmarking, or continuously improving them, is to apply a concentrated effort to a few processes, getting their future-state solutions defined before expending more resources on additional processes.

Xerox defined 64 different critical business processes for a major business unit and 76 additional ones at the enterprise level. In 1987, IBM defined 68 critical business processes at its San Jose, California location alone. On the other hand, Northern Telecom has defined only 13 critical business processes for the entire corporation. We believe that starting with just a few critical business processes, and completing them before addressing others, is an approach that is more in line with the resources—and amount of change—that most organizations can absorb.

Before you can define the measurements for a business process, the performance improvement team (PIT) needs to define where that business process begins and ends. This is necessary because the key measurements are based upon those two points. Defining what activities make up the business process is called *boxing in the process*. To get additional help in how to box in a process, we suggest you read *Business Process Improvement* by H. J. Harrington.

There are four major business process measurements:

1. *Effectiveness.* The degree to which the process has the right output at the right place, at the right time, at the right price. Often referred to as *quality.* It measures how well the process output meets all of its customer expectations.
2. *Efficiency.* A measurement of how well the process uses its resources. It includes all resources, such as people, time, space, equipment. Usually measured by productivity scales.
3. *Adaptability.* A measurement of the process flexibility in handling changing customer expectations, today's special and future requirements.
4. *Operational.* A measurement of how the process is performed. It takes the form of a flowchart that pictorially shows the process. It provides a picture of the different activities involved in the process.

Effectiveness Measurements

Effectiveness measurements are set up to determine if the process is producing the desired results. There are three steps to defining these measurement systems:

Step One: Determine your customers' needs and expectations.
Step Two: Specifically describe those needs and expectations in measurable terms.
Step Three: Define the way to collect and store measurement data.

The performance improvement team (PIT) must meet with the process's primary customers and determine what they need from the process. These needs and expectations typically relate to products and/or services. Attributes data such as accuracy, performance, reliability, and appearance are often collected. Customers will know what they want, but it may sometimes be difficult to put these wants into measurements. They will speak in general terms, such as "I want quick service" or "We want easy-to-use output." What the team must make out of these demands is measurable characteristics that can be evaluated—preferably before the output is delivered to the customer.

Since we have used the terms *needs* and *expectations* quite frequently, you should know the difference between the two.

This is a sample of the text for the definition, or these are more synonyms and usages that are commonly found in the English language.

Customer Needs—The minimum standard that customers will accept. They are the things that are defined in a specification or a contract.

Customer Expectations—The unspecified desires or needs that customers consider so obvious that they do not need to specify. In addition, they are things that customers would like to have, but that are not mandatory.

Think about what you *need* from a meal. You need proteins, carbohydrates, and fats. You need basic sustenance and calories to satisfy your hunger and keep you alive. Now what you might *expect* from the meal is that it be properly cooked, visually pleasing, and, of course, delightful to the taste buds. You can meet your nutrition *needs* with pills, water, and tofu—but that would not meet most people's *expectations*. As you can plainly see, there is a big difference between *needs* and *expectations*. Needs do not often change. But expectations do, so you should stay in constant contact with your current and future customer base to measure changing expectations.

There are many ways to measure how well an item meets or exceeds its customers' expectations. Some of the best techniques are:

- ▶ Market research
- ▶ Monitoring customer complaints
- ▶ Interviews with customers
- ▶ Focus groups
- ▶ Surveys and/or questionnaires
- ▶ Customer inspection of the product or service
- ▶ Feedback of customer sampling of incoming products and/or services
- ▶ Check sheets filled in by the customer and returned to the supplier

Efficiency Measurements

While *effectiveness* measurements reflect the *customers'* requirements, *efficiency* measurements reflect *stockholders'* requirements. As a nation, we have learned to live with poor efficiency. It is not popular to make things more efficient, because the common thought is that when you make things more efficient, you cut jobs. On the contrary, as you streamline your process you become more productive, allowing your organization to produce more at a reduced cost. As a result, more people can afford to buy your products—and this increased demand creates more jobs.

Efficiency should be taken very seriously, because it means great benefits to the organization and its customers. As you work to make your business processes more efficient, you will cut down on operating costs. This will lead to greater profit potential. The customer will benefit, because the organization will be able to pass on some of its savings in the form of lower prices. The employees should also benefit, because the organization should pass some of the savings on to the employees in the form of bonuses.

Requirements for efficiency focus on the use of money, time, and other resources. Improved efficiency means eliminating the errors that occur within the process and making better use of all the resources used. Each individual involved in the process must focus on providing error-free performance. The easiest way to get error-free performance is to design a process that makes errors difficult to make. But designing a process so that errors will not occur is just the starting point. An error-free process may still be a poor process. The process design must not only be capable of error-free output—it must also maximize the use of all resources. That's what process benchmarking is all about. Once these processes have been designed, the data system must continually feed back effectiveness and efficiency data, which are analyzed to make sure that the process is operating in top form.

Adaptability Measurements

The ability to adapt to special requests and the changing environment is what transforms good organizations into great ones. It is what puts organizations like Nordstrom department stores in the world-class category. Adaptable processes not only have the capacity to adjust to meet the average customer's expectations—they have intelligence designed into them so they will be able to accommodate individual special needs and expectations.

A good example of an organization that has capitalized on effectiveness and efficiency, only to lose on adaptability, is McDonald's. The restaurants produce very tasty hamburgers at a rapid rate. Customers get a good hot meal without having to wait. Unless, of course, you have special needs or expectations. For example, a customer who wants no onions is asked to step aside while others are served. The waiting period is not inordinate, but it does make that customer feel like he or she is disrupting the normal routine. Compare this with Wendy's, which focuses on adaptability. The average service time is slightly longer than for McDonald's, but Wendy's treats every customer equally—even those of us who can't stand onions.

Of the three key business process measurements—effectiveness, efficiency, and adaptability—adaptability is the most difficult to measure. As organizations around the world become more effective and efficient, the competitive edge will go to the ones that are most adaptable. You must make the effort required to measure the adaptability of your business processes. A few good ways to measure adaptability are:

▶ The percentage of time special requests are escalated, passed up to a higher level. (Each time a customer has to talk to a person who cannot solve the problem is wasted time for both the customer and the employee.)

▶ The average time it takes to get a special customer request processed, compared with standard requests. (Even though McDonald's takes only 5 to 10 minutes for a special order hamburger, this is still 10 to 20 times longer than the wait time for a regular order, and three times longer than the same service at Wendy's.)

▶ The percentage of special requests that are turned down.

Operational Measurements

It could be debated whether flowcharts are measurements or not. We choose to call them measurements, because measurements are used to define the item being improved, and a flowchart obviously provides a picture of the process being improved that is key to any exchange of data among the PIT's partners.

The level of detail in the item's flowchart usually depends on the amount of resources consumed by the activity. Cost, processing time, cycle time, error rates, and percentage of product flowing through the activity should be recorded for each activity. The complexity of most business process flowcharts and the amount of supporting data needed to do process improvement make it difficult to handle the information by hand-reported methods. We recommend that the PIT use a computer program to document the process flowchart and to store the supporting data. Typical software packages for this task are Work Draw—Business Redesign Kit and Envision.

For more information on business process measurements, see *Business Process Improvement* by H. J. Harrington.

Task 4—Define Product Measurements

Most of your end product's key measurements will come from product specifications. In some cases, you may also want to measure your product from the customer's standpoint.

Consider the following examples of product measurements that may not be part of the product specification:

- ▶ Ease of unpacking
- ▶ Ease of assembly
- ▶ User-friendliness
- ▶ Customer satisfaction level
- ▶ Cost of repair
- ▶ Safety

In other cases you may want to compare your own product and competitive products from an engineering and/or production standpoint:

- ▶ Ease of assembly
- ▶ Dimensional variation
- ▶ Workmanship
- ▶ Suppliers
- ▶ Technology
- ▶ Reworkability

Develop Product Flowchart

To help the PIT develop the measurement system for the product (the item), a flowchart of that product's manufacturing process should be developed. In this flowchart, you should list the control documents for the total process and for each operation. Examples of control documents include:

- ▶ Test procedures
- ▶ Reports
- ▶ Inspection procedures
- ▶ Customer feedback reports
- ▶ Engineering specifications

The flowchart should reflect each operation in the manufacturing process. For each flowcharted operation, the following typical data are often useful:

- ▶ First-time yields
- ▶ Processing time
- ▶ Defects per unit (percentage defective)
- ▶ Types of defects
- ▶ Value-added cost

Select Product Measurements

The flowchart will lead you to the point where you can begin to define specific measurements that you wish to use with your product. These measurements will allow you to unlock the hidden features in your competitor's products and your own, making improvements much easier and more efficient. In addition to the manufacturing process-related measurements, the PIT will need to define measurements that reflect the end-user's requirements. Typical end-user measurements are:

- ▶ As-delivered quality level
- ▶ Early-life failure rates
- ▶ Reliability
- ▶ Weight
- ▶ Useful life
- ▶ Time to repair
- ▶ Packaging protection level
- ▶ Appearance

Task 5–Define Equipment Measurements

With so much capital tied up in equipment, this form of measurement is crucial to an organization's long-term survival. When an organization wants to upgrade its equipment, it will compare different types of equipment that perform the same function. You might want to look at how different welders, drill presses, or computer software perform when compared with other equipment. This comparison is useful when the organization is considering replacing its present equipment, when a new equipment requirement is defined, or when the equipment is breaking down too often.

If you are replacing equipment, it is important to define how your present equipment performs so you can compare it with equipment that you are considering acquiring. Typical measurements are:

- ▶ Type(s) of operation(s) that it can perform
- ▶ Cost of equipment
- ▶ Drift
- ▶ Downtime
- ▶ Tool replacement time
- ▶ Tool replacement frequency
- ▶ Set-up time
- ▶ Space requirements
- ▶ Maintenance cost
- ▶ Output variation
- ▶ Output accuracy
- ▶ Resources required for operation
- ▶ Power consumption
- ▶ Process time

As you define equipment measurements, consult the equipment sales, operating, and maintenance manuals to obtain ideas on how the equipment's performance should be measured. However, avoid using the data in the equipment manuals. Sometimes the data are wrong. Also they often do not reflect equipment that has been used for a long time: with time, equipment may drift away from its original setting, and wear often decreases its accuracy.

Task 6–Define Manufacturing (Production) Process Measurements

Now that the PIT has a good understanding of the manufacturing process that is being improved, it can start to define key measurements. With manufacturing processes, measurements within the process can often be as important as measurements of the total process. These measurements will vary depending upon the particular item being evaluated. Typical manufacturing process measurements are:

- ► Safety problems per year
- ► Poor-quality cost
- ► Error rates
- ► Quality of output
- ► Customer return rates
- ► Cost per unit
- ► Rework cost
- ► First-pass yield
- ► Hours to produce a unit
- ► Equipment downtime
- ► Throughput yield
- ► Set-up time
- ► Capacity
- ► Maintenance cost

Task 7–Develop a Required Measurements Chart

Now that the PIT has evaluated the item being improved to determine which measurements are pertinent to improving its performance, develop a required measurements chart to summarize these findings (see Figure 8-4). We like to lay out the required measurements chart

Effectiveness Measurements	Type of Measurement
Errors per 10,000 inputs	Variables Data
Calls per day to get clarification data	Variables Data
Customer satisfaction	Attributes Data
Efficiency Measurements	
Cycle time	Variables Data
Processing time	Variables Data
Cost per cycle	Variables Data
Adaptability Measurements	
Percentage of special requests handled by salesperson only	Variables Data
Percentage of special requests granted	Variables Data
Physical Measurements	
None	

FIGURE 8-4. An example of a required measurements chart

using the four measurement categories discussed in Task 2. The required measurements chart defines the exact measurements that will be used to direct the waste elimination process, as well as the type of measurement (variables or attributes data).

Measurement Plan Summary

If you cannot measure, you cannot control. If you cannot control, you cannot manage. If you cannot manage, your organization is destined for failure.

Measurements are critical in all facets of life, but they become even more important in the performance improvement process. The war on waste is a conscious effort to learn how to improve yourself and/or your organization. Without a measurement system, you will not be able to do this, because you will have no idea how you are performing and where improvement opportunities exist. Even worse, a measurement system that is not consistent can often provide the organization with misleading data that result in bad management decisions. There are documented cases where incompatible measurement systems led to costly changes, only to end up hurting the performance of the item. But remember: measuring is expensive, so measure only what you need.

Learning about the different measurement systems involved with each category (business process, product and service, equipment, and manufacturing process) has given you a greater understanding not only of your current item, but also of all future ones.

Measurements are the military intelligence of the war on waste.

Introduction to Data Collection

Data + Analysis = Information
Information + Understanding = Knowledge

We have just defined which measurements need to be made. Now we are ready to define how the data will be collected. Without a plan that specifically defines what data need to be collected and how to collect them, the organization can generate a great deal of useless data. Worse, the organization can do a lot of work acquiring data that are not compatible with the original data, wasting everyone's resources. Incompatible data lead to misinterpretation that can cause costly process changes that do not produce the projected improvements and can even make the item perform worse than it did originally. A good data collection plan is worth a million times its weight in saved resources and reputation. Figure 8-5 is a flow diagram of the tasks required to develop a data collection plan.

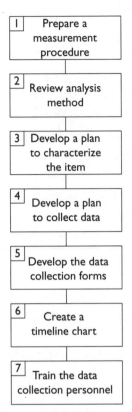

FIGURE 8-5. Flow diagram of the tasks required to develop a data collection plan

The data collection plan is a key part of the measurement system. It is also important to understand that averages can often get an organization into trouble. The average temperature in Chicago may be 68°F (very nice), but it would be a major mistake to visit Chicago in January wearing just a light suit coat. Usually it isn't averages that cause an organization to lose customers. Performance that falls at the extremes of the distribution is what makes customers upset. It is very important that the PIT understand the distribution of the data that are used to develop a future-state solution.

We have seen information technology used to improve an item's performance with no manual backup. As a result, when the computer goes down, the organization shuts down. For example, I recently checked into a hotel in Nashville. The computer was down, so the staff could not make room assignments. I waited for over two hours in the lobby and then had to call the hotel manager. The hotel's average registration cycle, I would estimate, was less than 10 minutes. Anything less than 10 minutes would have been acceptable, but two hours was not.

A word of caution: Don't design a data collection plan that would collect all the data that are out there. For most items, there are mountains of information available already, and more is being generated each day. If the PIT focuses on collecting all the information available, as soon as the analysis of the data selected is complete, more information will be available, and the cycle will never end. Prioritize the information you want to gather and the organizations you want to obtain it from.

Why Is the Data Collection Plan Important?

Obviously, if the data are important, then being able to properly collect data is also very important. The data collection plan becomes crucial for a plethora of reasons, but the two most important are *standardization* and *accuracy*.

Standardization

Standardization is key to collecting measurements. You must make sure that measurements are taken in exactly the same way, every time a measurement is taken. To ensure this conformity, you need to have a detailed measurement procedure or test procedure. This procedure must clearly show how measurements are to be taken, so they can be duplicated by anyone at any location. Standardizing the way in which the measurements are taken ensures validity of the data used to direct the improvement process.

Without a formal written procedure, there can be no assurance that the measurements will correspond to each other.

Imagine a firm that makes pencils—Mirizzi Pencil Company, whose motto is "Our Pencils Are the Strongest Pencils on Earth." Mirizzi takes great pride in the fact that its pencils have the lowest rate of breakage of any national brand of pencils. To keep this competitive advantage, Mirizzi has instituted a benchmarking study to measure how well its pencils deal with excessive force compared with other pencils. Mirizzi wants to make sure its pencils are consistently the last to break.

Think about all the different ways that the force could be applied and, therefore, the different measurements. The force could be applied with a hammer, a karate chop, or a highly calibrated tension instrument. The pencil could be supported at each end or the supports could be one inch apart. It would take 100 times the force to break a pencil with supports one inch apart than to break a pencil supported only at its ends. In each case, the measurements would be highly individualistic and completely irrelevant to each other.

The bottom line is that without standardization, Mirizzi Pencil Company would be wasting its time and might even make process changes that could be detrimental to the quality of its pencils. In order to avoid situations like this, you must completely document a measurement and data collection plan.

Accuracy

Accuracy in measurement varies in importance depending on what is being measured. Weight and age are two areas that are quite often reported with flagrant inaccuracy. Just try to determine the average weight of the people in your office by asking each one what he or she weighs and calculating the average. Then weigh each person on an accurate scale (plus or minus one pound) and calculate the average. We bet that the second average will be at least 15% higher. The important point here is that anything worth improving is worth accurate measurements.

Good equipment leads to good measurements. Ideally, you would like to have equipment that can measure ten times more accurately than the tolerance that you are trying to stay within. At a very minimum, you need equipment that is three times more accurate than the tolerance. For example, if your tolerance level is 3 mm, you need something that is accurate to 1 mm, and ideally to 0.3 mm. Without a proper measurement and data collection plan, instruments and equipment may not be accurate enough for your needs. Worse, they may be accurate enough at some test locations but not at others. For this reason, the equipment used to record measurements is usually specified in the data collection plan.

Task 8—Prepare a Measurement Procedure

What Equipment Will Be Used to Make the Measurements?

The measurement procedure should list the tools that will be used to make the measurements. (Using the pencil company as an example, the equipment used to make the measurements would be a Tinius-Olsen Stiffness Tester, Model 119.)

How Will the Measurements Be Made?

The measurement procedure should specifically define how to perform the measurement. (Again using the pencil example: The pencil will be supported in a 10-inch V-clamp, with facing edges 5 1/2 inch ± 1/8 inch apart, or using fixture no. 917634. The pencil will not be sharpened. The metal band that supports the eraser must be totally on the V-clamp. The probe and a flat side of the pencil must be at right angles to each other. The pressure rod should have a 1/8-inch radius, and the pressure should be applied at one ounce per second. The recorded measurement is the highest force reading on a Brady Force meter from the start of applying pressure until the pencil separates [breaks into two pieces].)

What Should the Sample Size Be?

The measurement procedure should define the number of different items that need to be analyzed for each measurement. The sample size should be kept to a minimum because of the cost to perform the evaluation. Unfortunately, for most parameters the PIT will need to know both the process average and the variation (sigma). This requires that larger sample sizes be specified, in order to calculate a numeric value for variation (sigma). In most cases, a minimum sample of 20 spaced over a time period is required, and larger sample sizes are preferred. The book *Total Quality Control* by Armand V. Feigenbaum can help you select your sampling plan.

When Will the Measurements Be Made?

Often the time of day, month, or year impacts the results. For example, if you were measuring the quantity of pencils produced per year, the quantity is often lower on the first day of the month than on the last.

Under What Conditions Will the Measurements Be Made?

Measurements are often influenced by external conditions. Typical aspects of the environment that need to be considered are:

- Temperature
- Humidity
- Lighting
- Noise levels
- Cleanliness
- Input voltage levels
- Materials

For example, error rates go up and productivity goes down when the activity is performed in high temperatures (95° F and above).

How Will the Data Be Recorded?

The measurement procedure should define how the data should be recorded. This includes the collection format and the required accuracy of the recorded data. For example, is it adequate to record 8:00 A.M.? Or do you need to know it was precisely 8:12 A.M.? Using the pencil example, is it adequate to record 32 lb.? Or do you need to know that it was exactly 31.95 lb.? Or is it necessary to specify 31.9523 lb.? Of course, the accuracy required for recording the data is dependent upon the accuracy of the measurement setup.

The PIT should prepare a measurement procedure for each measurement, defining the procedure for performing the measurement and for recording the data.

Task 9–Review Analysis Methods

As you begin to develop your data collection plan, consider how the data will be used and analyzed. The analysis method often impacts the amount of data that is required and when the data are recorded. There are many ways to analyze data. The following analysis methods are frequently used.

Line Graph—Used to display data. There are several kinds, including trend line graphs, bar graphs, and pie charts.

Data Matrix Analysis—A systematic way of organizing a set of data.

Pareto Analysis—A type of bar graph showing data classifications in descending order from left to right.

Control Charts—Used to determine when there is an abnormal change in the process and to project the expected variation in the process.

Histogram—A type of bar graph used to display a distribution of whatever is being measured.

Scatter Diagram—A two-dimensional graph consisting of points whose coordinates represent values of two variables under study.

Flowcharts—Provide a picture of the process activities and their inter-action.

Before moving on to the next task in this activity, review your list of measurements formalized earlier. For each measurement, select the analysis method that will be used to present the data. This is impor-tant, because the way you are going to analyze and present the data will have a large impact on how the data are collected.

A Major Data Analysis Consideration

Organizations lose customers most often because of exceptionally bad performance, not because of average performance. Most people and processes perform well most of the time, or they do not survive. For example, most people drive into their garage without hitting either side of their car. So if the garage opening is 8 feet wide and the car is 6 feet wide and if we were to measure the clearance between the car and the side of the garage 1,000 times, we would probably calculate an average clearance of one foot on each side. In fact, on occasion, the clearance on one side is much less than one foot. We know this because the paint on the side of the car was scratched on three occa-sions when there was no clearance and because one time we ripped the front bumper off as we backed the car out because we had a neg-ative clearance. This illustrates the fallacy in using averages when we benchmark our items.

In some cases, you will want to know the average value, the range (distance between minimum and maximum values), and the mathemat-ical variance. Mathematical variance is most often expressed as *sigma*. This means that you will want to analyze most of the data, taking into consideration how the actual measurement data are distributed.

Figure 8-6 is a normal distribution histogram. For more informa-tion about histograms and how to calculate sigma, see *Total Quality Control* by Feigenbaum. You will note that if a group of measurements

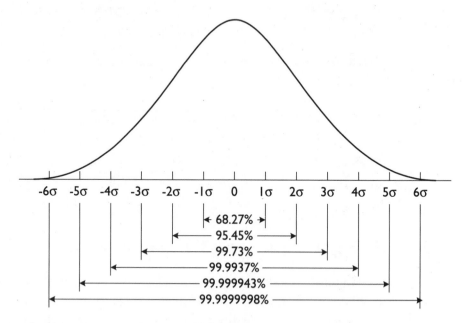

FIGURE **8-6. Normal distribution histogram**

forms a normal distribution, 68.27% of the measurements (infinite population) will be within ± 1 sigma band (limit), 95.45% will be within ± 2 sigma bands, and 99.73% will be within ± 3 sigma bands.

Using a frequency distribution approach to collecting and analyzing data, we can easily see why we hit the side of the garage 3 out of 1,000 times. In fact, we can statistically predict that we will hit the side of the garage 3.7 times out of 1,000—without making 1,000 or even 100 measurements. With a properly analyzed sample as small as 25 measurements, you can gain the degree of understanding required for most processes.

The excellence of an item often is not measured by its average alone, but also by its 3-sigma variation. Two drivers can have very different performances, even though the average clearance for each is one foot. If one driver's sigma value (standard variation) is 0.5 feet, he or she will hit the garage 46.5 times out of 1,000, whereas the driver whose sigma value is 0.33 feet will hit the garage only 2.7 times out of 1,000. Both drivers' average is one foot. What you really want is a process whose average is one foot and the ±6-sigma value is one foot, because then hitting the garage is no longer a concern because the car will hit the garage only 2 times out of 1,000,000 times.

Task 10–Develop a Plan to Characterize the Item

In this task we will develop a plan to characterize the item by:

- ▶ choosing a data-analysis method
- ▶ responding to the questions about how data collection, sampling, and data analysis will be conducted

Remember that in most cases, the PIT will need to know both the process average and how far the 3-sigma values are away from the process average.

Trend Analysis

For many measurements, the PIT will want to be able to project how the competition, and other sites within the organization, will be performing in the future. Performance projections can be based on past performance, activities currently under way, and new technological advances about to be released. These data are often needed because there is a time delay from when the database is established to when the improvements are implemented. The PIT would not want to recommend changes and have them implemented, only to find later that the item is still performing at a lower level than other leading organizations' items. It is very important to realize that the leading-edge organizations are always improving, continually raising the bar.

For this reason, the PIT should identify the measurements for which a trend chart should be developed. The PIT should make every attempt to collect real historical data on these measurements. Sometimes that is impossible, so informed judgment must prevail.

If historical data are not available, contact a number of informed sources for their best estimate of historical performance, based upon today's measured performance and their personal understanding of the item. Then use a scatter diagram to plot the individual estimates and today's measured performance. Using today's measured perfor- mance as a fixed point on the line, draw a best-fit curve through the estimated data point (see Figure 8-7).

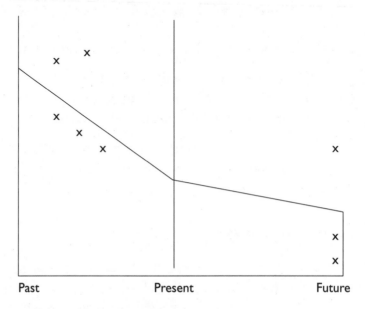

FIGURE **8-7. Past and future performance chart**

Repeat this process to project what the item's future performance would be if the proposed improvement were not implemented. Note that in the future projection only one future time is used. For example, each expert would be asked, "How will the item be performing in your organization three years from now?"

Past and future performance charts should be prepared for all major measurements, since they will become the basic data used for determining if a future-state solution will be implemented and for mea- suring the return on investment related to each change.

Choosing a Data-Analysis Method

Having recently reviewed data-analysis methods, you should be able to select the method that most effectively uses the data provided by your measurement system.

One of your biggest concerns should be how much data will be collected, since some of the methods do not handle small amounts of information well. For example, the scatter diagram needs larger amounts of data in order to be effective. Also, take into consideration which methods the PIT is particularly comfortable with. The PIT will be spending a large portion of its time analyzing data, so you want the process as user-friendly as possible.

Data Collection Questions

There are seven questions that should be answered in characterizing the item:

1. How are you going to measure?
2. How many are you going to measure?
3. How often are you going to measure?
4. What are you going to record?
5. What are you going to record the data on?
6. Who is responsible for collecting the data?
7. When and how are the collected data to be reported?

Characterize the Item

For clarity, we will review how a typical item would be characterized. Although the example is brief, it shows how to work through this process. For this example, we have chosen to look at order-entry cycle time and will analyze the data using control charts.

The following questions are used to aid the PIT in developing a data collection plan:

Question: How are you going to measure?

Answer: The salesperson will record the date and time of sale on each sales order. The order-entry clerk will time-and-date-stamp all orders with a black stamp as soon as the information has been entered into the computer.

Question: How many are you going to measure?
Answer: Record data for the first 35 orders processed.

Question: How often are you going to measure?
Answer: Month 1, Week 1; Month 2, Week 2; Month 3, Week 3; Month 4, Week 4.

Question: What are you going to record?
Answer: The data-entry supervisor will notify the data-entry team when to collect data. At the end of each day, the supervisor will collect the stamped orders and hold them for the analysts. Daily, the analysts will visit the order-entry department and record the date and time that the salesperson recorded on each order and the date and time that each order was entered into the computer.

Question: What are you going to record the data on?
Answer: The information is recorded on the order form when it is time and date stamped. This information will be transferred to a data record, Form 1075, by the analyst, so that the orders are not removed from the data-entry department.

Question: Who is responsible for collecting the data?
Answer: Analyst Scott Stefanik and order-entry supervisor Maureen Waters.

Question: When and how are the collected data to be reported?
Answer: Daily, the analysts will calculate the average daily cycle time and the range from the minimum to the maximum cycle time. This will be plotted on two graphs each day. Control limits for these graphs will not be established until the end of the data collection period.

While your characterization of items will differ for almost every item, this example provides you with insight and a reference for keeping you on the right track.

Task 11–Create a Timeline Chart

Before you begin to collect data, you should make an estimate of the time required to complete the remaining activities. Resources and time vary according to the complexity of the item and the concentration of effort applied.

For example, a benchmarking project can be as short as 10 weeks or as long as 18 months. Robert C. Camp states in his book, *Business Process Benchmarking*, that a typical business process benchmarking activity takes 3 people, working half their time, 9 to 12 months. Florida Power and Light Company, which makes extensive use of benchmarking, reports that its benchmarking cycle ranges between 6 and 10 months. Our experience indicates that it takes 2 to 4 months for a PIT to develop a future-state solution. The implementation can take as little as a few days or more than 18 months, when it involves new computer systems and/or changes to the information technology system in use.

The PIT should keep in mind the following questions as it develops the improvement plan:

- ► How many hours per week can the PIT devote to the project?
- ► What activities need to be done?
- ► What activities can be done concurrently?
- ► What activities are dependent upon resources outside the control of the PIT?

Each task will now be defined, so that you can list the estimated number of weeks necessary to accomplish each activity. The timeline chart should be recorded in *elapsed* time, not *processing* time. (For example, it could require 4 weeks of elapsed time to prepare the measurement plan, but only 40 hours of processing time. In this case you would record the time frame as 4 weeks.)

Now that you have an initial schedule, including the number of weeks necessary for the project, begin to assign actual dates to the beginning and completion points of each activity. This timeline will help immeasurably to simplify the often difficult coordination tasks.

Activity	Number of Weeks	
	Min	**Max**
1. Identify what to improve	————	————
2. Obtain management support	————	————
3. Develop the measurement plan	————	————
4. Develop the data collection plan	————	————
5. Review plan with location experts	————	————
6. Characterize the item	————	————
7. Identify corrective action	————	————
8. Develop an implementation plan	————	————
9. Gain management approval of the future-state solution	————	————
10. Implement future-state solution and measurement impact (dates not required now)	————	————

FIGURE **8-8. A timeline chart**

When choosing a start date for your timeline, it is best to use a "week ending Friday _ date _" format. This will help standardize measurement time frames. The timeline is a tool to simplify the process, not make it more difficult.

Data Collection Pitfalls

As you begin to collect data, avoid these common data collection pit-falls:
1. Lots of planning, but no action.
2. Data collection is assigned to a small committee, and the rest of the team does not get involved.
3. Insufficient resources are applied to collect, analyze, and report the data.
4. Too much data; no analysis and no assessment.

5. Too much analysis; never satisfied with analysis. ("Just one more cut on the data ....")
6. Incompatible data are combined. ("Apples" and "oranges" are counted as the same.)
7. Sample size is too small to make a legitimate conclusion.

Summary

In Chapter 8 you have accomplished two main objectives. You have developed two plans:

1. A plan to characterize (fully describe) your improvement item
2. A plan to collect information

By developing a plan to characterize your improvement item, you developed an approach that standardized the data-collection system. Through standardization you are now able to have accurate, reliable results. Just as important, the standardization allows repeatability of measurements—so that anyone could duplicate your process and get the same measurements.

The data-collection plan includes:

▶ A procedure detailing how to make each measurement and the sample size required to get meaningful results
▶ The data-analysis method that will be used for each measurement
▶ A plan to characterize your item's performance

This data-collection plan now makes up the heart of your improvement project file. All of the planning is now in place to obtain the information pertinent to improving an item's performance.

With your data-collection plan, you are now ready to move on to the next activity, which is using the data-analysis weapons to define improvement opportunities, then using the idea-generation and decision-making weapons to define how to take advantage of these opportunities.

Write it down. Written goals have a way of transforming wishes into wants, can'ts into cans, and plans into reality. Don't just think it—ink it.

—ANONYMOUS

Set challenge targets for your performance improvement activities. Motorola's prudent challenge is to improve 500% in 5 years on all measurements. Don't try to improve only 10% or 20%; go all the way. Make the most effective use of the performance improvement weapons.

Why go into something to test the waters? Go into it to make waves.

Additional Ammunition

Camp, Robert C. *Business Process Benchmarking: Finding and Implementing Best Practices* (Milwaukee, WI: ASQC Quality Press, 1995)

Envision, decision support toolkit software (Auburn, WA: Future Tech Systems, Inc.)

Feigenbaum, Armand V. *Total Quality Control*, revised edition (New York: McGraw-Hill, 1994)

Harrington, H. James. *Business Process Improvement: The Breakthrough Strategy for Total Quality, Productivity, and Competitiveness* (New York: McGraw-Hill, 1991)

Talley, Dorsey J. *Total Quality Management: Performance and Cost Measures* (Milwaukee, WI: ASQC Quality Press, 1991)

Work Draw—Business Redesign Kit, software (Pleasanton, CA: Edge Software, Inc.)

Glossary

5W's and 2H's—A rigid, structured approach that probes into and defines a problem by asking a specific set of questions related to a previously defined opportunity or problem statement. The 5W's and 2H's stand for
- W1—What?
- W2—Why?
- W3—Where?
- W4—Who?
- W5—When?
- H1—How did it happen?
- H2—How much did it cost?

Acceptable Quality Level (AQL)—The percentage or proportion of defects or defectives that is considered satisfactory quality performance for a process or product.

Activity-Based Costing (ABC)—A technique for accumulating product cost by determining all costs associated with the activities required to produce the output.

Activity Plan—A simple chart that shows a list of implementation activities listed in sequence. It identifies the individual responsible for a particular activity and the projected timing of that activity.

Advantage/Disadvantage Technique—Lists are made of advantages and disadvantages of each proposed solution. The solution with the most favorable ratio of advantages to disadvantages is assumed to be the best solution.

Advocate—An individual/group who wants to achieve change but does not have sufficient sponsorship.

Affinity Diagrams—A technique for organizing a variety of subjective data (such as options) into categories based on the intuitive relationships among individual pieces of information. Often used to find common points among concerns and ideas.

Appraisal Costs—The costs that result from evaluating already completed output and auditing the process to measure compliance with established criteria and procedures. To say it another way, appraisal costs are all the costs expended to determine if an activity was done right every time.

Area Activity Analysis (AAA)—A proven approach used by each natural work team (area) to establish efficiency and effectiveness measurement systems, performance standards, improvement goals, and feedback systems that are aligned with the organization's objectives and understood by the employees involved.

Area Graphs—Convenient methods of showing how 100% of something is apportioned. The most commonly used area graph is the pie chart.

Arrow Diagrams—A way to define the most effective sequence of events and control the activity in order to meet a specific objective in a minimum amount of time. It is an adaptation of PERT (Program Evaluation and Review Technique) or the CPM (Critical Path Method).

Ask "Why" Five Times—A systematic technique used to search for and identify the root cause of a problem.

Assumption Evaluation—Provides a way of redefining problem statements, analyzing solutions, and generating new ideas.

Attribute Control Chart—A plot of attributes data for some parameter of performance, usually determined by regular sampling of the product, service, or process as a function (usually) of time or unit number or other chronological variables. This is a frequency distribution plotted continuously over time, which gives immediate feedback about the behavior of a process. A control chart will have the following elements:
  ▸ Center line (CL)
  ▸ Upper control limit (UCL)
  ▸ Lower control limit (LCL)

Attributes Data—Counted data that can be classified as yes/no, accept/reject, black/white, or go/no-go. These data are usually easy to collect because they require only counting and not measuring the process, but they often require large samples.

Bar Graphs—Graphs with bands positioned horizontally (bars) or vertically (columns) that, by their lengths or heights, show variations in the magnitude of several measurements. The bars and columns may be multiple, to show two or more related measurements in several situations. They are also called column graphs but, to be technically correct, bar graphs have horizontal bars and column graphs have vertical columns.

Bathtub Curve—A picture of an item's failure rate versus time. It shows how the failure rate decreases during the item's early life to its intrinsic failure rate level and remains at the level until the item starts to wear out and its end-of-life rate begins to increase.

Bell-Shaped Curve—The shape of a normal distribution curve.

Best-Value Future-State Solution—A solution that results in the most beneficial new item as viewed by the item's stakeholders. It is the best combination of implementation cost, implementation cycle time, risk, and performance results (examples: return on investment, customer satisfaction, market share, risk, value-added per employee, time to implement, cost to implement, etc.).

Block Diagram—A pictorial method of showing activity flow through a process, using rectangles connected by a line with an arrow at the end of the line indicating direction of flow. A short phrase describing the activity is recorded in each rectangle.

Brainstorming—A technique used by a group to quickly generate large lists of ideas, problems, or issues. The emphasis is on quantity of ideas, not quality.

Brain Web—An unstructured cause-and-effect diagram. Also called a mind-flow or mind map.

Bureaucracy Elimination Method—An approach to identify and eliminate checks and balances activities that are not cost-justified.

Business Objective—Defines what the organization wishes to accomplish over the next 5-10 years.

Business Plan—A communication, planning, and business system that reaches and involves every employee in support of common goals and objectives. It is a three-way interactive process that defines direction, expectations, actions, and funding.

Cause-and-Effect Diagram—A visual presentation of possible causes of a specific problem or condition. The effect is listed on the right-hand side and the causes take the shape of fish bones. This is the reason it is sometimes called a fishbone diagram. It is also called an Ishikawa diagram.

c-Charts—Graphs that plot the number of defects per sample, with a constant sample size.

Central Tendency—A measure of the center of the distribution.

Certification—Designation that is issued to a single operation or piece of equipment, when the operation and/or equipment is producing products to specification when the documentation is followed, to an acceptable level of confidence. Typically, a Cpk (process capability index) of 1.4 is required to be certified.

Change Agent—Individual/group who is responsible for implementing the change.

Changee—Individual/group who must actually change. A changee is also called a change target.

Characteristic—The property of an entity or an item to identify or differentiate among entities or items.

Characterization—Process of evaluating any activity to understand how variations in the input and within the activity interact and how they affect the output. It is sometimes called interrelation mode analysis.

Checksheet—A simple form on which data are recorded in a uniform manner. The forms are used to minimize the risk of errors and to facilitate the organized collection and analysis of data.

Column Graphs—Graphs that have bands positioned vertically (columns) or horizontally (bars) that, by their heights or lengths, show variations in the magnitude of several measurements. The columns and bars columns may be multiple, to show two or more related measurements in several situations. They are also called bar graphs but, to be technically correct, column graphs have vertical columns and bar graphs have horizontal bars.

Comparative Analysis—A systematic way of comparing an item with another item to identify improvement opportunities and/or gaps. (It is the first three phases in the benchmarking process.)

Competitive Benchmarking—A form of external benchmarking that requires investigating a competitor's products, services, and processes. The most common way to do this is to purchase competitive products and services and analyze them to identify competitive advantages.

Consensus—An interactive process, involving all group members, where ideas are openly exchanged and discussed until all group members accept and support a decision, even though some of the groups' members may not completely agree with it. To reach a consensus often is time-consuming and often involves individual compromising.

Constants—Independent variables that are not allowed to vary during the experiment.

Control Chart—A tool that provides a picture of the way that a process is performing. It is a graphical chart with control limits and plotted values. The values are a statistical measure for a series of samples or subgroups of the process output. A solid line shows the mean (average) of the output.

Controllable Poor-Quality Costs—The costs that management has direct control over to ensure that only acceptable products and services are delivered to the customer. They are divided into three subcategories: prevention costs, appraisal costs, and non-value-added costs.

Cost Driver—Any factor that causes a change in cost of an activity.

Creative Thinking—A methodology designed to stimulate and encourage creativity and innovation within an organization and individuals.

Customer—The person or organization that receives the output of an area or process.

Customer-Dissatisfaction Poor-Quality Costs—The profits lost because customers buy competitive products because they perceive that the competitor's product is better quality or because the customer has had or knows someone who has had an unsatisfactory experience with the organization.

Customer-Incurred Poor-Quality Costs—The costs that the customer incurs when a product or service fails to perform to the customer's expectations. These could include loss of productivity while equipment is down, travel costs and time spent to return defective merchandise, and costs to repair after the warranty period.

Cycle Time—The actual time from the point when all of the input has been received by the process until an output has been delivered to the next process.

Cycle-Time Analysis—An approach to reduce the time that it takes to move an item through a process.

Decision-Making Matrix—A technique that allows for more methodical decisions. The team defines the desired results. Then it lists the criteria that are "givens" (must have) and "wants" (would like to have). It compares the alternative solutions against the "givens" and "wants" list and makes a risk analysis.

Delphi Narrowing Technique—A technique by which team members' priorities are used to reduce a list of alternatives to a few of the most important alternatives.

Dependent Variable—A parameter that can change as a result of changes in its independent variables.

Design of Experiments—Structured evaluations designed to yield a maximum amount of information at a defined confidence level at the least expense. They are a set of principles and formulas for designing statistically sound evaluations.

Direct Poor-Quality Costs—The costs that can be identified in the organization's ledger.

Equipment Poor-Quality Costs—The costs invested in equipment used to measure, accept, or control the products or services, plus the cost of the space the equipment occupies and its maintenance costs. This category also includes any costs related to preparing software to control and operate the equipment.

Error-Proofing—Designing the product and the processes so that it is very difficult for errors to occur.

Establish the Burning Platform—Define why the as-is process needs to be changed and prepare a vision that defines how the as-is pain will be lessened by the future-state solution.

Executive Error Rate Reduction (E^2R^2)—A way to establish acceptable executive behavior standards and measure compliance with them.

Experiment—A sequence of trials consisting of independent variables set at pre-designed levels, which lead to measurements and observations of the dependent variables.

Experimental Design—The building blocks of process definition, development, and optimization.

External Customers—People who receive output and are not part of the organization. They usually pay for the goods and/or services they receive from the organization.

External Error Costs—The costs incurred by the organization because the external customer is supplied with unacceptable products or services. These include the costs incurred because the appraisal system did not detect all of the errors before the product or service was delivered to the customer, plus the costs related to reliability problems.

Failure Mode and Effect Analysis—Identifies potential failures or causes of failures that may occur as a result of process design weaknesses.

Fast Action Solution Technique (FAST)—A breakthrough approach that focuses a group's attention on a single process for a one- or two-day meeting to define how the group can improve the process over the next 90 days. By the end of the meeting, management approves or rejects the proposed improvements.

Fishbone Diagram—A pictorial diagram showing cause-and-effect relationships among the factors that affect a process. It is also called a cause-and-effect diagram or an Ishikawa diagram.

Five S's or Five Pillars—A system designed to bring organization to the workplace. A translation of the original Five S terms from Japanese to English went like this:
- Seiri—Organization
- Seiton—Orderliness
- Seiso—Cleanliness
- Seiketsu—Standardized Cleanup
- Shitsuke—Discipline

Flowchart—A method of graphically describing a process (existing or proposed) by using simple symbols, lines, and words to display the sequence of activities in the process.

Force-Field Analysis—A visual aid for pinpointing and analyzing elements that resist change (restraining forces) or push for change (driving forces). This technique helps drive improvement by developing plans to overcome the restraining forces and make maximum use of the driving forces.

Function Diagrams—A systematic way of graphically displaying detailed tasks related to broader objectives or detailed issues related to broader issues.

Graphs—Visual displays of quantitative data that summarize a set of numbers or statistics.

Hard Consensus—When all members of the team absolutely agree with the outcome or solution.

High-Impact Team (HIT)—A methodology that designs and implements a drastic process change in a dozen days.

Histogram—A visual representation of the spread or distribution, using a series of rectangles (bars) of equal class sizes or widths. The heights of the bars indicate the relative number of data points in each class.

House of Quality—A matrix format used to organize various data elements, so named for its shape. This is the principal tool of Quality Function Deployment (QFD).

Ideagram—An unstructured cause-and-effect diagram. Also called mindflow or mind map.

Independent Variable—A variable that is controlled during an experiment.

Indirect Poor-Quality Costs—The costs that are incurred by the customer, costs that result from the negative impact of poor quality on future business or lost opportunity costs.

Inherent Process Capability—The range of variation that will occur from the predictable pattern of a stable process.

Initiating Sponsor—Individual/group who has the power to initiate and legitimize the change for all of the affected individuals.

Innovation—Converting ideas into tangible products, services, or processes.

Internal Customers—People within an organization who receive output from any area. Almost every person in an organization is an internal customer for someone else in the organization.

Internal Error Costs—The costs incurred by the organization as a result of errors detected before the organization's customer accepts the output. In other words, it is the costs the organization incurs before a product or service is accepted by the customer because someone did not do the job right the first time.

Interrelationship Diagrams—A way to graphically map out the cause-and-effect links among related items.

Interviewing—A structured discussion with one or more people to collect information related to a specific subject.

ISO—Term created by the International Organization for Standardization, from the Greek word *isos*, meaning "equal," to denote worldwide standards.

ISO 8402:1994—This document, titled *Quality Management and Quality Assurance—Vocabulary*, was prepared by the International Organization for Standardization (ISO) Technical Committee 176 and updated in 1994.

ISO 9000 Series—A set of standards released by the International Organization for Standardization, Zurich, Switzerland, that defines the fundamental building blocks for a Quality Management System and the associated accreditation and registration of QMSs.

Just-in-Time—A major strategy that allows an organization to produce only what is needed, when it's needed, to satisfy immediate customer requirements. Implemented effectively, the just-in-time concept will almost eliminate in-process stock.

Level (of a Variable)—The point at which an independent variable is set during a trial.

Line Graph—The simplest graph to prepare and use. It shows the relationship of one measurement to another over a period of time. Often this graph is continually created as measurement occurs. This procedure may allow the line graph to serve as a basis for projecting future relationships of the variables being measured.

Lost-Opportunity Poor-Quality Costs—The costs of profits lost through poor internal performance. These would include sales lost because the salesperson did not show up on time or did not do a good job of selling the service or because of engineering or manufacturing problems that caused products or services to not be available as initially scheduled.

Management Presentation—A special type of formal meeting of work groups and their managers with higher-level management.

Managing Organizational Change (MOC)—A methodology designed to lessen the stress and resistance of employees and management to individual critical changes. Sometimes called organizational change management (OCM).

Matrix Data Analysis—Takes the data displayed in a *matrix diagram* and makes it easy to visualize and compare.

Matrix Diagrams—A systematic way of selecting from large lists of alternatives. They can be used to choose among problems, root causes, or solutions. They're sometimes called decision matrices.

Milestone Graph—Shows the goals or target to be achieved by depicting the projected schedule of the process. A primary purpose is to help organize projects and coordinate activities.

Mind-Flow—An unstructured cause-and-effect diagram. Also called a mind map.

Mind Map—An unstructured cause-and-effect diagram. Also called a mind-flow or Brain Web.

Monte Carlo Analysis—An approach to varying process variables over a broad range of reasonable (and even unreasonable) options to simulate the variability in a process's key measurement.

Negative Analysis—A method used to define potential problems before they occur and develop countermeasures.

Nominal Group Technique (NGT)—A technique useful for situations where individual judgments must be tapped and combined to arrive at decisions.

Non-Value-Added Costs—The costs of doing activities that the customer would not want to pay for because they add no direct value for him or her. They can be divided into business-value-added, no-value-added, and bureaucracy costs. They also include appraisal costs.

Normal Distribution—Frequency distribution that is symmetrical about its mean or average.

On-Off Technique—A way to direct attention during a presentation, either to information on the screen or to the presenter. In other words, turn off the projector when you want attention focused on you and not on the screen.

Operational Process Capability—Determined by the manner in which the process is operated in respect to how this predictable pattern meets specification requirements.

Opportunity Cycle—A procedure for defining improvement opportunities and taking advantage of them by understanding them down to their root causes, defining and implementing improvement action, and measuring the effectiveness of the action taken. Preventive action is then taken to minimize the possibility of the condition recurring with that item or any other similar item.

Organizational Change Management (OCM)—A methodology designed to lessen the stress and resistance of employees and management to individual critical changes. This is sometimes called *managing organizational change (MOC)*.

Origin—The point where the two axes on an X-Y graph meet. When numbers are used, their values increase along both axes as they move away from the origin.

Other Point of View (OPV)—A method that aids in idea-generation and idea-evaluation by careful examination of the views of stakeholders involved. It is generally more effective when used early in the process, for idea generation as opposed to idea evaluation. It also tends to be more effective with small groups (two or three people) than with larger ones.

Pareto Diagram—A type of chart in which the bars are arranged in descending order from the left to the right. It is a way to highlight "the vital few" in contrast to "the trivial many."

p-Charts—A type of attribute control chart that shows the percentage of defective units, used when the sample size varies.

Performance Goals—Quantify the results that will be obtained if the business objectives are met.

Performance Improvement Plan (PIP)—A three-year plan designed to align the environment within an organization with a series of vision statements that drive different aspects of the organization's behaviors.

Performance Plan—A contract between management and the employees that defines the employees' roles in accomplishing the assigned tasks and the budget limitations that the employees have placed upon them.

Performance Standard—Defines the acceptable error level of each individual in the organization.

Pictogram—A diagram or graph in which picture objects convey ideas, information, etc.

Pictorial Graphs—A way to represent data using pictures. Pictograms are a type of pictorial graph in which a symbol is used to represent a specific quantity of the item being plotted. The pictogram is constructed and used like bar and column graphs.

Plan-Do-Check-Act (PDCA)—A structured approach for the improvement of services, products, and/or processes, developed by Walter Shewhart. Also known as the Shewhart cycle

Plus-Minus- Interesting (PMI)—An idea-evaluation weapon that analyzes the idea or concept by making a list of positive (+) and negative (-) things related to the idea or concept, with a third column, for recording "interesting" thoughts about the item being evaluated. A technique often used to evaluate an idea that may initially seem bad.

pn-Chart—A type of attribute control chart that shows the number of defective units, used when the sample size is constant.

Policy Deployment—An approach to planning in which organization-wide long-range objectives are set, taking into account the organization's vision, its long-term plan, the needs of the customers, the competitive and economic situation, and previous results.

Poor-Quality Cost (PQC)—A methodology that defines and collects costs related to resources (actual or potential) that are wasted or lost as a result of the organization's inability to do everything correct every time. It includes both direct and indirect costs.

Prevention Costs—All the costs incurred to prevent errors or, to say it another way, all the costs involved in helping the employee do the job right every time.

Primary Functions—Those functions for which the process was designed.

Problem-Tracking Log—A systematic way to categorize, monitor, and measure progress of the corrective action process. It is designed to ensure that the correct amounts of resources are applied to solving all important problems.

Process—A series of interrelated activities or tasks that take an input and provide an output.

Process-Analysis Diagram—An Ishikawa diagram for a process. It shows each step of the process and the factors contributing to it, indicating all cause-and-effect relationships. This allows systematic tracing of any problems to identify the source of those problems.

Process Benchmarking—A systematic way to identify superior processes and practices that are adopted for a process and adapted in order to reduce cost, decrease cycle time, cut inventory, and provide greater satisfaction for the internal and external customers.

Process Capability Study—A statistical comparison of a measurement pattern or distribution with the specification limits to determine if a process can consistently deliver products within those limits.

Process Decision Program Chart—A method that maps out the events and contingencies that may occur when moving from an identified problem to one or more possible solutions.

Process Flow Animation—A process model that shows the movement of transactions within the process and how outside functions impact the process's performance.

Process Improvement Team—A group of employees assigned to improve a process. It is usually made up of employees from different departments.

Process Performance Analysis—The collection of performance data (efficiency and effectiveness data) at the activities or tasks level of a flowchart that is used to calculate the performance of the total process.

Process Qualification—A systematic approach to evaluating a process to determine if it is ready to ship its output to an internal or external customer.

Process Redesign—A methodology used to streamline a current process with the objective of reducing cost and cycle time by 30% to 60% while improving output quality from 20% to 200%.

Process Reengineering—A methodology used to radically change the way a process is designed by developing an aggressive vision of how it should perform and using a group of enablers to prepare a new process design that is not hampered by the present process's paradigms. Used when a 60% to 90% reduction in cost or cycle time is required.

Process Simplification—A methodology that takes complex tasks, activities, and processes and dissects them to define less complex ways of achieving the defined results.

Process Simulation—A technique that pictorially represents the processing of resources, products, and services in a dynamic computer model.

Process Stability—State that exists when a predictable pattern of statistically stable behavior is demonstrated by a sequence of observations made and plotted on appropriate charts with all interpretation rules being satisfied.

Process Variation Analysis—A way of combining the variation that occurs in each task or activity in a process in order to produce a realistic prediction of the total variation that will occur in the total process.

Project—A temporary endeavor undertaken to create a unique product or service (source: Project Management Body of Knowledge, PMBOK).

Project Communications Management—A subset of project management that includes the processes required to ensure timely and appropriate generation, collection, dissemination, storage, and ultimate disposition of project information.

Project Cost Management—A subset of project management that includes the processes required to ensure that the project is completed within the approved budget.

Project Human Resource Management—A subset of project management that includes the processes required to make the most effective use of the people involved with the project.

Project Integration Management—A subset of project management that includes the processes required to ensure that the various elements of the project are properly coordinated.

Project Management—The application of knowledge, skills, tools, and techniques to project activities in order to meet or exceed stakeholders' needs and expectations from a project.

Project Quality Management—A subset of project management that includes the processes required to ensure that the project will satisfy the needs for which it was undertaken.

Project Risk Management—A subset of project management that includes the processes required to identify, analyze, and respond to project risk.

Project Scope Management—A subset of project management that includes the processes required to ensure that the project includes the correct work elements required to complete the project successfully.

Project Strategy—A system of networking experimental designs in order to:
- Achieve the goal
- Know if the goal cannot be achieved and there is a need to change the process.

Project Time Management—A subset of project management that includes the processes required to ensure timely completion of the project.

Pugh Technique—This technique compares the alternatives with the present process. First, the performance improvement team generates a list of key process characteristics. Then it compares each alternative solution, characteristic by characteristic, with the present process. If the proposed solution will provide better results than the present process, it is given a plus (+); if the results will be the same, an "s" is recorded; if it will provide worse results, it is given a minus (-).

Qualification—Acceptable performance of a complete process consisting of many operations that have already been individually certified. For a process to be qualified, each of the operations and all of the equipment used in the process must be certified. In addition, the process must have demonstrated that it can repeatedly produce products or services that meet specifications.

Quality Function Deployment—A structured process for taking the "voice of the customer," translating it into measurable customer requirements, translating the customer requirements into measurable counterpart characteristics, and deploying those requirements into every level of the product and manufacturing process design and all customer service processes.

Quality Management—All activities of the overall management function that determine the quality policy, objectives, and responsibilities and implement them by means such as quality planning, quality control, quality assurance, and quality improvement within the QMS. (ISO 8402: 1994)

Quality Management System/ISO 9000 (QMS)—The organizational structure, procedures, processes, and resources required to determine the quality policy, objectives, planning, control, assurance, and improvement that impact, directly or indirectly, the products or services provided by the organization.

Quality Manual—A document stating the quality policy and describing the Quality Management System of an organization. (ISO 8402: 1994)

Quality Plan—A document setting out the specific quality practices, resources, and sequence of activities relevant to a particular product, project, or contract. (ISO 8402: 1994)

Quality System—The organizational structure, procedures, processes, and resources needed to implement quality management. (ISO 8402: 1994)

Relationship Diagram—Graphic that directs the emphasis to people and the interactions among teams from different functional units. It helps a team visualize the process steps and brainstorm process-improvement ideas. The diagram also fosters a common understanding of the overall process. Sometimes known as a relational map.

Reliability Management System—The organizational structure, procedures, processes, and resources needed to design, analyze, and control the design and manufacturing processes so that there is a high probability of an item performing its function under stated conditions for a specific period of time to meet specified standards.

Resource Driver—Describes the basis for assigning cost from an activity cost pool to products or other cost objects.

Resultant Poor-Quality Costs—The costs that result from errors. These costs are called resultant costs because they result directly from management decisions made in the controllable poor-quality costs category. They are divided into two categories: internal error costs and external error costs.

Reverse Engineering—The process of purchasing, testing, and disassembling competitors' products in order to understand the competitors' design and manufacturing approaches, then using these data to improve the organization's products.

Root Cause Analysis—The process of identifying the various causes affecting a particular problem, process, or issue and determining the real reasons that caused the condition.

Run Charts—A graphic display of data used to assess the stability of a process over time or over a sequence of events (such as the number of batches produced). The run chart is the simplest form of control chart.

Scatter Diagrams—A graphic tool used to study the relationship between two variables. A scatter diagram is used to test for possible cause-and-effect relationships. It does not prove that one variable causes the other, but it does show whether a relationship exists and, if so, reveals the character of that relationship.

Secondary Functions—Those functions that support the primary functions or are of secondary importance.

Shewhart Cycle—The same as the Plan-Do-Check-Act (PDCA) cycle.

Simulation—A means of experimenting with a detailed model of a real process or system to determine how the process or system will respond to change in its structure, environment, or underlying assumptions.

Simulation Modeling—Using computer programs to represent the item (activity, process, or system) under study in order to predict how it will perform or to control how it is performing.

Situation-Description Technique (5W's and 2H's)—A rigid, structured approach that probes into an opportunity or a problem and defines it by asking a specific set of questions related to a previously prepared opportunity or problem statement. The 5W's and 2H's stand for:
- ▶ W1—What?
- ▶ W2—Why?
- ▶ W3—Where?
- ▶ W4—Who?
- ▶ W5—When?
- ▶ H1—How did it happen?
- ▶ H2—How much did it cost?

Six-Sigma Program—A program designed to reduce error rates to a maximum of 3.44 errors per million units, developed by Motorola in the late 1980s.

Six-Step Error-Prevention Cycle—A process to prevent problems rather than to fix them.

Six-Step Problem-Solving Cycle—A basic procedure for understanding a problem, correcting the problem, and analyzing the results.

Six-Step Solution-Identification Cycle—A procedure for defining how to solve a problem or take advantage of an opportunity.

Soft Consensus—When some members of a team would prefer a different solution but are willing to support the decision of the team.

Solution-Analysis Diagram—Graphic depiction of a situation designed to analyze all the possible effects of a proposed solution or cause.

Spider Diagrams/Radar Charts—Graphics used to show a number of parameters of one item in one figure or to compare one or more sets of data. Often used to indicate the status quo (current state) against the vision (future state).

Sponsor—The individual or group with the power to sanction or legitimize a project or program.

Stakeholder—Individuals or groups with a common interest in an entity and/or environment in which they operate. Stakeholders are typically customers, owners, employees, suppliers, management, employees' families, and society.

Stakeholder Analysis Plan—A system to identify "key stakeholders."

Standard Deviation—An estimate of the spread (dispersion) of the total population based upon a sample of the population. The Greek letter sigma (σ) is used to designate the estimated standard deviation.

Statistical Process Control (SPC)—Using data for controlling processes, making outputs of products or services predictable. A mathematical approach to understanding and managing activities. It includes three statistical quality tools: design of experiments, control charts, and characterization.

Statistical Stability—A statistical comparison of the variation of equipment or processes over time against allowable variation.

Statistics—A mathematical approach to evaluating and analyzing situations. Some people say it's common sense put to numbers.

Storyboard—A series of pictures and accompanying narrative that is used to define how something is done or what is going on related to a problem or situation.

Strategy—The approach that will be used to meet the performance goals.

Stratification—The process of classifying data into subgroups based on characteristics or categories. It is the breakdown of the whole (total area of concern) into related subgroups.

Survey—A systematic way to collect information about a specific subject by interviewing people. Often, the interview takes the form of a series of questions that are presented to a target audience in written or oral form.

Sustaining Sponsor—Individual or group with political, logistical, and economic proximity to the individuals who will need to change as a result of some activity or project.

System—The organizational structure, responsibilities, procedures, and resources needed to perform a major function within an organization or to support a common business need.

Tactic—Defines the action that is required to implement a strategy.

Total Cost Management—A comprehensive management philosophy for proactively managing an organization's total resources (material, capital, and human resources) and the activities that consume those resources.

Total Productivity Management—A methodology designed to direct the organization's efforts at improving productivity without decreasing quality. It is designed to eliminate waste by involving employees, effective use of information technology, and automation.

Total Quality Management—A methodology designed to focus an organization's efforts on improving quality of internal and external products and services. ISO 8402 defines it as "A management approach of an organization, centered on quality, based on the participation of all its members and aiming at long-term success through customer satisfaction and benefits to the members of the organization and to society."

Tree Diagram—A systematic approach that helps the user think about each phase or aspect of solving a problem, reaching a target, or achieving a goal.

Trial—An observation made with all of the variables set at pre-designed levels and held constant during the duration of the observation.

Trivial Many—Approximately 20% of the errors are caused by 80% of the problems. This 80% is called "the trivial many." The 80% of the problems that have a minimum impact on an organization.

u-Charts—A type of attribute control chart that plots the number of defects per unit with a varying sample size.

Value-Added Analysis (VA)—A procedure for analyzing every activity within a process, classifying it as value-added or non-value-added, and then taking positive action to eliminate or at least minimize the non-value-added activities or tasks.

Variable Control Chart—A plot of variables data of some parameter of a process's performance, usually determined by regular sampling of the product, service, or process as a function (usually) of time or unit numbers or other chronological variable. This is a frequency distribution plotted continuously over time, which gives immediate feedback about the behavior of a process. A control chart will have the following elements:
- Center line (CL)
- Upper control limit (UCL)
- Lower control limit (LCL)

Variables Data—The kind of data that is always measured in units, such as inches, feet, volts, amps, ohms, centimeters, etc. Measured data give you detailed knowledge of the system and allow for accurate assessment of small, frequent samples.

Vision—A description of the desired future state of an organization, process, team, or activity.

Vision Statement—A group of words that paints a clear picture of the desired business environment in a specific number of years in the future. A vision statement should consist of two to four sentences.

Vital Few—Approximately 80% of the errors are caused by 20% of the problems. This 20% is called "the vital few." The 20% of the problems that have the maximum impact on an organization.

Voice of the Customer—The customer's expression of his or her requirements, in his or her own terms.

Work Flow Monitoring—An online computer program that is used to track individual transactions as they move through the process, in an effort to minimize process variation.

World-Class Operations Benchmarking—A form of external benchmarking that extends the benchmarking approach outside the organization's direct competition to involve organizations in dissimilar industries.

X-bar-R Control Chart—An important statistical tool that can be used to signal problems very early and thus enable action to be taken before large volumes of defective output have occurred.

X-Y Axes Graph—A pictorial presentation of data on sets of horizontal (X) and vertical (Y) lines called a grid. The data are plotted on the grid according to the specific numerical values assigned to the horizontal and vertical axes.

Zmin—The distance between the process mean and the nearest specification limit (upper or lower) measured in standard deviation (sigma) units.

Performance Improvement Weapons

This appendix lists more than 1001 Performance Improvement Weapons.

Select wisely the weapons you use. All of these are good weapons, if applied to the right opportunity under the right circumstances. On the other hand, most of them can have a negative impact on the organization if they are used incorrectly or if the circumstances are not right.

This is our list of the weapons, and I am sure it is incomplete. If you have others that should be added to the list, please send them to us along with a short definition of the weapon and, if possible, an explanation of how the weapon is used. Send them to:

H. James Harrington
16080 Camino Del Cerro
Los Gatos, CA 95032-4844
USA
E-mail: James.Harrington@ey.com

1. 5W's and 2H's Method
2. 6-3-5 Method
3. 7-S Model
4. A Delta T
5. Accelerated Solution Environment (ASE)
6. Accelerated System Development
7. Accountability Matrix
8. ACORN Test
9. Acquisition Streamlining
10. Action-and-Effect Diagram
11. Action Diagramming
12. Action Planning
13. Action Readiness Chart
14. Activity Accounting
15. Activity Analysis
16. Activity-Based Budgeting
17. Activity-Based Costing
18. Activity-Based Management
19. Activity Chart
20. Activity Cost Matrix
21. Activity Cost Pool Definitions
22. Activity Network Diagram
23. Activity-On Arrow
24. Activity-On Node
25. Actual Cost of Work Performed
26. Add-On/Replacement Matrix
27. Affect-Task Concept Balancing
28. Affinity Analysis
29. Affinity Diagrams
30. Algorithms
31. Alignment Processes
32. Amoeba Units
33. Analogy and Metaphor
34. Analysis and Segmentation of Customer Views

35. Analysis of Customer Wants
36. Analysis of Variance
37. Annual Strategic Quality Plans
38. Anova
39. Application Construction
40. Application Context Diagram
41. Application Development Alternative
42. Application Evolution
43. Application Installation
44. Application Prototype
45. Application Screen Flow
46. Application Structuring and Identification
47. Application Testing
48. Architecture for Managing Corporate Culture
49. Architecture Interaction Diagram
50. Area Activity Analysis (AAA)
51. Area of Impact
52. Arrow Diagrams
53. Ask "Why" Five Times
54. Assess Change Management Enablers and Barriers
55. Assimilation Capacity Audit Procedures
56. Assimilation Capacity Audit Software
57. Assimilation Capacity Consultation
58. Association Diagram
59. Association Matrix
60. Association Programming
61. Assumptions Evaluation
62. Attribute Control Charts
63. Attribute Identification
64. Audience Analysis
65. Auditing
66. Audits by Top Management
67. Automation
68. Autonomous Work Teams
69. Auxiliary
70. Balance Sheet
71. Bar Chart
72. Barriers-and-Aids Analysis
73. Baseline Load Factor
74. Basic Quality Functions
75. Basili Data Collection Analysis
76. Batch Procedure Design
77. Bayes' Theorem
78. Bayesian Estimates
79. Behavior Model
80. Behavior Modification
81. Behavior of a System
82. Behavior Pattern
83. Behavioral Analysis
84. Benchmarking
85. Benefits Assessment
86. Best-Value Future-State Solution
87. Big-Picture Analysis
88. Binomial
89. Black Box Testing
90. Block Diagram
91. Blue-Collarization
92. Bottom-Up Testing
93. Box Plot
94. BPI Measurement Methods
95. Brainstorming
96. Brainwriting Pool
97. Breakdown Tree
98. Budget Attainment Analysis
99. Bureaucracy Elimination Methods
100. Business Area Data Modeling
101. Business Engineering
102. Business Plan
103. Business Process Improvement Concepts
104. Business Process Improvement Measurement Methods
105. Business Process Innovation
106. Business Process Reengineering
107. Business Process Simulation
108. Business Strategy Analysis
109. Business Systems Planning (BSP)
110. Business Transaction Identification
111. Buzz Group
112. c Charts
113. Canonical Synthesis
114. Capacity and Staff Planning
115. Career Development
116. Career Planning
117. Cascade Processes

118. CASE (Computer-Aided Software Engineering)
119. Case Study
120. Cash Bonuses
121. Catastrophe Effects Diagram
122. Causal-Loop Analysis
123. Causal-Loop Diagram
124. Cause/Effect Graphing
125. Cause-and-Effect Diagrams (Fishbone Diagrams)
126. Cause-and-Effect Diagrams with Cards (CEDAC)
127. Change Agent Evaluation
128. Change Agent Selection Form
129. Change History Survey
130. Change Impact Evaluation
131. Change Implementation Monitoring
132. Change Knowledge Assessment
133. Change Leader Readiness Assessment (CLR)
134. Change Management Architecture Consultation
135. Change Program Portfolio (CPP)
136. Change Project Analysis
137. Change Project Evaluation Service
138. Change Resistance Scale
139. Change Synergy Evaluation
140. Checklist
141. Checksheets
142. Checkerboard Method
143. Checksheet Design
144. Circle of Influence
145. Circle of Knowledge
146. Circle of Opportunity
147. Circle Response
148. Class Relationship Diagram
149. Classification of Characteristics
150. Cluster Analysis
151. Cluster Factor Assessment
152. Cluster Organizations
153. Coaching
154. Coaching Styles Inventory
155. Code Generation
156. Cognitive Architecture
157. Cognitive Health
158. Cognitive Quality of Worklife
159. Cognitive Technologies
160. Cognitively Balanced Jobs and Careers
161. Collaboration Technology
162. Communicating Change: Constituency Analysis
163. Communicating Styles Survey
164. Communication
165. Communication Management and Planning
166. Communications Planning
167. Company-Based Training
168. Company-Wide Quality Control
169. Comparative Analysis
170. Comparison Matrix
171. Competency Gap Assessment
172. Competency Model
173. Competitive Analysis
174. Competitor Product Disassembly Research
175. Computer-Aided Design (CAD)
176. Computer-Aided Engineering (CAE)
177. Computer Augmentation of Cooperative Work
178. Computer Forms of Cooperative Work
179. Computer Model
180. Computer Simulation
181. Computer-Supported Cooperative Work
182. Concept Diagram
183. Concept Ontology
184. Conceptual Data Model
185. Conceptual Process Partitioning Model
186. Concurrent Engineering
187. Conditional Probability
188. Conditions-of-Doing Effects
189. Conference Room Test
190. Confidence Intervals
191. Configuration Management
192. Conflict Management Guidelines
193. Conjoint Analysis
194. Connectivity Analysis
195. Consensus Building
196. Consensus Decision Making
197. Consensus Design

198. Conservation Analysis
199. Constant
200. Consultation Map
201. Consultation Net Analysis
202. Context Diagramming
203. Contextual Leadership
204. Contingency Diagram
205. Contingency Planning
206. Contingency Reserve
207. Continuum of Team Goals
208. Contract Negotiation
209. Control Charts
210. Conventional True Value (of a Quantity)
211. Coordination Technology
212. Corrective Evolution
213. Correlation Analysis
214. Cost/Benefit Analysis
215. Cost-Cycle Time Analysis
216. Cost-Driven Analysis
217. Cost-Effectiveness Programs
218. Cost Flow Diagramming
219. Cost of Conformity
220. Cost of Lost Opportunity
221. Cost of Low Standards
222. Cost of Nonconformity
223. Cost of Poor Quality
224. Cost-of-Quality Analysis
225. Cost-Time Analysis
226. Cost-Time Charts
227. Could Cost
228. Countermeasures Matrix
229. Crawford Slip Method
230. Creative Brainstorming
231. Creative Thinking
232. Creativity Assessment
233. Criteria Filtering
234. Critical Dialogue
235. Critical Incident
236. Critical Path Method (CPM)
237. Critical Success Factor Analysis
238. Critical-to-Quality Analysis
239. Cross-Functional Hobbying
240. Cross-Functional Management
241. Cross Unit
242. Cross-Unit Promotion Paths

243. CRUD Matrix
244. CSA/SD
245. Culture Alignment Assessment
246. Culture Assessment
247. Culture Audits
248. Culture Consistency Evaluation
249. Cumulative Hazard Sheet
250 Current State Analysis
251. Current Systems Investigation
252. Customer Acquisition/Defection Matrix
253. Customer Analysis
254. Customer Data Analysis and Action Plans
255. Customer-First Questions
256. Customer Interface Training
257. Customer Leadership Establishment Chart
258. Customer Loss Analysis (Cost Impact)
259. Customer Needs Table
260. Customer Partnerships
261. Customer Phone Calls (Management and Employees)
262. Customer-Related Measurements
263. Customer Requirements Mapping
264. Customer Reviews
265. Customer Round Tables
266. Customer Satisfaction Analysis
267. Customer Simulated Testing
268. Customer Surveys
269. Customer Understanding Tour
270. Customer Visits
271. Cycle-Time Analysis
272. Cycle-Time Flowchart
273. Cycle-Time Reduction Methods
274. Cycle-Time Reporting
275. Daily Life Protocol
276. Data Access Modeling
277. Data Analysis
278. Data Collection Strategy
279. Data Flow Diagramming
280. Data Gathering by Document Review
281. Data Gathering by Interview
282. Data Gathering by Samples and Surveys
283. Data Gathering by Secondary Research
284. Data Stratification

370. Equilibrium
371. Equilibrium Value
372. Error Guessing
373. Error-Proofing
374. Error-Proofing Fixtures and Methods
375. Event-On Node
376. Events Log
377. Executable Module
378. Executive Error Rates Reduction
379. Executive Improvement Teams (EITs)
380. Executive Information Needs Analysis
381. Executive Needs Analysis
382. Exemplary Facilities
383. Expanded Uncertainty
384. Expert Decision Systems and Knowledge Bases
385. Expert System Voice Determination Matrix
386. Exponential Decay or Growth
387. Exponential Formula for Reliability
388. EXPRESS
389. Facilitative Management
390. Facilitator Training
391. Facilitators
392. Facilities Planning
393. Facility Layout Diagram
394. Factor Analysis
395. Factorial Design
396. Factorial Experiment (General)
397. Fail-safe Planning
398. Failure Analysis
399. Failure Mode and Effect Analysis
400. FAST (Fast Action Solution Technique)
401. Fault Diagnosis
402. Fault Modes, Effects, and Criticality Analysis (FMECA)
403. Fault Tree Analysis
404. Fewer Good Suppliers
405. Field Reporting
406. Financial Analysis
407. Financial Reporting
408. Finish-No-Earlier-Than Constraint
409. Finish-to-Finish Dependency
410. Finish-to-Start Dependency
411. Finite Element Analysis (FEA)
412. First-Order Delay
413. Fishbowls
414. Five S's
415. Flattening the Organization
416. Flowcharting
417. Flow Diagram
418. FOCUS
419. Focus Groups
420. Focused Process Improvement
421. Focused Restructuring
422. Fog Index
423. Foolproof Engineering Methods
424. Force-Field Analysis
425. Forced Association
426. Forced Choice
427. Forms Design
428. Foundation Immersion Reinforcement
429. Fractional Factorial Experiments
430. Frequency Distribution
431. Fresh Eye
432. Function Diagrams
433. Function Execution by Mass Work Events
434. Functional Map
435. Fundamental Process Sequence
436. Fury Logic
437. Future State Business Process Model
438. Future State Vision
439. Futures Wheel
440. Gain Sharing
441. Gantt Chart
442. Gap Analysis
443. General Ledger Analysis and Consolidation
444. Geometric Dimensioning and Tolerancing
445. Geometric Sample/Directional Sample
446. Global Model
447. Goal Control Process
448. Goal Gap
449. Goodness of Fit of a Distribution
450. Gozinto Chart
451. Grace Latin Square Model
452. Graphical Evaluation and Review Technique (GERT)

537. Life-Cycle Impact Assessment
538. Life-Cycle Inventory Analysis
539. Line Chart
540. Line Management
541. Linear Relationship
542. Linear Responsibility Chart
543. Linking Diagram
544. List Reduction
545. Listening
546. Logic Diagram
547. Logical Database Design
548. Logical Relationship
549. Long-Range Quality Planning
550. Loss Function
551. Maintainability
552. Maintainability Analysis
553. Maintainability Assessment
554. Major Process and Infrastructure Alignment
555. Major Program Status
556. Management by Objectives
557. Management by Objectives Achievement Measurement
558. Management by Walking Around
559. Management Improvement Teams (MIT)
560. Management of Change
561. Management Presentations
562. Management Process Alignment
563. Management Review and Approval
564. Management Self-Audits
565. Management's Seven Tools
566. Manufacturability Assessment
567. Market Analysis
568. Markov Analysis
569. Mastery Timeline
570. Matrix Charts/Decision Matrices
571. Matrix Data Analysis
572. Matrix Diagram
573. Matrix Management
574. Measurement Matrix
575. Meeting Management
576. Mental Imaging
577. Mentorship Coverage Map
578. Meta-Action Diagram
579. Meta-Modesty

580. Metrics Analysis
581. Microdiagnostics
582. Middle-Up-Down Management
583. Milestones Chart
584. MIL-Q-9858A Compliance
585. Mind Flow
586. Mind Maps
587. Mission Statement
588. Mission Statement Checklist
589. Mission Statement Wordsmithing
590. Mistake Proofing
591. Mobilization Processes
592. Model (Organizational Effectiveness)
593. Model Building
594. Modeling
595. Module Structure Diagram
596. Monastic Management
597. Monetary Awards
598. Monte Carlo Analysis
599. Monte Carlo Sampling
600. Monthly Assessment Schedule
601. Morphological Analysis
602. Morphological Forecasting
603. Multi-Level Continuous Sampling
604. Multinomial
605. Multiple-Attribute Decision Modeling
606. Multiple Correlation
607. Multiple Rating Matrix
608. Multiple Regression
609. Multiple Sampling
610. Multi-Skills Maintenance
611. Multi-Skills Operator
612. Multi-Stage Cluster Sampling
613. Multi-Stage Sampling/Nested Sampling
614. Multi-Vari Strategy
615. Multivariable Analysis
616. Multivariable Chart
617. Multivariate Frequency Distribution
618. Multi-Voting
619. Mutually Exclusive Relationships
620. Needs Analysis
621. Needs-Seed
622. Negative Analysis
623. Negative Binomial
624. Negative Loop

625. Network Analysis
626. Neural Net Emotion Detection
627. Neural Nets and Classifier Search Engines
628. New Employee Selection
629. New Performance Standards
630. Nominal Group Techniques
631. Nominal Prioritization
632. Nondestructive Testing
633. Non-linear Relationships
634. Non-Value-Added Activity and Bureaucracy Elimination Methods
635. Non-Verbal Communications
636. Normal Probability Distribution
637. No-Value-Added Analysis
638. np Charts
639. Numerical Prioritization
640. Object Behavior Scenario
641. Object Interaction Diagram
642. Objectives Matrix
643. Observation
644. On-Line Conversion Design
645. Ontological Programming
646. Operating Characteristic Curve
647. Operating Efficiency
648. Operation Verification
649. Operational Alternatives Analysis
650. Operational Definitions
651. Opportunity Analysis
652. Order of Magnitude Estimate
653. Organization Chart
654. Organization Design
655. Organization Design and Structure
656. Organization Fractality
657. Organization Mapping
658. Organization Model
659. Organization Readiness Chart
660. Organization Relationship Map
661. Organization Taguchi
662. Organizational Alignment
663. Organizational Analysis
664. Organizational Breakdown Structure (OBS)
665. Organizational CAD
666. Organizational Change Enablers
667. Organizational Change Management (OCM)
668. Organizational Change Management Evaluation Process
669. Organizational Change Management Process Model
670. Organizational Change Management Techniques
671. Organizational/Human Resource Enablement Sessions
672. Organizational Improvisation
673. Organizational Knowledge Matrix
674. Organizational Neurosis
675. Organizational Performance Lever
676. Organizational Performance Lever (OPL) Dashboard
677. Organizational Prototyping
678. Orthogonal Arrays
679. Orthogonal Polynomial
680. Other Points of View (OPV)
681. Outsourcing
682. Overload Index
683. p-Charts
684. Package Application
685. Package Evaluation
686. Package Integration Strategy
687. Package Software Evaluation
688. Package Validation Testing
689. Pain Management Strategies
690. Pain-Sharing Matrix
691. Pair Matching Overlay
692. Paired Comparison
693. Panel Debate
694. Paperwork Simplification Techniques
695. Paradigm
696. Paradox Analysis
697. Paradoxon in Smallest Work Unit
698. Parametric Estimating
699. Pareto Diagrams
700. Participative Management
701. Participatory Cabaret
702. Participatory Research Assembly
703. Participatory Town Meeting
704. Pay for Knowledge System
705. Pay for Performance

706. Peer Evaluations
707. People Enabler Detailed Analysis
708. Perfection Evolution
709. Performance Improvement Plan
710. Performance Index
711. Performance Planning and Evaluation
712. Performance Qualification
713. Performance Standard
714. Periodic Systematic Sample
715. Personal Power Survey
716. Personal Resilience Questionnaires
717. Personality Profile (Keirsey-Bates)
718. PERT Charting
719. Pessimistic Time
720. Phillips 66
721. Physical Database Design
722. PIC-A-Solution
723. Pictograph
724. Pie Chart
725. Pin Cards Technique
726. Plan-Do-Check-Act Cycle
727. Plan-Results Matrix
728. Plus Minus Interesting
729. Point-Scoring Evaluation
730. Poisson
731. Policy Deployment
732. Polygon
733. Polygon Overlay
734. Poor-Quality Cost
735. Positive Loop
736. Potential Problem Analysis (PPA)
737. Practical Intelligence Matrix
738. PRE–Control
739. Precedence Diagramming Method (PDM)
740. Prediction Intervals
741. Predried Sample
742. Presentation
743. Principal Component
744. Principal Component Analysis
745. Prioritization Matrices
746. Prioritization Through Ratings
747. Problem Analysis
748. Problem-Selection Matrix
749. Problem Solving
750. Problem-Solving Unit
751. Problem Specification
752. Problem-Tracking Logs
753. Problematic Behavior
754. Process Action Diagram
755. Process Analysis and Improvement
756. Process Analysis Technique (PAT)
757. Process Benchmarking
758. Process Capability Analysis
759. Process Capability Studies
760. Process Decision Program Chart
761. Process Deployment Automation
762. Process Design Program Charts
763. Process Documentation
764. Process Empowerment Rooms
765. Process Engineering
766. Process Evaluation
767. Process Flow Controls
768. Process Flow Diagram
769. Process Improvement Teams (PITs)
770. Process Mapping
771. Process Modeling
772. Process Qualification
773. Process Redesign
774. Process Reengineering
775. Process-Selection Matrix
776. Process Simplification Techniques
777. Process Visioning
778. Process Walk-Through Methods
779. Process Window Definitions
780. Product Cycle Controls
781. Product Liability
782. Product Metamorphic Transposition Matrix
783. Productivity Processes
784. Proficiency Testing
785. Program Evaluation and Review Technique (PERT) Charting
786. Program Group Dependency Diagram
787. Project Management
788. Project Management Knowledge Base
789. Project Plan
790. Project Planning Log
791. Project Prioritization Matrix
792. Project Role Map

793. Projection Analysis
794. Prototype Test Checklists
795. Prototyping
796. Pugh Technique
797. Purposing Matrix
798. Qualitative Analysis
799. Qualitization of Systems
800. Quality Area Improvement
801. Quality Assessment
802. Quality Assurance Manual
803. Quality Assurance Planning
804. Quality Chart
805. Quality Circle
806. Quality College
807. Quality Communication
808. Quality Company Policies
809. Quality Control Circles (QCC)
810. Quality Data Collection and Reporting System
811. Quality Engineering Methods and Training
812. Quality Function Deployment
813. Quality Integration
814. Quality Loop
815. Quality Loss Function
816. Quality Management System (ISO 9000)
817. Quality Manuals
818. Quality of Management
819. Quality of Service
820. Quality Policy
821. Quality Policy Deployment
822. Quality Principle
823. Quality-Related Costs
824. Quality Spiral
825. Quality Surveillance
826. Quality Survey
827. Quality Visions
828. Quantitative Analysis
829. Questionnaires
830. Radar Chart
831. Random Numbers Generator
832. Range Chart
833. Ranking Matrix
834. Rating Matrix
835. Recall
836. Reduced Inspection
837. Redundancy Techniques
838. Reengineering Project
839. Regression Analysis
840. Regression Testing
841. Regularized Structure Reading Diagram
842. Relations Diagram
843. Relationship Map
844. Reliability Analysis
845. Reliability Block Diagram
846. Reliability-Centered Maintenance
847. Reliability Model
848. Reliability Predictions
849. Remote Maintenance/ Telemaintenance/Online Maintenance
850. Report Design
851. Reproducibility Standard Deviation
852. Requests for Corrective Action (RCA)
853. Requirements-and-Measure Tree
854. Requirements Matrix
855. Requirements of Society
856. Research Assembly
857. Resource and Activity Driver Analysis
858. Resource Histogram
859. Resource Life Cycle
860. Resource Requirements Matrix
861. Response Data-Encoding Form
862. Response Matrix Analysis
863. Responsibility Assignment Matrix
864. Responsibility Charting
865. Responsibility Matrix
866. Restructuring of the Quality Assurance Organization
867. Retainage
868. Reverse Brainstorming
869. Reverse Engineering
870. Reverse Thinking
871. Ringi Elimination
872. Risk Assessment
873. Risk Control
874. Risk Management Plan

875. Risk/Opportunity Management Process
876. Risk Space Analysis
877. Risk Taking
878. Room Collection Theory of Organizations
879. Root-Cause Analysis
880. Rotating Roles
881. Round Robin Brainstorming
882. Rules of Probability, Combinatorics
883. Run Chart
884. Run-It-By
885. Rural Industriality
886. Safe-Life Concept
887. Safety Management
888. Sample Inspection
889. Sampling Method
890. SAP ABAP/4
891. SCAMPER
892. Scatter Diagrams
893. Scenario Writing
894. Scientific Management
895. Screen Design
896. Screening Inspection
897. Security and Access Controls Design
898. Selection Matrix
899. Selection Window
900. Self-Assessment
901. Self-Explaining Work Processes
902. Self-Managed Work Teams
903. Self-Management Enablement Skills
904. Self-Recording Products
905. Semantic Intuition
906. Sensitivity Analysis
907. Sequential Sampling
908. Serial Equity
909. Servability/Serviceability
910. Set-Up Time Reduction
911. Seven Basic Tools
912. Shared Meeting Wall
913. Shelf Life
914. Shewhart PDCA Cycle
915. Ship-to-Stock Cost
916. Should-Cost Estimates
917. Significance Test
918. Simple Correlation
919. Simple English
920. Simple Language Analysis
921. Simplification Analysis (Process, Paperwork, and Language)
922. Simulation Modeling
923. Simulation Techniques
924. Simultaneous Equations
925. Situation Analysis Diagrams
926. Situational Feed-Forward Diagram
927. Situational Feedback Diagram
928. Six Sigma System
929. Six-Step Error-Prevention Cycle
930. Six-Step Problem-Solving Cycle
931. Six-Step Solution-Identification Cycle
932. Skeletal Action Diagram
933. Skill-Based Compensation
934. Skip Lot Inspection
935. Skunk Works
936. Slope (of a variable on a graph)
937. SMOOTH Function
938. Snake Chart
939. Social Computation
940. Social Connectionism
941. Social Expert Systems
942. Social Interaction Patterns
943. Social Process Balancing
944. Social Process Model
945. Sociogram
946. Sociotechnical Design
947. Software Configuration Management Version
948. Software Quality Assurance
949. Solace System
950. Solicitation Planning
951. Solution Analysis Diagrams
952. Solution Matrix
953. Solutions Evaluation
954. Source Inspection
955. Spider Diagram
956. Sponsor Commitment Evaluation
957. Sponsor Evaluation
958. Staffless Organizations
959. Stakeholder Association Matrix
960. Stakeholder Identification Analysis (SIA)

961. Stakeholder Mapping
962. Stakeholder Needs Analysis
963. Standard Deviation
964. Standardization
965. Starbursting
966. Statistical Design of Experiments
967. Statistical Estimation
968. Statistical Methods (Control Charts)
969. Statistical Process Control (SPC)
970. Statistical Thinking
971. Stem-and-Leaf Display
972. Sticking Dots
973. Stimulus Analysis
974. Stock Purchase Plans
975. Storyboarding
976. Strategic Alliances Planning
977. Strategic Business Review
978. Strategic Information Systems Plan (SISP)
979. Strategic Plan
980. Stratification
981. Stratified Sampling
982. Stratum Chart
983. Stress Testing
984. Structural Methodology for Process Improvement
985. Structural Reading
986. Structure Charts
987. Structured Analysis/Structured Design (SASD)
988. Structured Customer Surveys
989. Structured Design (SD)
990. Structured Interview
991. Structured Walk-Through
992. Suggestion Programs
993. Supplier Design Involvement
994. Supplier Partnerships
995. Supplier Process Audits
996. Supplier Qualification
997. Supplier Quality Incentive Plans
998. Supplier Ratings
999. Supplier Seminars
1000. Supplier Surveys
1001. Supply Chain Management
1002. Supply Chain Terminology

1003. Surveying
1004. SWOT Analysis
1005. Symbolic Flowchart
1006. Synergy Survey
1007. System
1008. System Analysis Diagram
1009. System Diagram
1010. System Impact Analysis
1011. Systematic Sampling
1012. Systems Assurance
1013. TABLE Function
1014. Tactical IS Plan
1015. Taguchi Techniques
1016. Target Costing
1017. Target Goal Setting
1018. Target Resistance Evaluation
1019. Task Analysis
1020. Task Team (TT)
1021. Team Building
1022. Team Meeting Evaluation
1023. Team Mirror
1024. Team Process Assessment
1025. Team Recognition
1026. Team Resilience Questionnaire
1027. Teams-Group Process
1028. Technical Vitality
1029. Technology Enablement Sessions
1030. Technology Impact Analysis
1031. Test Objectives Definition
1032. Test of Hypotheses
1033. Test Plan Design
1034. Test to Failure
1035. Thematic Content Analysis
1036. Third-Order Delay
1037. Three-Job Week
1038. Tiger Teams
1039. Time Box
1040. Timeline Chart
1041. Time Management
1042. Time-Scaled Network Diagram
1043. Time Series Analysis
1044. Time Study Sheet
1045. Tolerance Intervals
1046. Top-Down Flowchart
1047. Top-Down Testing

1048. Total Business Management (TBM)
1049. Total Cost Management
1050. Total Productivity Management
1051. Total Quality Management
1052. Total Resource Management (TRM)
1053. Total Technology Management (TTM)
1054. Traceability
1055. Training Evaluations
1056. Transition Enablers and Barriers Assessment
1057. Tree Diagrams
1058. Trend Analysis
1059. Triple Ranking
1060. Truth Table
1061. Two-Dimensional Survey Grid
1062. Two-Directional Bar Chart
1063. Two-Stage Sampling
1064. Type I Error Probability
1065. Type II Error Probability
1066. u Charts
1067. Ubiquitous Computing
1068. Undesirable Behavior
1069. User Involvement
1070. User's Quality Costs
1071. Value-Added Process Career
1072. Value Analysis
1073. Value Analysis and Control
1074. Value Analysis Engineering
1075. Value Chain Model
1076. Value Conversation
1077. Value Engineering
1078. Value-/Non-Value-Added Cycle Time Chart
1079. Value Orientation
1080. Value Propositions
1081. Value Sensitivity Analysis
1082. Variable Control Charts
1083. Variance Analysis
1084. Vendor Appraisal/Supplier Evaluation
1085. Venn Diagram
1086. Venture Business Consult
1087. Venture Development Workshop
1088. Verification
1089. Virtual Teams
1090. Visible Management
1091. Visioning
1092. Visual Controls
1093. Voice of Customer Interaction Matrix
1094. Voice of the Customer
1095. Voice of the Customer Gathering Displays
1096. Voice of the Process
1097. Weighted Voting
1098. What-If Analysis
1099. White Collar Production Management
1100. Why/How Charting
1101. Why/Why Diagram
1102. Wiebull Chart
1103. Wildest Idea Technique
1104. Window Analysis
1105. Wishful Thinking
1106. Work Breakdown Structure
1107. Work Cells
1108. Work Coordination and Workflow Software
1109. Work Coordination Software
1110. Work-Flow Analysis
1111. Work-Flow Control
1112. Work-Flow Diagram
1113. WorkRight
1114. Work Simplification
1115. Work Teams
1116. X Bar and R Charts
1117. XDOM
1118. Yield Chart
1119. Zero Stock

Index

ERNST & YOUNG LLP/SYSTEMCORP INC.

GUIDED TOUR

Included with this book is Ernst & Young LLP's/SystemCorp Inc.'s Multimeida Guided Tour CD-ROM called "WOW" (The War on Waste).

System Requirements
- Windows 3.1 or higher
- Sound Blaster or similar sound card
- CD-ROM Drive
- 8MB RAM
- 4MB free disk space

Installation Instructions:
1. Start Windows.
2. Load Guided Tour CD-ROM into CD-ROM drive.
3. Select Run from the file or Start menu.
4. Type in **<drive>:\setup** where **<drive>** is the drive letter of your CD-ROM drive.
5. Follow instructions given in setup program.

CONTENTS OF CD-ROM GUIDED TOUR

Segment 1. Overview of WOW

Part 1. Battle Plans
  Section A. Specialized Battle Plans
  Section B. Mass-Destruction Battle Plans
  Section C. Strategic Battle Plans
Part 2. Data-Analysis Weapons
  Section D. Specialized Data-Analysis
  Weapons
  Section E. Mass-Destruction Data-Analysis
  Weapons
  Section F. Strategic Data-Analysis Weapons
Part 3. Idea-Generation Weapons
  Section G. Specialized Idea-Generation
  Weapons
  Section H. Mass-Destruction Idea-
  Generation Weapons

Part 4. Decision-Making Weapons
  Section I. Specialized Decision-Making
  Weapons
  Section J. Mass-Destruction Decision-
  Making Weapons
Part 5. Action/Execution Weapons
  Section K. Specialized Action Weapons
  Section L. Mass-Destruction Weapons
  Section M. Strategic Action Weapons

Segment 2. Author's Biographies

Segment 3. Other Books in this Series

Segment 4. Work Draw—This is an
  advance process modeling application
  developed by Edge Software Inc.

ANY QUESTIONS?

In you need any technical assistance or for more detailed product information or any of the programs demonstrated, contact **SystemCorp** at (514) 339-1067.
   Fax a copy of this page to get a 10% discount on any of our products.

SOFTWARE AND INFORMATION LICENSE